Reader's Companion to F. Scott Fitzgerald's *Tender Is the Night*

Matthew J. Bruccoli
with Judith S. Baughman

UNIVERSITY OF SOUTH CAROLINA PRESS

Endsheet Decorations by Edward Shenton
(by permission of Charles Scribner's Sons)

Copyright © 1996 University of South Carolina

Published in Columbia, South Carolina, by the
University of South Carolina Press

Manufactured in the United States of America

Bruccoli, Matthew Joseph, 1931–
    Reader's companion to F. Scott Fitzgerald's Tender is the night /
by Matthew J. Bruccoli; with Judith S. Baughman.
        p.   cm.
    Includes bibliographical references.
    ISBN 1-57003-078-2
    1. Fitzgerald, F. Scott (Francis Scott), 1896–1940. Tender is the
night.   2. Fitzgerald, F. Scott (Francis Scott), 1896–1940. Tender
is the night—Criticism, Textual.   I. Baughman, Judith.   II. Title.
PS3511.I9T4515 1996
813′.52–dc20   95-4408

Still for Scottie
When the saint passes, the feast is over.

Contents

Acknowledgments

M any people were coerced into collaborating on this project. My special obligations are to Arlyn Bruccoli and Dmitri Nabokov. Mrs. Bruccoli vetted the time scheme, edited the Introduction and Explanatory Notes, and disparaged the quality of my writing. Mr. Nabokov—who was well trained by his parents— solved note problems that defeated me, especially those related to Switzerland.

My research assistants at the University of South Carolina performed heroically: Tracy S. Bitonti, Justin Giroux, Cy League, and Tony Perrello. Robert W. Trogdon earned a battlefield commission.

These colleagues at the University of South Carolina answered question after question: Ward Briggs, James Hardin, George Holmes, Eugene H. Kaplan, Isaac Jack Levy, Amy Millstone, William Mould, Faust Pauluzzi, Kenneth Perkins, David Rembert, and John Winberry. Joel Myerson argued with me. Bert Dillon, chairman of the USC Department of English, granted all my requests for more aid.

These scholars marked copies of Tender Is the Night and advised me about annotation policy: Horst H. Kruse (Westfälische Wilhelms-Universität), Ursula Kruse (Münster), Ahmed Nimieri (University of Khartoum), and Kiyohiko Tsuboi (Okayama University)—as did my undergraduate and graduate students at the University of South Carolina.

These librarians and archivists generously responded to my queries: Dean George Terry (University Libraries, USC); Gary

Geer (Reference, Cooper Library, USC); James Brooks, Jo Cottingham, Rhonda Felder, Arthelia Ford, and Linda Holderfield (Interlibrary Loan, Cooper Library, USC); Daniel Boice (Caroliniana Library, USC); William Cagle and Anthony W. Shipps (Lilly Library, Indiana University); Charles Mann (Pennsylvania State University Library); John Delaney and Alice V. Clark (Princeton University Library); Robert Grattan (American Library in Paris); Dottie Farrar and Ginger Reiman (Bagaduce Music Lending Library); the staff of the Archives Department (*l'Equipe*); William R. Day Jr. (Alan Mason Chesney Medical Archives, Johns Hopkins Medical Institutions); G. M. Baylis and Sarah Paterson (Imperial War Museum); Jane Gottlieb (Julliard School Library); Evelyne Lüthi-Graf (Commune de Montreux); R. Giraud (Bibliothèque Municipale de Nice); Jean Claude Garetta (la Bibliothèque de l'Arsenal, Paris); Jacques Delarue (la Sureté Nationale, Paris); Susan P. Walker (United States Military Academy); and Edmund Berkeley Jr. (Joseph M. Bruccoli Great War Collection, Alderman Library, University of Virginia).

These scholars, editors, and association officers provided crucial help: Maguy Allegri (Société d'Économie Mixte Pour les Événements Cannois); Cécile Alziary and Annie Sidro (Comité des Fêtes, des Arts et des Sports de la Ville de Nice); William E. Baxter (American Psychiatric Association); Frank Bond (Western Front Association); Ronald R. Butters (*American Speech*); Marie Thérèse Caloni (Les Editions de la Table Ronde); Gerald Cohen (University of Missouri—Rolla); J. P. Durier and M. Casile (Société des Auteurs, Composeurs et Editeurs de Musique); Charles Egleston (*English Short-Title Catalogue*); Joan Hall (*Dictionary of American Regional English*); Antonio Illiano (University of North Carolina); J. H. Marshall (*Oxford English Dictionary*); Linda Patterson Miller (Pennsylvania State University, Ogontz); Prince S. Obolensky (Union de la Noblesse Russe); Stephen J. Perrault and Thomas F. Pitoniak (Merriam-Webster); Randy Roberts (University of Missouri, Columbia); Charles Scribner III (Charles Scribner's Sons); Todd Stebbins (William Penn College); Frank Wall (Royal Canadian Legion); and Lydia Zelaya (Macmillan Publishers).

The following organizations and institutions also assisted me:

Austrian Institute (New York); Austrian National Tourist Office (New York); Chanel, Inc. (Paris and New York); Cultural Services of the French Embassy (Washington, D.C.); and Hermès, Inc. (Paris and New York).

Some of the many others who responded to my pleas were Eric Roman (who vetted the French in this edition), Bart Auerbach, Alain Decaux (Académie Française), Honoria Murphy Donnelly, Annie Duchanaud, William Emerson, George Greenfield, Peter B. Hénault, Joseph Hopkins, Caroline Hunt, Denis Jeambar (Point), Michael Lazare, John Hanson Mitchell, Ghislaine Roman, Mr. and Mrs. V. Roman, Anthony Rota (Bertram Rota, Ltd.), Mary Jo Tate, Calvin Tomkins, Henri Troyat (Académie Française), C. Webster Wheelock, and Fred Zentner (Cinema Bookshop).

My discussions with Fredson Bowers when we were planning the Cambridge Edition of the works of F. Scott Fitzgerald influenced the emendation policy advocated here.

See the dedication.

Diagram of the Development of *Tender Is the Night*

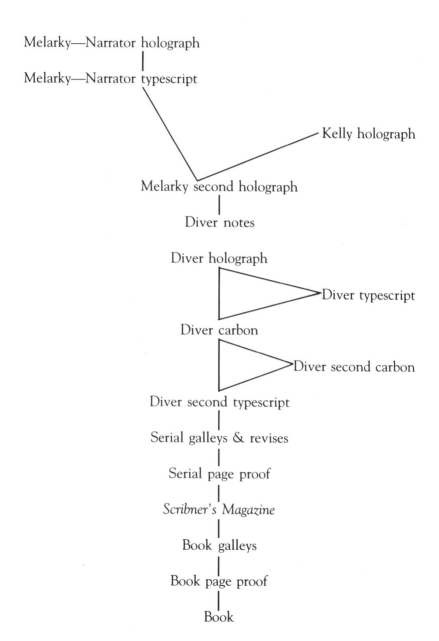

Melarky holograph
|
Melarky typescript

Melarky—Narrator holograph
|
Melarky—Narrator typescript

Kelly holograph

Melarky second holograph
|
Diver notes

Diver holograph

Diver typescript

Diver carbon

Diver second carbon

Diver second typescript
|
Serial galleys & revises
|
Serial page proof
|
Scribner's Magazine
|
Book galleys
|
Book page proof
|
Book

Reader's Companion to F. Scott Fitzgerald's
Tender Is the Night

Introduction

This volume is not a critical study: it does not analyze the putative meanings of *Tender Is the Night*.[1] The functions of this vade mecum are to encourage useful reading of the novel by explaining or identifying the references that F. Scott Fitzgerald expected fit readers to recognize, and to correct the errors—especially in the time scheme—that distract readers and damage the work. Competent fiction writers know what they are doing—or trying to do. Otherwise reading fiction would be a waste of time.

1. Composition

On 1 May 1925, three weeks after publication of *The Great Gatsby*, F. Scott Fitzgerald wrote to Scribners editor Maxwell Perkins: "The happiest thought I have is of my new novel—it is something really NEW in form, idea, structure—the model for the age that Joyce and Stien are searching for, that Conrad didn't find."[2]

By late April 1926 Fitzgerald informed Harold Ober, his agent: "The novel is about one fourth done and will be delivered for possible serialization about January 1st. It will be about 75,000 words long, divided into 12 chapters, concerning tho this is absolutely confidential such a case as that girl who shot her mother on the Pacific coast last year."[3]

The novel was to be about Francis Melarky, an American in his twenties who murders his domineering mother while they are traveling in Europe. The matricide version occupied Fitzgerald, with many interruptions, from 1925 to 1930. There were five drafts—

1

three in third-person and two with a narrator—but no draft progressed beyond four chapters. Francis Melarky and his mother arrive on the Riviera; he is taken up by attractive American expatriates Seth and Dinah Piper (Roreback) and the alcoholic Abe Grant (Herkimer); Francis, a movie technician, visits a Riviera movie studio, and he acts as a second in a duel; then Melarky, the Grants, and the Pipers go to Paris. There is a flashback opening chapter in which Melarky is beaten by the police in Rome. Many of these incidents are recognizable in *Tender Is the Night*.

The character of Francis Melarky was loosely based on Theodore Chanler, a young expatriate American composer—who was not involved in a violent crime. The Pipers are recognizable as Sara and Gerald Murphy (see Explanatory Notes, Dedication), the Fitzgeralds' close friends at Cap d'Antibes and later. Abe Grant is a portrait of Ring Lardner (see Explanatory Notes, 12.1). The Pipers and Grant were developed into the Divers and Abe North in the published novel.

Trans-Atlantic travel and the effects of Europe on Americans were the subjects of Fitzgerald short stories during the time he was working on the novel. As George Anderson demonstrates (see Appendix D), themes, descriptions, and phrases were transplanted from the novel drafts to stories or from stories to the novel. In June 1929 Fitzgerald reported to Perkins: "I am working night + day on novel from new angle that I think will solve previous difficulties."[4] This "new angle" was a plot utilizing movie director Lew Kelly and his wife Nicole, who are going to Europe for an extended vacation. Fitzgerald wrote two manuscript chapters set on shipboard. Also aboard the ship is a young actress named Rosemary who hopes to impress Kelly. No transcript survives for the Kelly chapters, which indicates that Fitzgerald abandoned the angle. There is evidence that Fitzgerald returned to the Melarky material early in 1930, assembling 127 typescript pages from the previous drafts.

Zelda Fitzgerald's collapse and hospitalization in Switzerland, commencing in April 1930, interrupted work on the novel; and it provided Fitzgerald with material about which he felt strongly, superseding the unfelt Melarky plot. A signal to Fitzgerald's new concerns is provided by "One Trip Abroad," a story written in August 1930, while Zelda was at Les Rives de Prangins clinic on

Lake Geneva, Switzerland. This story published in *The Saturday Evening Post* in October is a forecast of *Tender*. An attractive young American couple, Nicole and Nelson Kelly, go to France intending to study music and painting; but they are caught up in dissipation and become patients in a Swiss clinic.

The Fitzgeralds returned to America in September 1931. In January 1932 Fitzgerald reported to Perkins: "At last for the first time in two years + 1/2 I am going to spend five consecutive months on my novel. I am actually six thousand dollars ahead Am replanning it to include what's good in what I have, adding 41,000 new words + publishing. Don't tell Ernest or anyone— let them think what they want—you're the only one whose ever consistently felt faith in me anyhow."[5] Work was interrupted by Zelda Fitzgerald's February relapse and hospitalization at the Phipps Psychiatric Clinic of Johns Hopkins Hospital in Baltimore. Fitzgerald's plot outline ("Sketch"), chronologies, and character sketches were prepared in Montgomery, Alabama, early in the year or at "La Paix," the house he rented in May 1932 at Towson, Maryland, near Baltimore. In August 1932 he made this entry in his *Ledger*: "The Novel now plotted + planned, never more to be permanently interrupted."[6]

Les Rives de Prangins" *Zelda's room + bath are around the corner [second floor?]*

Fitzgerald's note on the Swiss clinic where Zelda Fitzgerald was treated (Bruccoli Collection, University of South Carolina).

His wife's illness determined Fitzgerald's final approach to the novel. The details of Nicole Diver's illness were based on Zelda Fitzgerald's illness, as shown by the chart comparing the two case histories, although the incest factor in Nicole's collapse was apparently invention. Zelda Fitzgerald's illness supplied more than factual background for *Tender*: it provided the emotional focus of the novel. Diver's response to Nicole's illness derives from Fitzgerald's feelings about his wife's collapse and relapses.

In the published novel the major departures from the "Sketch" have to do with the nature of Nicole's insanity and Diver's political ideas. She does not manifest a homicidal mania in *Tender*, nor does she commit a murder that Diver conceals. Diver is not a communist in the novel; he is apolitical. Nothing in the surviving drafts indicates that Fitzgerald tried to develop these ideas.

The criticism has been made that Dick Diver is not a convincing figure as a psychiatrist. It is true that he is not surrounded with medical details, but *Tender* is not about psychiatry. Fitzgerald's note under "Method of Dealing with Sickness Material" indicates that the paucity of medical details was deliberate: "Only suggest from the most remote facts. Not like doctor's stories."

Fitzgerald's memo on the three-part structure establishes that the point-of-view shifts in the novel were planned from the inception of work. Book I shows the Divers through Rosemary's adoring eyes. It is brilliant surface, with hints of the corruption beneath the facade Diver maintains. "From outside mostly" provides the rationale for the introductory flashback. Although Fitzgerald reconsidered the flashback structure after the book was published, the plans and drafts show that he did not alter the structural plan during the writing of *Tender*. In Book II the reader is taken behind the barricade of charm to learn Nicole's case history as Diver did. Book III provides Diver's attempts to work out his destiny—to break the bond with Nicole, to cure her, and to save himself.

The preliminary planning material supports the conclusion that *Tender* is not just the result of work Fitzgerald began in 1932; the published novel is the product of a cumulative process, salvaging the seemingly wasted work on the Melarky drafts. The dominant theme—the deterioration of a personality under the distractions and dissipations of expatriate life in its most attractive form—endured throughout the process of composition.

4

General Plan

Pp. 5–21: Notes for the Third Version of *Tender Is the Night*, working title "Dick Diver" (Princeton University Library).

The novel should do this. Show a man who is a natural idealist, a spoiled priest, giving in for various causes to the ideas of the haute Burgoise, and in his rise to the top of the social world losing his idealism, his talent and turning to drink and dissipation. Background one in which the leisure class is at their truly most brilliant + glamorous such as Murphys.

The hero, born in 1891, is a man like myself brought up in a family sunk from haute burgoisie & petit burgoisie, yet expensively educated. He has all the gifts, ~~and at~~ and ~~twenty three he seems to have~~ goes through Yale almost succeeding but not quite but getting a Rhodes scholarship which he caps with a degree from Hopkins, + with a legacy goes abroad to study psychology in Zurich. At the age of 26 all seems bright. Then he falls in love with one of his patients who has a curious homicidal mania toward men caused by an event of her youth. Aside from this she is the legendary promiscuous

woman. He "transfers" to himself & she falls
in love with him, a love he returns.

After a year of non-active service in the
war he returns and marries her. ⟨+ is madly⟩ She is
an aristocrat of half American, half
European parentage, young, mysterious &
lovely, <u>a new character</u>. He has cured her
by pretending to a stability & belief in
the current order which he does not have,
being in fact a communist – liberal – idealist,
⟨a moralist in revolt⟩
But the years ~~have~~ of living under patronage
ect. & among the burgeoise have seriously
spoiled him and he takes up the marriage
as a man divided ~~in~~ himself. During the
war he has taken to drink a little & it
continues as secret drinking after his
marriage. The difficulty of taking care of
her is more than he has imagined and
he goes more and more to pieces, always
keeping up a wonderful face.

At the point when he is socially the
most charming and inwardly ~~the most~~
corrupt he meets a young actress on the

[margin top right:] ⟨& in love with her & utterly consecrated to completing the cure⟩

7

during which he is in Rome with the actress having a disappointing love affair too late he is beaten up by the police & returns to find that instead of taking great cure she has

Riverra who falls in love with him. With considerable difficulty he contains himself out of fear of all it would entail since his formal goodness is all that is holding his disintegration together. ~~But~~ He knows too that he does not love her as he has loved his wife. Nevertheless the effect of the repression is to throw him toward all women during his secret drinking when he has another life of his own which his wife does not suspect, or at least he thinks she doesn't. ~~He ignores~~ On one of his absences ~~he~~ committed a murder and in a revulsion of spirit he tries to conceal it and succeeds. It shows him however that the game is ~~almost~~ up and he will have to perform some violent & Byronic act to save her for he is losing his hold on ~~them~~ & himself.

He has known slightly for some time a very strong ~~and young~~ & magnetic ~~young animal~~ man and now he deliberately brings them together. When he finds under circumstances of jealous

agony that it has succeeded he departs
knowing that he has cured her. He sends
his neglected son
the boy into soviet Russia to educate him
as a
and comes back to America to be a
quack thus having accomplished both
his burgeoise sentimental idea in the
case of his wife and his ideales in
the case of his son, + now being only himself
a shell to which nothing matters but
survival ~~+ death with th~~ as long as
possible with the old order.

~~Characters~~

~~We have~~.

~~(9) The hero, treated 1st entirely from without~~
~~and then entirely from within~~

Technique:

~~Our first shall plot to a ten, fifteen parts.~~
~~narrative~~

(*further sketch)   5.   Approach

The Drunkard's Holiday will be a novel
of our time showing the break up of a
fine personality. Unlike The Beautiful
and Damned the break-up will be
caused not by flabbiness but really
tragic forces such as the inner conflicts
of the idealist and ~~the~~ the compromises
forced upon him by circumstances.

The novel will be a little over
a hundred thousand words long, composed
of fourteen chapters, each 7,500 words long,
five chapters each in the first and
second part, four in the third — one
chapter or its equivalent to be composed
of retrospect.

most actresses by being

The actress was born in 1908. Her
career is like Lois or Mary Hay —
that is, she is ^differs from a lady, simply seeking
of vitality, health, sensuality. Rather
gross as compared to the heroine, or
rather will be gross for at present her
youth covers it. Mimi — Lupe Velez.

We see her first at the very
beginning of her career. She's already
made one big picture

We follow her from age 17 to age 22

The Friend was born in 1896. He is
a wild man. He looks like Tunti and
like that dark communist at the meeting.
He is half Italian, + half american. He
is a type who hates all sham + pretense.
(See the Long + type who was like Foss Wilson)
He is one who would lead tribesmen or
communists — utterly aristocratic, King
or nothing. He fought three years ~~again~~ in
the French foreign legion in the war and
then painted a little and then fought
the Riff. He's just back from there on his
first appearance in the novel and seeking
a new outlet. He has money + this French
training — otherwise would be a revolutionist.
He is a fine type, useful or destructive but
his mind is not quite as good as the
hero's. Touch of Percy Pyne, Denny Holden also

We see him from age 28 to age 33

Summary of Part III (1st half.)

The Divers, as a marriage, reach the end of their resources. Medically Nicole is _nearly_ cured but Dick has given out + is sinking toward alcoholism and discouragement. It seems as if the completion of this ruination will be the fact that cures her — almost mystically. However this is merely hinted at. Dick is still in control of the situation and thinks of the matter practically. They must separate for both their sakes. In wild bitterness he thinks of one tragic idea but controls himself and manages a saner one instead.

His hold is broken, the transference is broken. He goes away. He has been used by the rich family and cast aside.

Part III is as much as possible seen through Nicole's eyes. All Dick's stories such as are _absolutely_ nessessary: Edwaele, father, auto catastrophe (child's eyes perhaps), strappen quarrel?, girls on Riviera, must be told without pulling in his reactions or feelings. From now on he is mystery man, at least to Nicole with her guessing at the mystery.

Dick

The hero was born in 1891. He is a well-formed rather athletic and fine looking fellow. Also he is very intelligent, widely read — in fact he has all the talents, including especially great personal charm. This is all planted in the beginning. He is a superman in possibilities, that is, he appears to be at first sight from a bourgeois point of view. However he lacks that tensile strength — none of the ruggedness of Brancusi, Leger, Picasso. For his external qualities use anything of Gerald, Ernest, Ben Finny, Archie McLeish, Charley McArthur or myself. He looks, though, like me.

The faults — the weakness such as the social-climbing, the drinking, the desperate clinging to one woman, finally the neurosis, only come out gradually.

We follow him from age 34 to age 39.

DICK

September 1891   Born

     "   1908   Entered Yale

June   1912   Graduated Yale aged 20

June   1916   Graduated Hopkins. Left for Vienna (8 mo. there)

June   1917   Was in Zurich after 1 year and other work. Age 26

June   1918   Degree at Zurich. Aged 26

June   1919   Back in Zurich. Aged 27

September 1919   Married--aged 28 (after his refusing fellowship at University in neurology and ̶p̶a̶t̶h̶ pathologist to the clinic. Or does he accept?

July   1925   After 5 years and 10 months of marriage is aged almost 34

Story starts

July 1929   After 9 years and 10 months of marriage is aged almost 38.

Nicole's Age

Always one year younger than century.

Born July 1901

    courtship for two and one half years before that, since she
was 13.

Catastrophe   June 1917   Age almost 16

Clinic.   Feb. 1918   Age 17

                       To middle October bad period
                       After armistice good period

                       He returns in April or May 1919

                       She discharged in June 1, 1919. Almost 18

                       Married September 1919. Aged 18

Child born August 1920

Child born June   1922

    2nd Pousse almost immediately to October 1922 and thereafter

    Frenchman (or what have you in summer of 1923 after almost
        4 years of marriage.

In July 1925 when the story opens she is just 24

    (One child almost 5 (Scotty in Juan les Pins)

    One child 3 (Scotty in Pincio)

In July 1929 when the story ends she is just 28

The heroine was born in 1901. She is beautiful on the order
of Marlene Dietrich or better still the Norah--Kiki Allen girl with
those peculiar eyes. She is American with a streak of some foreign
blood. At fifteen she was raped by her own father under peculiar
circumstances--work out. She collapses, goes to the clinic and there
at sixteen meets the young doctor hero who is ten years older. Only
her transference to him saves her--when it is not working she reverts
to homicidal mania and tries to kill men. She is an innocent,
widely read but with no experience and no orientation except what he
supplies her. Portrait of Zelda--that is, a part of Zelda.

We follow her from age 24 to age 29

Method of Dealing with Sickness Material
(1) Read books and decide the general type of case
(2) Prepare a clinical report covering the years 1916-1920
(3) Now examine the different classes of material selecting not too
many things for copying.
     (1) From the sort of letter under E
     (2) " " " " " " F
        (In this case using no factual stuff)
     (3) From the other headings for atmosphere, accuracy and
material being careful not to reveal basic ignorance
of psychiatric and medical training yet not being glib.
Only suggest from the most remote facts. Not like doctor's
stories.

Must avoid Faulkner attitude and not end with a novelized Kraft-
Ebing--better Ophelia and her flowers.

Classification of the Material on Sickness

A. Accounts

B. Baltimore

C. Clinics and clipping

D. Dancing and lst Diagnoses

E. Early Prangins--to February 1931

F. From Forel (include Bleuler Consultation)

H. Hollywood

L. Late Prangins

M. My own letters and comments

R. Rosalind and Sayre Family

S. Squires and Schedule

V. Varia

Parallel between actual case and case in novel

(Actual case)	(Case in novel)
Various outbursts	McKisco + Paris outbursts
2nd pousse after 10 mos	2nd pousse after 1 child 1923 "after this comes" conclusion
Reunion	Marriage
Clinic for 5 mos recovery for husband	Clinic recovery love for Dick
Clinic for 10 mos serious Diagnosis Schizophrene See novel. Tendencies ect.	Clinic for 1 yr serious for ten mos Diagnosis Schizophrene
Collapses	Collapses
Projects on husband	Projects on everyone
Invents homosexuality	Invents rape by unknown
She sees herself failing	She succumbs to him
A woman of 29 has a rivalry complex for success + power competing with her husband	A girl of 16 has a father complex (abnormally built up by her father), a well-screened degenerate

Dates for Zurich not checked.

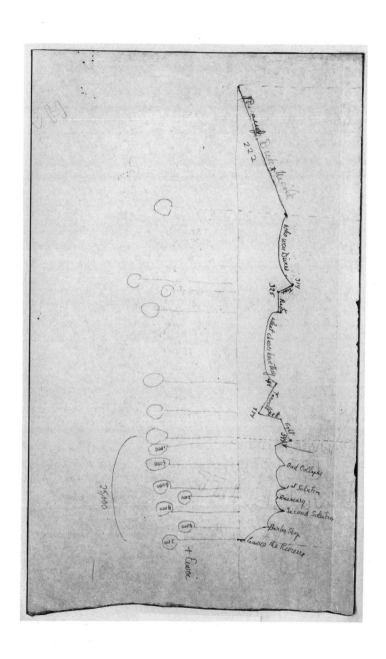

19

To call him

    I Dick

    II Dr. Diver   }   in the three parts

    III Diver

Long rythin based on Ettés
full excuse + Thank you &
Aquila's I mean

Part I   from outside Mostly

    II   Nicole from Dick

    III   Dick

Later Stones have not been
thoroughly combed.

The treatment of this theme became more penetrating as Fitzgerald worked his way from the matricide plot to the Nicole-Dick material.

The first complete draft of the Dick Diver version—entitled "The Drunkard's Holiday"—was assembled from revised typescripts of the Melarky version (corresponding to Book I, Chapters 1–12; Book II, Chapters 22–23) and from new manuscript for the rest of the novel. Fitzgerald did not type. All of his first drafts were written in holograph and turned over to typists. He revised his work through layers of typescripts and carbon copies. It was not unusual for him to revise retyped drafts for *Tender* three times. Since the manuscript chapters were being typed while Fitzgerald was working ahead, he might be revising typescript and writing new manuscript chapters on the same day.

When Fitzgerald was in the late stages of composition—probably during summer 1933—Perkins and Fitzgerald decided to serialize the novel in four monthly installments (January–April 1934) of *Scribner's Magazine*. Serialization would bring Fitzgerald additional income and publicize the forthcoming book. On 25 September Fitzgerald reported to Perkins: ". . . things have gone ahead of my schedule, which you will remember, promised you the whole manuscript for reading November 1, with the first one-fourth ready to shoot into the magazine (in case you can use it) and the other three-fourths to undergo further revision. I now figure that this can be achieved by about the 25th of October. I will appear in person carrying the manuscript and wearing a spiked helmet."[7] The twelve long chapters of the typescript, retitled "Doctor Diver's Holiday A Romance," correspond to the sections of the serial, which were being set in type for *Scribner's Magazine* by 27 October 1933.

In March 1935—nearly a year after the publication of the novel—Fitzgerald wrote to Perkins:

> It has become increasingly plain to me that the very excellent organization of a long book or the finest perceptions and judgment in time of revision do not go well with liquor. A short story can be written on a bottle, but for a novel you need the mental speed that enables you to keep the whole pattern in your head and ruthlessly sacrifice the sideshows as Ernest did in "A Farewell to Arms." If a mind is slowed up

the last letter she had from him he was
practising medicine in Geneva, New York, and
Nicole got the impression that he had really
settled down and a woman to keep house
for him. Nicole looked up Geneva in an
atlas and found it was in the heart of
the Finger Lakes section and considered a
pleasant town. Perhaps he stayed there
like Grant at Galena again, but his latest
note was postmarked from Hornell which is
some distance from there; in
any case he is certainly in that section
of the country, in one town or another

Fitzgerald's manuscript draft for the end of *Tender Is the Night* (Princeton University Library).

ever so little it lives in the individual part of a book rather than in a book as a whole; memory is dulled. I would give anything if I hadn't had to write Part III of "Tender is the Night" entirely on stimulant. If I had one more crack at it cold sober I believe it might have made a difference. Even Ernest commented on sections that were needlessly included and as an artist he is as near as I know for a final reference.[8]

Fitzgerald's admission about writing Part III (almost certainly referring to the third serial installment) "entirely on stimulant" means that he drank during his work on this section—but not necessarily that he was drunk while he was writing these chapters or the rest of *Tender Is the Night.*

2. Editing and Publication

The setting copy for the serial galleys consists of revised carbons and revised ribbon-copy typescripts. Fitzgerald revised the serial galleys so extensively that the second, third, and fourth installments were reset. He was a compulsive reviser of his work and defied publishing practice by treating proofs as an opportunity to perfect his prose and especially to alter the effect of his words as they would appear in print. Fitzgerald's proof revisions demonstrate his concern for the details of his text. He enjoined Alfred Dashiell, managing editor of *Scribner's Magazine,* and Perkins against tampering with his system of using italics for emphasis only: "PLEASANT NICE THOUGHTS IT WOULD BREAK MY HEART IF THE PROOF READERS ARE STICKING BACK ALL THOSE ITALICS I TWICE ELIMINATED STOP IN THE FIRST PROOF THEY HAD ALL THE FRENCHMEN TALKING IN ITALICS = SCOTT"[9]

The Dashiell / Fitzgerald correspondence shows that the *Tender* serial was edited on a tight schedule: 29 December 1933—Dashiell sends Fitzgerald second installment proof; 2 January 1934—Dashiell sends revised second installment proof; 12 January—Dashiell sends third installment proof; 6 February—Fitzgerald returns "first half of Section IV."[10] In addition to queries on the galleys, Dashiell provided editorial queries in letters or in list form. Fitzgerald acted on some of these suggestions and disregarded others (see Emendations). On 13 February Dashiell called

Cover for the first installment of the novel and the first page of the serialization, with art by Edward Shenton.

attention to word repetition: *reserved* at 337.32 / 338.1 and *off* at 359.5–6; but Fitzgerald did not alter these readings.

There is surprisingly little editorial correspondence for *Tender;* much of the Fitzgerald-Perkins editorial discussion was probably conducted by phone. On 18 January 1934 Perkins advised omitting the shooting in the Gare Saint-Lazare (serial installment 2) from the book, but Fitzgerald disagreed (see Explanatory Note, 109.17–110.9). When Perkins endorsed Dashiell's decision that the episode in which Dick rescues Mary North Minghetti and Lady Caroline from the Cannes police would have to be cut to eight hundred words in the fourth installment for space reasons, Fitzgerald argued for its retention (see Explanatory Note, 391.1–396.17).

The drafts from manuscript through typescript setting copy for the serial include an account of Tommy Barban and Nicole swimming on the beach of "Monsieur Irv," a Chicago gangster living on the Riviera. This material was deleted in the serial galleys and remained unpublished until Malcolm Cowley used it in his 1951 edition.

Three substantial cuts were made between the serial and book publication: The serial includes a fuller account of Abe North's day in the Ritz bar (Book I, Chapter 23; see Appendix C). The serial material about the young man who jumps from the ship on which Dick is returning to Europe (Book II, Chapter 19) was omitted (see Appendix C). The serial material about Diver's involvement with a woman in Innsbruck (Book II, Chapter 18) was condensed (see Appendix C).

Edmund Wilson had read *Tender* in typescript; in a letter postmarked 12 March 1934 Fitzgerald discussed the cuts and revisions:

> Despite your intention of mild critisism in our conversation, I felt more elated than otherwise—if the characters got real enough so that you disagreed with what I chose for their manifest destiny the main purpose was accomplished (by the way, your notion that Dick should have faded out as a shyster alienist was in my original design, but I thot of him, in reconsideration, as an "homme épuisé", not only an "homme manqué". I thought that, since his choice of a profession had accidentally wrecked him, he might plausibly have walked out on the profession itself.)

Any attempt by an author to explain away a partial failure in a work is of course doomed to absurdity—yet I could wish that you, and others, had read the book version rather than the mag. version which in spots was hastily put together. The last half for example has a *much* more polished facade now. Oddly enough several people have felt that the surface of the first chapters was *too* ornate. One man even advised me to "coarsen the texture", as being remote from the speed of the main narrative!

In any case when it appears I hope you'll find time to look it over again. Such irrevelencies as Morton Hoyt's nose dive and Dick's affair in Innsbruck are out, together with the scene of calling on the retired bootlegger at Beaulieu, + innumerable minor details. I have driven the Scribner proofreaders half nuts but I think I've made it incomparably smoother.[11]

The fifth draft of *Tender* conflates serial galleys, revised galleys, revised typescript, and new typescript. These documents representing several layers of revision constituted the latest printer's copy for the serial text. Incomplete marked page proof survives for the *Scribner's Magazine* installments (pp. 168–174, 207–229; corresponding to Book II, Chapters 10–23).

First Installment. January 1934.
Pp. [1]–8, [60]–80

Serial section	corresponds to	book
I		I, 1–5
II		I, 6–11
III		I, 12–18

Second Installment. February 1934.
Pp. [88]–95, 139–160

Serial section	corresponds to	book
IV		I, 19–25
V		II, 1–9

Third Installment. March 1934.
Pp. [169]–174, 207–229

Serial section	corresponds to	book
VI		II, 10–13
VII		II, 14–15
VIII		II, 16–21
IX		II, 22–23

Fourth Installment. April 1934.
  Pp. [252]–258, [292]–310

Serial section	corresponds to	book
X		III, 1–3
XI		III, 4–6
XII		III, 7–13

The book galleys were completely reset from the serial install-ments *without changes*, probably in the naive expectation of expe-diting book publication, but Fitzgerald revised or rewrote on the proofs anyhow. The surviving galleys for the last third of Book II and all of Book III are covered with revisions; Fitzgerald cut up most of these galleys and patched them together. Galleys for Book II, Chapters 18–22, and III, 2–7, were so densely revised that it was impossible to correct the type; new galleys were set from type-script. There is no complete set of revised book galleys.

3. Reception

Tender Is the Night was published on 12 April 1934; despite the expectation that had been aroused during Fitzgerald's nine-year pause after *The Great Gatsby*, the reviews of the novel were restrained. In the June number of the *North American Review*, Herschel Brickell mentioned "the kind of violent arguments that have been going on about *Tender Is the Night*"; [12] since there was no controversy in print—only disagreement—the "violent argu-ment" presumably raged orally among readers. Disagreement about the merits and flaws of the novel has continued since 1934.

Discussions of the novel habitually return to the initial recep-tion of *Tender*, a topic which provides its own controversy. One of the commonplaces of Fitzgerald criticism is that *Tender* failed in 1934 because the critics ganged up on it and dismissed the novel as politically irrelevant. As Cowley explained in 1951, "It dealt with fashionable life in the 1920s at a time when most read-ers wanted to forget that they had ever been concerned with fri-volities; the new fashion was for novels about destitution and revolt. . . . most reviewers implied that it belonged to the bad old days before the crash. . . ." [13] John O'Hara shared Cowley's conclusion:

```
                    CHARLES SCRIBNER'S SONS
                      PUBLISHERS, IMPORTERS AND BOOKSELLERS
                             597 Fifth Avenue
                               NEW YORK

  No.              DATE October 15, 1934          CLAIMS FOR DAMAGES OR SHORT-
                                                  AGES MUST BE MADE IMMEDIATELY
                                                       ON RECEIPT OF GOODS.

                                                       TERMS: NET CASH
                                                  PAYABLE WITH EXCHANGE ON
  Sold To    Mr. F. Scott Fitzgerald                     NEW YORK


                                                  No.
  Sent Per
```

QUANTITY	DESCRIPTION	EDUCATIONAL	TRADE	TOTAL
	To excess cost of corrections on:			
	TENDER IS THE NIGHT			
	Cost of composition and electrotyping	712.07		
	Cost of corrections		318.56	
	Allowance - 20% of $712.07, according to agreement		142.41	$176.15

The invoice for Fitzgerald's revisions in the book (Princeton University Library).

> . . . after *The Great Gatsby* he had toiled and sweated over
> *Tender Is the Night*, which I considered far and away his best
> novel. As a favor to Fitzgerald I had read proof on *Tender Is
> the Night*, galleys and page proofs, and I was shocked and
> probably frightened by what the critics and the public had
> done to it and to him. People from whom he had the right
> to expect respectful treatment were condescending or
> worse. . . .[14]

According to this influential interpretation the critics com-
pounded their socio-political prejudice with obtuseness by claiming to find difficulty with the simple flashback structure. The
reviewers were allegedly abetted by the reading public, which rejected Fitzgerald in favor of social tracts. Depending upon whether
one is listening to a revisionist or anti-revisionist, the accord be-

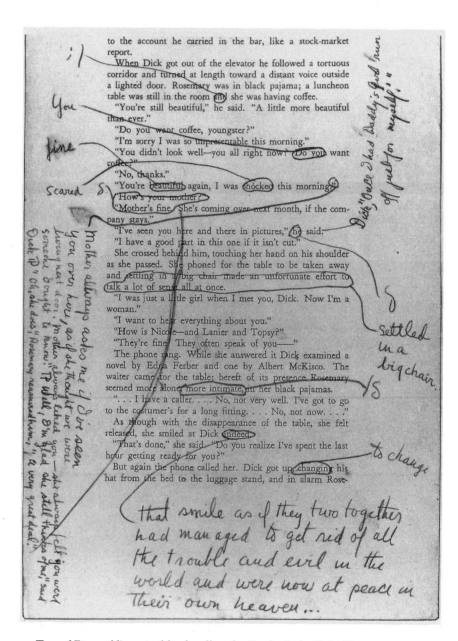

Two of Fitzgerald's revised book galleys for *Tender Is the Night* (Princeton University Library).

went into the room next to them and told a collapsed psychiatrist that he was better, always better, and the man tried to read his face for conviction, since he hung on the real world only through the reassurance he could find in the resonance, or lack of it, in Doctor Diver's voice. After that Dick discharged a shiftless orderly and it was time for luncheon. Meals with the patients were a chore he approached with apathy. The gathering, which of course did not include residents at the Eglantine or the Beeches, was conventional enough at first sight but over it brooded always a heavy melancholy. Such doctors as were present kept up a conversation but most of the patients, as if exhausted by their morning's endeavor, or depressed by the company, spoke little, and ate looking into their plates.

Luncheon over, Dick returned to his villa. Nicole was in the salon wearing a strange expression. He scented trouble and asked quickly: "What is it, dear?"

"Read that." She tossed him a letter. It was from a woman recently discharged, though with skepticism on the part of the faculty. It accused him in no uncertain terms of having seduced her daughter who had been at her mother's side during the crucial stage of the illness. It presumed that Mrs. Diver would be glad to have this information and learn what her husband was really like.

Dick read the letter again. Couched in clear and concise English he yet recognized it as the letter of a manic. Upon a single occasion he had let the girl, a flirtatious little brunette, ride into Zurich with him upon her request, and in the evening had brought her back to the clinic. On the way back, in an idle, almost indulgent way, he kissed her. Later, she tried to carry the affair further but he was not interested and subsequently, perhaps consequently, the girl had come to dislike him, and taken her mother away before the proper time.

"This letter is deranged," he said casually. "I had no relations of any kind with that girl. I didn't even like her."

"Yes, I've tried thinking that," said Nicole.

"Surely you don't believe it?"

"I've been sitting here."

He sank his voice to a reproachful note and sat beside her. "This is absurd. This is a letter from a mental patient."

"I was a mental patient."

He stood up and spoke more authoritatively.

"We're not going to have any nonsense, Nicole. Go and round up the children and we'll start."

In the car, with Dick driving, they rounded the lake, following its little promontories, catching the burn of light and water in the windshield, tunnelling through cascades of evergreen. It was Dick's particular car, a Renault so dwarfish that they all stuck out of it except the children, between whom Mademoiselle towered mast-like in the rear seat. They knew every kilometer of the road—where they would smell the pine needles and the black stove smoke, a high sun with a face traced on it beat fierce on the straw hats of the children.

Nicole was silent; Dick could make nothing of her straight hard gaze. Often he felt lonely with her, and frequently she tired him with the flood of personal revelations she reserved exclusively for him, "I'm like this—I'm more like that," but this afternoon he would have liked her to rattle on in staccato for a while and give him glimpses of her thoughts. The situation held most threat of trouble when she backed up into herself and closed the doors behind her.

31

tween the opinion makers and readers either revealed to Fitzgerald what was wrong with the structure of *Tender*, their response or befuddled his critical judgment so that he subsequently attempted to restructure *Tender* in straight chronology.

Like many biographical-critical explanations of Fitzgerald's literary conduct, these alternatives combine fact with romantic invention. Fitzgerald's most ambitious novel sold disappointingly in its own time; yet three printings totaling 14,595 copies was not a catastrophic sale in 1934. The reception hurt and puzzled Fitzgerald, but it is not demonstrable that he was the victim of a critical conspiracy. The majority of the notices were favorable, and there was little complaint about the setting or the flashback. Some of the mainly favorable reviews patronized Fitzgerald, but critics had patronized him in the Twenties.

Examination of the best-selling novels of 1934 provides no support for the notion that readers of the Depression rejected *Tender* because they preferred proletarian fiction: Hervey Allen's *Anthony Adverse,* Caroline Miller's *Lamb in His Bosom* (Pulitzer Prize), Stark Young's *So Red the Rose,* James Hilton's *Good-bye, Mr. Chips,* Margaret Ayers Barnes's *Within This Present,* Sinclair Lewis's *Work of Art,* Phyllis Bottome's *Private Worlds,* Mary Ellen Chase's *Mary Peters,* Alice Tisdale Hobart's *Oil for the Lamps of China,* and Isak Dinesen's *Seven Gothic Tales.* The three top sellers of the year were historical novels, and the number-four novel was Hilton's sentimental story about a schoolmaster.

People who lament the commercial failure of *Tender* usually ignore the circumstance that Fitzgerald had never written a prodigious seller: *This Side of Paradise* sold about 41,000 copies in 1920; *The Beautiful and Damned* sold about 50,000 copies in 1922; and *The Great Gatsby* about 23,000 copies in 1925. During his lifetime Fitzgerald was much better known as a magazine story writer than as a novelist.

Four days after publication, John Chamberlain commented in *The New York Times* on the responses of his fellow reviewers:

> The critical reception of F. Scott Fitzgerald's "Tender Is the Night" might serve as the basis for one of those cartoons on "Why Men Go Mad." No two reviews were alike; no two had the same tone. Some seemed to think that Mr. Fitzgerald was writing about his usual jazz age boys and girls; others that

he had a "timeless" problem on his hands. And some seemed to think that Doctor Diver's collapse was insufficiently documented.[15]

Of twenty-four reviews by influential critics or by critics appearing in influential American periodicals, nine were favorable, six were unfavorable, and nine were mixed.[16] Gilbert Seldes, who was Fitzgerald's friend, recognized *Tender* as "a great novel": "He has gone behind generations, old or new, and created his own image of human beings. And in doing so has stepped again to his natural place at the head of the American writers of our time."

Three reviews commented on the flashback:

> C. Harley Grattan, "The integral significance of the opening pages of the book has been missed by most reviewers."
> Edward Weeks, "Don't make up your mind until you have read past page 151!"
> John Chamberlain, "At this point one could almost guarantee that 'Tender Is the Night' is going to be a failure. But, as a matter of fact, the novel does not really begin until Rosemary is more or less out of the way."

Cowley's *New Republic* review analyzed Fitzgerald's apparent indecision between writing a psychological or a social novel—Fitzgerald thought of it as a dramatic novel. Then Cowley offered a theory that acquired currency: that as the novel developed through its several versions during the years of writing, the early sections crystallized so that Fitzgerald was unable to unify them with the later sections.

Two reviews complained about the expatriate material from the Twenties. The unsigned *News-Week* review was headlined "A Sinful, Ginful Tale" and noted that "it is a long time since the decay of American expatriates on the Riviera was hot news." In *The Daily Worker*, the journal of the American Communist Party, Philip Rahv admonished: "Dear Mr. Fitzgerald, you can't hide from a hurricane under a beach umbrella."

Seven reviewers (Mary Colum, Henry Seidel Canby, Clifton Fadiman, J. Donald Adams, Horace Gregory, William Troy, and Edith Walton) expressed reservations about the credibility of Dick Diver and his crack-up. In *The New Yorker* Clifton Fadiman cited the absence of a psychoanalytic approach to Diver:

> Dick's rapid acceptance of his failure, for instance, is not
> convincing; there must have been some fundamental weak-
> ness in his early youth to account for his defeatism. . . .
> The events of the narrative, tragic as they are, are insuffi-
> cient to motivate his downfall. It is the failure to reach far,
> far back into his characters' lives that helps prevent this
> novel from being the first-rate work of fiction we have been
> expecting from F. Scott Fitzgerald.

Fadiman also complained about the sloppy copy-editing and listed
thirteen errors. Henry Seidel Canby in *The Saturday Review of
Literature* also criticized Fitzgerald for inadequate or unclear cau-
sality:

> What begins as a study of a subtle relationship ends as the
> accelerating decline into nothingness of Dr. Driver [sic]—not
> for no reason, but for too many reasons, no one of which is
> dominant. This book may be life with its veil over causality,
> but it is not art which should pierce that veil.

J. Donald Adams's review in the Sunday *New York Times Book
Review* charged that Nicole and Rosemary were unconvincing and
that Dick's collapse was contrived. The following day Chamberlain interrupted his *Times* review of Faulkner's *Dr. Martino* to de-
fend the effectiveness of Diver's characterization:

> It seemed to us that Mr. Fitzgerald proceeded accurately, step
> by step, with just enough documentation to keep the drama
> from being misty, but without destroying the suggestiveness
> that added to the horror lurking behind the surface. . . .
> And when he does collapse, his youth is gone, it is too late
> to catch up with the Germans who have been studying new
> cases for years. This seems to us to be a sufficient exercise in
> cause-and-effect. Compared to the motivation in Faulkner, it
> is logic personified.

The two reviews in the papers in Fitzgerald's hometown, St.
Paul, Minnesota, were strongly negative.[17] Both James Gray
("This is a big, sprawling, undisciplined, badly coordinated book")
and H. A. MacMillan ("the obscure manner in which the narrative is developed") denounced the structure. The unsigned review
in *The Princeton Alumni Weekly* commented on the structural dis-
agreements engendered by the novel: "*Tender Is the Night* lacks
unity in the ordinary sense of the word; the debate of the review-

ers is concerned with whether or not Mr. Fitzgerald has achieved a unity less conventional but not less serviceable."[18]

The most thorough defense of Fitzgerald's structure appeared in *The Modern Monthly*, a Marxist journal, some three months after publication of *Tender*. C. Hartley Grattan observed:

> The integral significance of the opening pages of the book has been missed by most reviewers. Almost to a man they have complained that the stress laid upon Rosemary, the beautiful cinema star, is unjustified by the future action of the story, that the pages devoted to building her up are really wasted effort, and that they "throw the reader off." Rather I should say that in these pages Fitzgerald is presenting the type of girl who, in the past, has always been foreordained to absorption into the world of his characters. . . . Seen through his eyes, however, what glamour remains can legitimately be exploited and by the same token, the tragedy of its actuality can be all the more accentuated.

After quoting Fitzgerald's explication of Nicole's spending habits ("For her sake trains began their run at Chicago. . . .), Grattan concluded his review:

> This is perceptive writing and I should like to stress for the benefit of those austere individuals who see in the bourgeois world nothing but filth and corruption the significance of the words "feverish bloom" and "grace." Only a person utterly insensitive to the grace and beauty of the way of life open to the leisured will fail to see that even in decay these people are infinitely charming, insidiously beguiling to all but seagreen incorruptibles.

The attacks on the verisimilitude of Diver's decline probably troubled Fitzgerald more than anything else the critics wrote. On 23 April he sent H. L. Mencken—who had not reviewed *Tender*—an eloquent defense of the novel's construction:

> . . . . I would like to say in regard to my book that there was a deliberate intention in every part of it except the first. The first part, the romantic introduction, was too long and too elaborated, largely because of the fact that it had been written over a series of years with varying plans, but everything else in the book conformed to a *definite intention* and if I had to start to write it again tomorrow I would adopt the same plan, irrespective of the fact of whether I had, in this

case, brought it off or not brought it off. That is what most
of the critics fail to understand (outside of the fact that they
fail to recognize and identify anything in the book) that the
motif of the "dying fall" was absolutely deliberate and did not
come from any diminution of vitality, but from a definite
plan.

That particular trick is one that Ernest Hemmingway and
I worked out—probably from Conrad's preface to "The Nig-
ger"—and it has been the greatest "credo" in my life, ever
since I decided that I would rather be an artist than a career-
ist. I would rather impress my image (even though an image
the size of a nickel) upon the soul of a people than be
known, except in so far as I have my natural obligation to
my family—to provide for them. I would as soon be anonymous as Rimbaud, if I could feel that I had accomplished
that purpose—and that is no sentimental yapping about being disinterested. It is simply that having once found the intensity of art, nothing else that can happen in life can ever
again seem as important as the creative process.[19]

This statement indicates that Fitzgerald's subsequent proposal to
reorganize the novel resulted from his desire to reinforce the docu-
mentation of Diver's decline by putting together all the information about him—not from his decision that the flashback structure
was confusing (see Section 4).

Fitzgerald took satisfaction from the anonymous 1935 review
in the *Journal of Nervous and Mental Disease,* which concluded:
"an achievement which no student of the psychobiological sources
of human behavior, and of its particular social correlates extant
today, can afford not to read."[20]

Tender Is the Night was published in England in September
1934, and the located reviews[21] resembled the American recep-
tion. D. W. Harding asserted in *Scrutiny* that Fitzgerald had not
supplied any cause for Diver's crack-up; yet he admits that he had
been moved against his will by Diver's fate, and he concludes by
echoing Fitzgerald's style: ". . . I am prepared to be told that this
attempt at analysis is itself childish—an attempt to assure myself
that the magician didn't really cut the lady's head off, did he? I
still believe there was a trick in it." The trick usually goes under
the name of genius.

Reviewers who questioned the convincingness of Diver's crack-up may really have been troubled by the chronological flaws in *Tender*. It is difficult for the reader to gauge the step-by-step deterioration of the hero because the time signals are inadequate and contradictory (see Time Scheme).

4. *"The Author's Final Version"*

Fitzgerald brooded over the stillbirth of *Tender Is the Night* and came to blame the opening section written from Rosemary's point of view. Shortly after publication he inscribed a copy for novelist Joseph Hergesheimer:

> Dear Joe:
> You talked to someone who didn't like this book—I don't know who, or why they didn't. But I could tell in the Stafford Bar that afternoon when you said it was "almost impossible to write a book about an actress" that you hadn't read it thru because the actress fades out of it in the first third + is only a catalytic agent.
> Sometime will you open it at the middle, perhaps at page 155 + read on for five or ten minutes—? If it were not for my sincere admiration of your judgement I would forgo this plea. You were not the only one repelled by the apparent triviality of the opening—I would like this favorite among my books to have another chance in the chrystal light of your taste
> Ever yrs
> F Scott Fitzgerald
> Page 155—*et sq.*[22]

In May 1936 Fitzgerald wired publisher Bennett Cerf:

> WOULD YOU CONSIDER PUBLISHING TENDER IS THE NIGHT IN THE MODERN LIBRARY IF I MADE CERTAIN CHANGES TOWARD THE END WHICH I SEE NOW ARE ESSENTIAL COMMA IT WOULD MAKE ALL THE DIFFERENCE IN THE SPLIT UP OF THE TWO PRINCIPAL CHARACTERS STOP OR DO YOU THINK THAT ONCE PUBLISHED A NOVEL IS FOREVER CRYSTALIZED. PLEASE ANSWER CAMBRIDGE ARMS CHARLES STREET BALTIMORE MARYLAND. . . .[23]

Cerf's response is unknown, but in August Fitzgerald sent him a general explanation of the proposed alterations:

Dear Bennett:

The revision job would take the form, to a large extent, of a certain new alignment of the scenes—without changing their order in any case. Some such line as this:

That the parts instead of being one, two, and three (they were one, two, three and four in the magazine serial) would include in several cases sudden stops and part headings which would be to some extent explanatory; certain pages would have to be inserted bearing merely heads. Part two, for example, should say in a terse and graceful way that the scene is now back on the Riviera in the fall after these events have taken place, or that, This brings us up to where Rosemary first encounters the Divers. Those examples are not accurate to my intention nor are they at all couched as I would have them, but that's the general idea. (Do you remember the number of subheads I used in "This Side of Paradise"—at that time a rather novel experiment, the germ of which I borrowed from Bernard Shaw's preface headings to his plays; indeed that was one of the few consciously original things in "This Side of Paradise".)

There would be certain changes but I would supply the equivalent line lengths. I have not my plan with me; it seems to be in Baltimore. But I know how printing costs are. It was evolved to have a very minimum of replacement. There is not more than one complete sentence that I want to eliminate, one that has offended many people and that I admit is out of Dick's character: "I never did go in for making love to dry loins." It is a strong line but definitely offensive. These are all the changes I contemplated with in addition some minor spelling corrections such as would disturb nothing but what was within a printed line. There will be no pushing over of paragraphs or disorganization of the present set-up except in the aforesaid inserted pages. I don't want to change anything in the book but sometimes by a single word change one can throw a new emphasis or give a new value to the exact same scene or setting.[24]

At this point he intended to retain the flashback structure but wanted to insert signals alerting the reader to narrative shifts. Again, Cerf's response has not been located, but he obviously did not encourage the project.

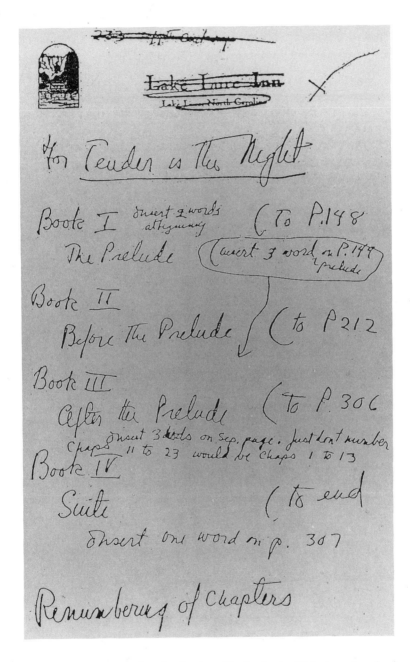

Fitzgerald's 1936–1937 plan for dividing *Tender Is the Night* into four books, probably intended for the *Modern Library* (Princeton University Library).

When Fitzgerald knew that his Metro-Goldwyn-Mayer contract would not be renewed, he wrote Perkins in December 1938 proposing several publishing ideas intended to revive his reputation—including an omnibus volume of three novels:

> But I am especially concerned about *Tender*—that book is not dead. The *depth* of its appeal exists—I meet people constantly who have the same exclusive attachment to it as others had to *Gatsby* and *Paradise,* people who identified themselves with Dick Diver. It's great fault is that the *true* beginning—the young psychiatrist in Switzerland—is tucked away in the middle of the book. If pages 151–212 were taken from their present place and put at the start the improvement in appeal would be enormous. In fact the mistake was noted and suggested by a dozen reviewers. To shape up the ends of that change would, of course, require changes in half a dozen other pages.[25]

Perkins tactfully declined, and there was no further discussion of the revision.

At the time of Fitzgerald's death on 21 December 1940 his books included a copy of *Tender Is the Night* in which he had written on the front endpaper: "This is the <u>final version</u> of the book as I would like it." This disbound book re-orders the chapters in straight chronological order, beginning with Dick Diver's arrival at Zurich in 1917. The plan for restructuring the novel into five sections is in Fitzgerald's *Notebooks:*

Analysis of Tender:
I   Case History 151–212 61 pps. (change moon) p.212
II Rosemary's Angle 3–104 101 pps. P. 3
III Casualties 104–148, 213–224 55 pps. (-2) (120 + 121)
IV Escape 225–306 82 pps.
V   The Way Home 306–408 103 pps. (-8) (332–341)[26]

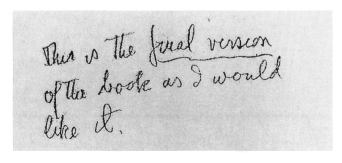

(Princeton University Library)

Plan of Cowley's Restructured Edition
First Edition Corresponds to "The Author's Final Version"

Book I:	1	Book II:	2	
	2		3	
	3		4	
	4		5	
	5		6	
	6		7	
	7		8	
	8		9	
	9		10	
	10		11	
	11		12	
	12		13	
	13	Book III:	1	
	14		2	
	15		3	
	16		4	
	17		5	
	18		6	
	19		7	
	20		8	
	21		9	
	22		10	
	23		11	
	24	Book III:	12	
	25		13	
Book II:	1	Book I:	1	
	2		2	
	3		3	
	4		4	
	5		5	
	6		6	
	7		7	
	8		8	
	9		9	
	10	Book II:	1	
	11	Book III:	14	
	12	Book III:	15 & Book IV:1	
	13	Book IV:	1	
	14		2	
	15		3	
	16		4	
	17		5	
	18		6	

	19		7
	20		8
	21		9
	22		10
	23		11
Book III:	1	Book V:	1
	2		2
	3		3
	4		4
	5		5
	6		6
	7		7
	8		8
	9		9
	10		10
	11		11
	12		12
	13		13

Fitzgerald made some forty corrections or revisions in this copy (see Appendix B). On p. 160 of Book II, Chapter 5, Fitzgerald wrote: "This is my mark to say that I have made final corrections up to this point."[27] The note suggests that he lost interest in the endeavor—or at least that he broke off revising and never resumed.

In 1951, during the early stage of the Fitzgerald revival, Scribners published Malcolm Cowley's edition of *Tender* "With the Author's Final Revisions." In addition to Fitzgerald's revisions, Cowley corrected scores of proofreading errors, stating rightly that the errors in the first edition "had a cumulative effect on readers and ended by distracting their attention. . . ."[28]

In his 1951 introduction Cowley claimed that the revised edition improved *Tender*: "By rearranging the story in chronological order Fitzgerald tied it together. He sacrificed a brilliant beginning and all the element of mystery, but there is no escaping the judgment that he ended with a better constructed and more effective novel."[29] The revised edition had a limited impact, receiving a few unenthusiastic reviews. Charles Poore commented in *The New York Times* that "It takes a case history that he had transmuted into art and prosaically tries to bring it back closer to what might be a case historian's heart's desire."[30] Budd Schulberg concurred in *The New York Times Book Review:* "Logic and clarity have been gained, but at the cost of irony, beauty and a dramatic suspense. . . . I believe that Fitzgerald's first esthetic instincts were sound, as usual, and that he was panicked by failure and disappointment."[31] John Chamberlain, who had defended the novel in 1934, gave the Cowley redaction one sentence: "The reshuffling of the components of 'Tender is the Night' into more strictly chronological order does improve the novel."[32] The publication of "The Author's Final Version" was not a literary event.

Although Ernest Hemingway had expressed strong criticism of *Tender* in 1934, he had come to admire the "magic" of the prose. When he read the revised edition in 1951, he wrote Cowley:

> Scribner's sent the new edition of Tender Is The Night yesterday and I have read it until page 206.
>
> Truly I did not want the reforms to turn out as I was afraid they might. But I am afraid the whole idea was just a bad idea of Scott's.
>
> In the straight chronological order the book loses the magic completely. Starting off with a case history there is no secret to discover and no mystery and all sense of a seemingly magical world (the world of Sara and Gerald Murphy) being destroyed by something that is unknown is lost.
>
> By the time the bath-room incident comes off the reader knows everything which was to come as a shock. In the form it is now it is simply a pathological and not a nice one at that. It has all the dullness of all stories of the insane and where it had the charm of the strange mixture that was Scott it is now about as much fun to read as The Snake Pit.
>
> I know you did it for Scott and it was what he wanted. But I think if he had been completely sane I could have argued him out of it.
>
> It is just like takeing the wings off a butterfly and arrangeing them so he can fly straight as a bee flies and loseing all the dust that makes the colors that makes the butterfly magical in the process.[33]

In the once-influential *The Rhetoric of Fiction* (1961), Wayne C. Booth made a case for restructuring *Tender:*

> The achievement of the revision is, in short, to correct a fault of over-distancing, a fault that springs from a method appropriate to other works at other times but not to the trag-

edy Fitzgerald wanted to write. His true effect could be obtained only by repudiating much of what was being said by important critics of fiction about point of view and developing a clean, direct, old-fashioned presentation of his hero's initial pre-eminence and gradual decline.[34]

The defenders of the revised version miss the point about how *Tender Is the Night* was written—how every serious work of fiction is written. As Fitzgerald wrote he knew what he had already written and what he intended to write next. The circuity of the novel became fixed as it grew on paper. Everything connected. To shuffle the chapters is to break the circuits.

When Fredson Bowers and Matthew J. Bruccoli were planning their interrupted critical edition of *Tender Is the Night* in 1989, Bowers prepared an evaluation of the claims that "The Author's Final Version" embodied Fitzgerald's best and final intentions. The Bowers document was not written for publication, but it is so powerfully reasoned that sections merit inclusion here:

> Literary history has other instances of authors being influenced by outside opinion to change their original conceptions of the presentation or content of a work. It is interesting that not one of these has gone unchallenged by posterity. Self-censorship is sometimes a prominent reason for a change in authorial expression, but closely related to this is the influence of outside opinion that has succeeded in convincing an author, however reluctantly, that if his book is to succeed to his hopes it must undergo some major alteration. An author's reliance on such outside opinion as to a book's reception instead of his own creative force that produced the version under criticism has not always been found—as remarked—to be in his ultimate best interest. Most authors are right in the end when they trust to their instincts and their original creative plan. We may take this as applying with particular weight to Fitzgerald's acceptance of what the critics believed to be a serious flaw. The depth of his acceptance of the flashback as "a serious fault" cannot be estimated—how much he convinced himself in his desire for a reversal of the book's initial reception remains unknown. What is of textual importance to an editor is the distinction between the internal forces that generated Fitzgerald's recognition of the desirability of removing the lengthy incident of the governess at Innsbruck and the external forces that (post-creation) led

him to want to ensure the future success of the novel by convincing himself that the critics' view of the flashback was correct. . . .

One other consideration is appropriate. When a narrative has been structured in a particular way, the balance of the treatment rests on it accordingly. The account of the earlier events in Switzerland and of the ironic consequences up to the opening on the beach is written with the technique of a catching-up of the narrative. Merely to rearrange the sequence of events to a chronological order does violence to the balance of the opening and then in a sense réprise in the original book. There can be little question that if Fitzgerald had reordered the events at some stage in the composition, even so late as the book's galley proofs, the early events would have been differently narrated, since there could be no reliance on the reader's understanding of them resulting from his view of the Divers in their introduction on the Riviera. *Tender* is not so mechanically conceived and executed as to yield to post-creation restructuring in such an important matter that has dictated the treatment both of start and of middle. In the sense of "might-have-been" we can envisage a novel that Fitzgerald himself had composed, or revised, to read in chronological order, but it would be a fundamentally different novel from what results in the Cowley edition when the middle is bodily transferred to the beginning without the necessary reworking. This is no doubt special pleading, but the concept is true. Scribners exhibited the right attitude when the firm re-issued in paperback the originally conceived (and in fact the only published) version as a substitute for Cowley's extrapolation of Fitzgerald's letter to Perkins and his note in his private copy. This is one instance where an author's own version must be respected despite his after-the-event wishes. To choose the Cowley ordering as the base-text for a critical edition would be an act of violence to the inner coherence of authorial conception and execution. The pressure that Fitzgerald felt to popularize his novel was illegitimate. His capitulation to what he conceived of as public opinion, no matter how rationalized, should not be permitted to tear apart the living fabric of the novel as he wrote it.[35]

The longevity of "The Author's Final Version" was decided by reader preference. Scribners reprinted it through 1959 but let it go out of print to no outcry.[36] Cowley's edition was first published in England in 1953 and reprinted in the widely distributed Penguin paperbacks between 1955 and 1978. "The Author's Final Version" is out of print in America and England in 1995.

Notes

1. This introduction necessarily draws heavily on my *The Composition of Tender Is the Night* (Pittsburgh: University of Pittsburgh Press, 1963). Facsimiles are reproduced from *Tender Is the Night*, 5 vols.; Part 4 of *F. Scott Fitzgerald Manuscripts*, ed. Bruccoli (New York and London: Garland, 1991).
2. 1 May 1925. *F. Scott Fitzgerald: A Life in Letters*, ed. Bruccoli (New York: Scribners, 1994), p. 108. Fitzgerald's letters and manuscripts are transcribed here as written.
3. *A Life in Letters*, pp. 140–141. In January 1925 Dorothy Ellingson, a sixteen-year-old San Francisco girl, murdered her mother; Fitzgerald knew of this crime only from newspaper reports.
4. c. June 1929. *Dear Scott/Dear Max: The Fitzgerald-Perkins Correspondence*, ed. John Kuehl and Jackson R. Bryer (New York: Scribners, 1971), p. 156.
5. c. 15 January 1932. *A Life in Letters*, p. 208.
6. *F. Scott Fitzgerald's Ledger: A Facsimile* (Washington, D.C.: Bruccoli Clark/NCR Microcard Editions, 1972), p. 186.
7. *A Life in Letters*, p. 235.
8. 11 March 1935. *A Life in Letters*, pp. 277–278.
9. To Maxwell Perkins, 15 March 1934. *Correspondence of F. Scott Fitzgerald*, ed. Bruccoli and Margaret M. Duggan (New York: Random House, 1980), p. 332.
10. Scribners Archives, Princeton University Library.
11. *A Life in Letters*, p. 250.
12. 237, pp. 569–570.
13. Introduction, *Tender Is the Night: With the Author's Final Revisions* (New York: Scribners, 1951), p. x.
14. "Hello Hollywood Good-Bye," *Holiday*, 43 (May 1968), 54–55, 125–126, 128–129.
15. "Books of the Times" (16 April 1934), 15.
16. —Mary M. Colum, *Forum and Century*, 91 (April 1934), 219–223; + Burton Rascoe, *Esquire*, 1 (April 1934), 133, 159; + Edward Weeks, *Atlantic Monthly*, 153 (April 1934),

17; +Harry Hansen, *New York World-Telegram* (12 April 1934), 25; +Gilbert Seldes, *New York Evening Journal* (12 April 1934), 23; ±Hal Borland, *Philadelphia Public Ledger* (13 April 1934), 9; +John Chamberlain, *New York Times* (13 April 1934), 17; ±Lewis Gannett, *New York Herald Tribune* (13 April 1934), 15; ±Fanny Butcher, *Chicago Tribune* (14 April 1934), 10; —Henry Seidel Canby, *Saturday Review of Literature*, 10 (14 April 1934), 630–631; ±Clifton Fadiman, *New Yorker*, 10 (14 April 1934), 112–115;—Edith H. Walton, *New York Sun* (14 April 1934), 30; ±J. Donald Adams, *New York Times Book Review* (15 April 1934), 7; ±Horace Gregory, *New York Herald Tribune Books* (15 April 1934), 5; +Cameron Rogers, *San Francisco Chronicle* (15 April 1934), 4D; +John Chamberlain, *New York Times* (16 April 1934), 15; ±*Time*, 23 (16 April 1934), 77; —Philip Rahv, *Daily Worker* (5 May 1934), 7; —William Troy, *Nation*, 138 (9 May 1934), 539–540; +Herschel Brickell, *North American Review*, 237 (June 1934), 569–570; ±Edith H. Walton, *Forum and Century*, 91 (June 1934), iv–v; ±Malcolm Cowley, *New Republic*, 79 (6 June 1934), 105–106; +C. Hartley Grattan, *Modern Monthly*, 8 (July 1934), 375–377; —Gertrude Diamant, *American Mercury*, 33 (October 1934), 249–251; —*News-Week*, 3 (14 April 1934), 39–40. Most of these reviews are reprinted in Jackson R. Bryer, ed. *F. Scott Fitzgerald: The Critical Reception* (New York: Franklin, 1978).

17. Gray, *St. Paul Daily News* (12 April 1934), I, 8; MacMillan, *St. Paul Daily News* (22 April 1934), magazine section, 4.

18. 34 (4 May 1934), 665.

19. *A Life in Letters*, pp. 255–256.

20. 82 (July 1935), 115–117.

21. Peter Quennell, *New Statesman & Nation*, 7 (28 April 1934), 642; E. B. C. Jones, *New Statesman & Nation*, 8 (22 September 1934), 364–366; D. W. Harding, *Scrutiny*, 3 (December 1934), 316–319; *Spectator*, 153 (21 September 1934), 410; *Times Literary Supplement* (27 September 1934), 652.

22. University of Virginia Library. See *in their time/1920–1940* (Bloomfield Hills & Columbia: Bruccoli Clark, 1977), # 118.

23. 16 May 1936. *A Life in Letters*, pp. 300–301. See Andrew B. Myers, " 'I Am Used to Being Dunned': F. Scott Fitzgerald

and the Modern Library," *Columbia Library Columns*, 25 (February 1976), 28–39.

24. 13 August 1936. *A Life in Letters*, pp. 306–307.

25. 24 December 1938. *A Life in Letters*, p. 374.

26. Page 212 of the first edition is the last page of Book II, chapter 10, and is marked for deletion in Fitzgerald's copy. Pages 332–341 describe the Divers' visit to the Minghetti establishment at Book III, chapter 4, but are not marked for deletion in Fitzgerald's copy. The only *moon* between page 151 and page 212 is at 158.11: "moon over that mountain."

27. Princeton University Library.

28. Introduction, p. xiii.

29. Introduction, pp. xiv–xv.

30. "Books of the Times" (15 November 1951), 26.

31. "Prodded by Pride and Desperation" (18 November 1951), 5, 38.

32. "A Reviewer's Notebook," *Freeman*, 2 (19 November 1951), 121–122.

33. 10 November 1951. Bruccoli, *Fitzgerald and Hemingway: A Dangerous Friendship* (New York: Carroll & Graf, 1994), p. 224.

34. (Chicago: University of Chicago Press, 1961), p. 195.

35. Bruccoli Collection, Cooper Library, University of South Carolina.

36. The plates for the revised edition were inadvertently used for three printings in the Contemporary Classic/Scribner Library series in 1970–1971.

Explanatory Notes

He observed, that all works which describe manners, require notes in sixty or seventy years, or less. . . .
—James Boswell, *The Life of Samuel Johnson*

It is impossible for an expositor not to write too little for some, and too much for others. He can only judge what is necessary by his own experience; and how long soever he may deliberate, will at last explain many lines which the learned will think impossible to be mistaken, and omit many for which the ignorant will want his help. These are censures merely relative, and must be quietly endured. I have endeavoured to be neither superfluously copious, nor scrupulously reserved, and hope that I have made my authour's meaning accessible to many who before were frighted from perusing him, and contributed something to the publick, by diffusing innocent and rational pleasure.
—Samuel Johnson, *Preface to Shakespeare*

None of the above is important unless everything is important in writing.
—Ernest Hemingway, commenting on the text of *Tender Is the Night*

E very novel is a product of its time. *Tender Is the Night* was written between 1925 and 1934 by a man born in 1896. The purpose of this enchiridion is to assist readers in understanding F. Scott Fitzgerald's intentions as conveyed by the details of *Tender Is the Night*. Genius is purposeful, although writers err. Masterpieces are deliberate. Details are meaningful.

Tender Is the Night is an under-rated masterpiece because it has become harder to read. The classic American novels of the twentieth century are, year by year, becoming harder to read. New generations of readers—students, teachers, civilians—do not know the same things that the authors knew and expected their readers to know. Culture is the body of knowledge through which people communicate: more than recognition of data, it is shared emotional response to names, places, events, songs, titles. Vladimir Nabokov stated that a familiarity with the Moscow-St. Petersburg railroad cars was necessary for a proper reading of *Anna Karenin;* and his edition of Pushkin's *Eugene Onegin* provides a standard for annotators.

Annotation is a form of explication: it assumes that the meanings intended by the author through the real details and references in a work of fiction can be at least explained. Yet annotation cannot resuscitate the emotions associated with an authorial reference. Thus the note for *Beaumont Hamel* (74.5) does not evoke a sense of the useless heroic slaughter of the Somme battles. Moreover, annotation is to some degree subjective; it conveys the note-maker's own responses to the material, which are shaped by his own knowledge or experience.

Tender Is the Night is the most difficult of Fitzgerald's novels because of its concentration of meaningful detail—some of it inaccurate. Fitzgerald possessed a delicate sense of time and place that enabled him to evoke evanescent experience. Although he wanted to get details right, he nonetheless got them wrong. Yet even when he was not certain where he or his characters actually were, he knew how it felt to be there; moreover, he had the ability to convey the colors, the moods, the rhythms of experience.

With other authors a concentration of errors usually indicates that the work is not worth serious attention because the writer is incompetent or irresponsible. In the case of Fitzgerald the errors in part resulted from his unfulfilled expectations: he required and expected editorial help that was not provided. Fitzgerald's Scribners editor, the legendary Maxwell Perkins, was an indifferent line editor and proofreader. He was concerned with the structure and effectiveness of the whole novel; however, even if Perkins or his associates had been attentive to details, the job of checking them would have been impeded by Fitzgerald's compulsive revising and rewriting in proof.

Consequently, *Tender Is the Night* requires that the good reader be able to recognize Fitzgerald's details and also be able to correct the details. Uninitiated readers are puzzled by the references they don't recognize. Initiated readers are distracted by the references they recognize as wrong. * The confusing chronology in the novel troubles all careful readers, regardless of their cultural backgrounds (see Time Scheme).

The entries for these explanatory notes were selected from copies of *Tender Is the Night* marked by undergraduate and graduate students, high-school and college teachers, "general readers"— and, especially, teachers of Fitzgerald's works at foreign universities. It is a purpose of this companion to make the meanings of *Tender Is the Night* accessible to readers in other countries; accordingly, Americanisms and other aspects of the American language have been defined.

There will be objections that some of these explanatory notes are unnecessary: "Everybody knows that." I don't know what *Everybody* knows, but it is damned little in Anno Television 50. There are critics who proclaim that reliance on facts interferes with "the free play of critical insights." They are advised to play elsewhere.

All page-line references to *Tender Is the Night* are to the first printing of the first edition (New York: Scribners, 1934). In cases where a note explains a reading that should be emended by word substitution (not spelling correction), both the original reading and the necessary emended reading are cited. There is a complete

---

* Clifton Fadiman's 1934 review in the *New Yorker* noted errors in the first edition: "It would be picayune indeed to list these proof-reader's oversights were it not that the inhabitants of Mr. Fitzgerald's world, who pride themselves on their impeccability, should never arouse in the reader's mind the slightest suspicion of their competence in fields— such as liquor, resort geography, and mental disease—that are staked out as their very own. It is perfection or nothing, as in a set by Mr. Belasco." A 1995 reviewer could not assume a general identification of theatre producer David Belasco.

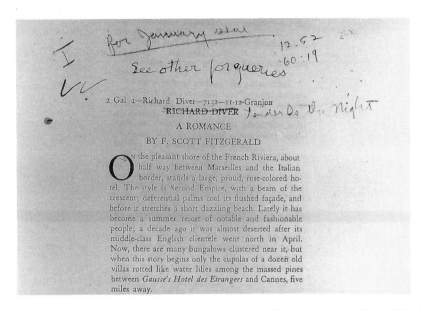

2 Gal 1—Richard Diver—7132—11-12-Granjon
~~RICHARD DIVER~~ *Tender Is the Night*

A ROMANCE

BY F. SCOTT FITZGERALD

ON the pleasant shore of the French Riviera, about half way between Marseilles and the Italian border, stands a large, proud, rose-colored hotel. The style is Second Empire, with a beam of the crescent; deferential palms cool its flushed façade, and before it stretches a short dazzling beach. Lately it has become a summer resort of notable and fashionable people; a decade ago it was almost deserted after its middle-class English clientele went north in April. Now, there are many bungalows clustered near it, but when this story begins only the cupolas of a dozen old villas rotted like water lilies among the massed pines between *Gausse's Hotel des Etrangers* and Cannes, five miles away.

Galley proof for First Serial installment; the title change is not in Fitzgerald's hand (Bruccoli Collection, University of South Carolina).

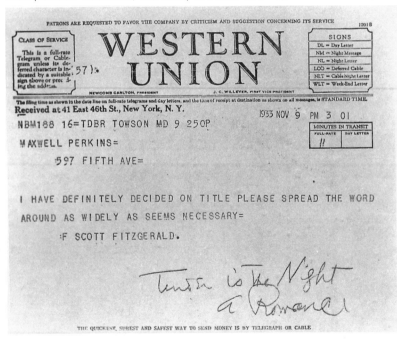

The title is written in Maxwell Perkins's hand (Princeton University Library).

Emendations section that lists *all* requisite emendations, including spelling and punctuation corrections. Both the Explanatory Notes and the Emendations section use standard abbreviations: MS (manuscript—a document in Fitzgerald's hand); TS (secretarial typescript—Fitzgerald did not type); and RTS (revised typescript—a typed draft revised in Fitzgerald's hand).

Epigraph/Title

English romantic poet John Keats (1795–1821), Fitzgerald's favorite poet, wrote his ode "To a Nightingale" in 1819. In August 1940 Fitzgerald wrote his daughter about this poem "which I can never read through without tears in my eyes" (*F. Scott Fitzgerald: A Life in Letters*, ed. Bruccoli [New York: Scribners, 1994], p. 460). The lines selected by Fitzgerald from the fourth stanza express the poet's yearning to escape from painful reality:

1

My heart aches, and a drowsy numbness pains
  My sense, as though of hemlock I had drunk,
Or emptied some dull opiate to the drains
  One minute past, and Lethe-wards had sunk:
'Tis not through envy of thy happy lot,
    But being too happy in thine happiness,—
      That thou, light-winged Dryad of the trees,
      In some melodious plot
    Of beechen green, and shadows numberless,
      Singest of summer in full-throated ease.

2

O, for a draught of vintage! that hath been
  Cool'd a long age in the deep-delved earth,
Tasting of Flora and the country green,
  Dance, and Provençal song, and sunburnt mirth!
O for a beaker full of the warm South,
Full of the true, the blushful Hippocrene,
    With the beaded bubbles winking at the brim,
      And purple-stained mouth;
That I might drink, and leave the world unseen,
    And with thee fade away into the forest dim:

3

Fade far away, dissolve, and quite forget
  What thou among the leaves hast never known,

The weariness, the fever, and the fret
  Here, where men sit and hear each other groan;
Where palsy shakes a few, sad, last gray hairs,
    Where youth grows pale, and spectre-thin, and dies;
      Where but to think is to be full of sorrow
        And leaden-eyed despairs;
    Where Beauty cannot keep her lustrous eyes,
      Or new Love pine at them beyond to-morrow.

4

Away! away! for I will fly to thee,
  Not charioted by Bacchus and his pards,
But on the viewless wings of Poesy,
  Though the dull brain perplexes and retards:
Already with thee! tender is the night,
    And haply the Queen-Moon is on her throne,
      Cluster'd around by all her starry Fays;
        But here there is no light,
    Save what from heaven is with the breezes blown
      Through verdurous glooms and winding mossy ways.

5

I cannot see what flowers are at my feet,
  Nor what soft incense hangs upon the boughs,
But, in embalmed darkness, guess each sweet
  Wherewith the seasonable month endows
The grass, the thicket, and the fruit-tree wild;
    White hawthorn, and the pastoral eglantine;
      Fast fading violets cover'd up in leaves;
        And mid-May's eldest child,
    The coming musk-rose, full of dewy wine,
      The murmurous haunt of flies on summer eves.

6

Darkling I listen; and, for many a time
  I have been half in love with easeful Death,
Call'd him soft names in many a mused rhyme,
  To take into the air my quiet breath;
Now more than ever seems it rich to die,
    To cease upon the midnight with no pain,
      While thou art pouring forth thy soul abroad
        In such an ecstasy!
    Still wouldst thou sing, and I have ears in vain—
      To thy high requiem become a sod.

7

Thou wast not born for death, immortal Bird!
No hungry generations tread thee down;
The voice I hear this passing night was heard
In ancient days by emperor and clown:
Perhaps the self-same song that found a path
Through the sad heart of Ruth, when, sick for home,
She stood in tears amid the alien corn;
The same that oft-times hath
Charm'd magic casements, opening on the foam
Of perilous seas, in faery lands forlorn.

8

Forlorn! the very word is like a bell
To toll me back from thee to my sole self!
Adieu! the fancy cannot cheat so well
As she is fam'd to do, deceiving elf.
Adieu! adieu! thy plaintive anthem fades
Past the near meadows, over the still stream,
Up the hill-side; and now 'tis buried deep
In the next valley-glades:
Was it a vision, or a waking dream?
Fled is that music:—Do I wake or sleep?

Tender Is the Night was a late decision; the working titles
were "The Drunkard's Holiday," "Richard Diver," and "Dr.
Diver's Holiday." The subtitle "A Romance" indicates that Fitzgerald regarded his book as a work of emotional and sensory
appeal.

Title Page DECORATIONS BY EDWARD SHENTON

Edward Shenton's "line technique" pen-and-ink illustrations
for the *Scribner's Magazine* serial were so effective that it was decided to include them in the book (also see endpapers). Shenton
wrote Fitzgerald in the late fall of 1933:

> I just finished reading the final installment and will start the
> drawings this week. I wish I could tell you precisely how your
> novel affected me. Nothing comes readily to hand, except
> the kind of glib phrases, reviewers use. The pattern of disin-
> tegration you've created, is so subtle, adroit, so techinically
> proficient—and so completely moving—that the book seems

Four of Shenton's "decorations" for the novel.

to have a new form; something entirely it's own.—That's not what I mean, at least only partially. It's a swell job! Any writer would give his right arm and both legs to have done it. It's the best thing that's been written since "The Great Gatsby"—(This is going to become a "fan-letter" if I don't curb it). *

Shenton (1895–1977) illustrated nearly one hundred books, including Hemingway's *Green Hills of Africa* (1935), Faulkner's *The Unvanquished* (1938), and Marjorie Kinnan Rawlings's *The Yearling* (1938). He was also a muralist and the author of ten books.

Dedication GERALD AND SARA / MANY FETES

American expatriates Gerald (1888–1964) and Sara (1883–1975) Murphy were the Fitzgeralds' close friends on the Riviera and thereafter. The Murphys' "Villa America" at Cap d'Antibes provided a partial model for the Divers' "Villa Diana" (see Explanatory Notes, 36.12). The assumption that the Murphys were the models for the Divers—or even that *Tender Is the Night* is a roman à clef about the Murphys—is misleading. Certain of the Divers' social qualities were drawn from the Murphys, but the circumstances of the Divers' lives ultimately derived from the Fitzgeralds. Fitzgerald wrote Sara Murphy on 15 August 1935:

> In my theory, utterly opposite to Ernest's, about fiction i.e. that it takes half a dozen people to make a synthesis strong enough to create a fiction character—in that theory, or rather in despite of it, I used you again and again in *Tender*:
> "Her face was hard + lovely + pitiful"
> and again
> "He had been heavy, belly-frightened with love of her for years"
> —in those and in a hundred other places I tried to evoke not *you* but the effect that you produce on men—the echoes and reverberations—a poor reason for what you have given by your living presence, but nevertheless an artist's (what a word!) sincere attempt to preserve a true fragment rather than a "portrait" by Mr. Sargent. And someday in spite of all the affectionate skepticism you felt toward the brash young man you

Correspondence of F. Scott Fitzgerald, ed. by Bruccoli and Margaret M. Duggan (New York: Random House, 1980), p. 319.

Gerald and Sara Murphy at Plage de la
Garoupe (Honoria Murphy Donnelly).

Gerald Murphy raking the beach at
Plage de la Garoupe.

Sara Murphy sunning her pearls.

The model for Gausse's Hôtel des Étrangers.

met on the Riviera eleven years ago, you'll let me have my little corner of you where I know you better than anybody—yes,
even better than Gerald (*A Life in Letters*, p. 288).

The dedication refers to the Murphys' hospitality, i.e., many fes-
tivities: see Honoria Murphy Donnelly with Richard N. Billings,
Sara & Gerald: Villa America and After (New York: Times Books,
1982); Calvin Tomkins, *Living Well Is The Best Revenge* (New
York: Viking, 1971); *Letters from the Lost Generation: Gerald and
Sara Murphy and Friends,* ed. Linda Patterson Miller (New Bruns-
wick, N.J.: Rutgers University Press, 1991).

Book I, Chapter 1

3.10   **Gausse's Hôtel des Étrangers** Literally, hotel for for-
          eigners. Based on the Grand-Hôtel du Cap at the tip
          of Cap d'Antibes. The name *Gausse* was taken from
          Princeton professor and dean Christian Gauss.

3.14–15   **the purple alp that bounded Italy** It is about twenty-
          eight miles (forty-five kilometers) from Cap d'Antibes
          to the Maritime Alps.

4.1–2   **Merchantmen** Vessels engaged in the transportation of
          cargo; freighters.

4.2   **bus boy** Servant who sets and clears tables—an underwaiter.

4.5   **Maures** Mountains on the western end of the Riviera.

4.6   **Provençal** Referring to Provence, the area in southeast France between Nice and Languedoc.

4.9   **victoria** A horse-drawn carriage with a folding top.

5.14   **nannies** Female—usually British—servants who take care of young children.

5.28   **tights** Close-fitting legless bathing suit, as differentiated from the swimming shorts usually worn by men in the Twenties, often with sleeveless tops.

6.1   **four-beat crawl** Swimming stroke in which the swimmer's mouth emerges from the water every fourth arm rotation.

6.12   **Oxford drawl** Affected pattern of upper-class speech acquired at Oxford University.

6.13   **flotte at Golfe-Juan** The French fleet anchored in the Mediterranean between Cannes and Cap d'Antibes.

6.30   **peignoir** A dressing gown or robe (French).

8.11   **Campion** Malcolm Cowley suggested that this name is a pun on the slang term *camping*—behaving effeminately.

8.12   **Sorrento** Resort on the Bay of Naples, southern Italy.

8.17   **McKisco** Albert McKisco's name probably echoes Robert McAlmon's. McAlmon (1896–1956) was an American expatriate writer Fitzgerald disliked.

8.20   **Rosemary Hoyt** Character based on Lois Moran (1909–1990), a movie actress Fitzgerald admired in Hollywood in 1927. He used her personal, familial, and professional characteristics in creating Rosemary. There was no sexual relationship between Fitzgerald and Moran, who stated that her mother was present at all their Hollywood meetings.

Book I, Chapter 2

12.1   **Abe North** The American humorist and short-story writer Ring W. Lardner (1881–1933), on whom Abe

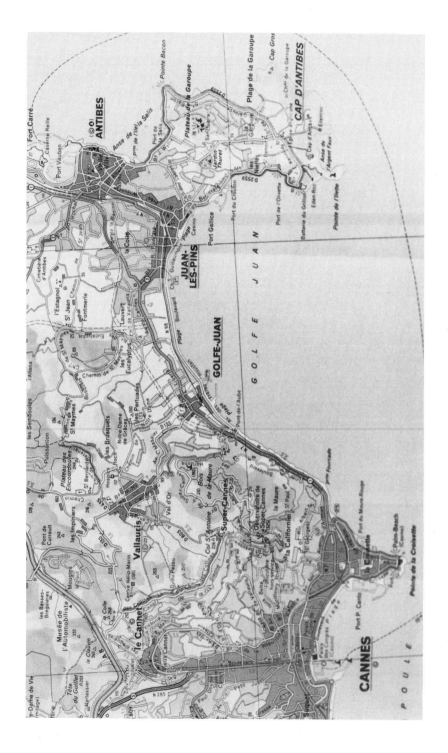

The Riviera.

North was based, had become Fitzgerald's close friend when they both resided in Great Neck, Long Island, during 1922–1924. Like North, Lardner was an alcoholic. Fitzgerald's memorial essay "Ring" (*New Republic*, 76 [11 October 1933], 254–55) expresses regret that Lardner undervalued and partly wasted his genius: "Proud, shy, solemn, shrewd, polite, brave, kind, merciful, honorable—with the affection these qualities aroused he created in addition a certain awe in people. His intentions, his will, once in motion, were formidable factors in dealing with him—he always did every single thing he said he would do. Frequently he was the melancholy Jaques, and sad company indeed, but under any conditions a noble dignity flowed from him, so that time in his presence always seemed well spent."

12.5–6   **Antheil** George Antheil (1900–1959), American composer of experimental works including the *Ballet Mécanique* (1926).

12.6–8   **Joyce . . . 'Ulysses'** Fitzgerald met James Joyce (1882–1941), the Irish expatriate writer whose novel *Ulysses* (1922) developed the stream-of-consciousness technique, in Paris in June 1928.

13.25   **robin-breasted sailing boat** Boat having wind-filled red sails.

14.12   **Dick Diver** It is impossible to determine whether Fitzgerald was aware that these words have the slang meaning of one who performs fellatio. His editors' tolerance for the name is evidence of their innocence in this regard.

Book I, Chapter 3

15.6   **table d'hôte** A set meal; not selected from the menu.

16.11–12 **'Daddy's Girl'** The fictional movie *Daddy's Girl* is based on the tearjerker *Stella Dallas* (United Artists, 1925), in which Lois Moran had her first important role. *Stella Dallas* was made from Olive Higgins Prouty's novel about a lower-class woman who gives up her daughter

Lois Moran—the model for Rosemary Hoyt—with Ronald Colman as her father in *Stella Dallas*.

Ring W. Lardner, on whom Fitzgerald based Abe North.

to her husband's socially prominent family. The title *Daddy's Girl* has connections with the incest theme in *Tender Is the Night*.

16.15 **Earl Brady** Irish-American movie director Rex Ingram (1893–1950), who had a studio at La Turbie on the Riviera during the Twenties, was the model for Brady and for Lew Kelly, the movie-director protagonist of the second version of the novel (see Introduction).

16.26–29 **No stimuli . . . clamor of Empire** Fitzgerald gently mocks American travelers by equating nationalistic fervor with the reassurance of overheard fragments of American speech.

17.11–12 **The Pont du Gard at Arles [the Pont du Gard at Nîmes** Part of a Roman aqueduct built c. 19 B.C. that brought water into Nîmes; Fitzgerald mistakenly placed it at Arles. Both Arles and Nîmes are in southern France.

17.12 **amphitheatre at Orange** Built by the Romans in the second century A.D., it held 10,000 spectators; Orange is in southern France.

17.13 **Chamonix** Winter resort in the French Alps.

17.21 **cabbies. . . hacks** Taxicab drivers . . . vehicles for hire.

17.22 **Casino** A cabaret or nightclub, not a gambling house (see 353.11).

17.24–25 **a "season"** A time of the year when fashionable people assemble.

18.9 **Café des Alliés [Café des Allées** The Allées de la Liberté is a tree-shaded area along the Boulevard de la Croisette in Cannes. Fitzgerald confused the words *Alliés* (Allies) and *Allées* (tree-lined avenues).

18.9 **the Croisette** Boulevard de la Croisette, the main boulevard along the Mediterranean in Cannes.

18.11–12 **the Nice Carnival Song** Each year the city of Nice commissioned a carnival song. The "Chanson Officielle du Carnaval de Nice 1925" was "Nice en Folie" by A. Pyns and D. J. Mari.

Director Rex Ingram, the source for Earl Brady.

Rex Ingram's studio at La Turbie.

18.12–13 **"Le Temps"** National evening newspaper published in Paris.

18.13 **"The Saturday Evening Post"** Popular American weekly magazine; Fitzgerald, who contributed many short stories to this magazine during the 1920s and 1930s, was known as a *Saturday Evening Post* author.

18.14 **citronnade** Lemonade (French).

18.24 **vaudeville** A variety show consisting of acts with different performers.

18.30 **a Russian czar of the period of Ivan the Terrible** Ivan the Terrible was ruler of Russia from 1533 to 1584. Impoverished refugees from the 1917 Russian revolution worked as chauffeurs in France, and Fitzgerald is indicating that the chauffeur is a former aristocrat.

18.32 **Monte-Carlo** An opulent gambling resort in Monaco, a one-half-square-mile Riviera principality.

19.1 **Buddhas' eyes** The jewels from statues of Buddha.

19.2 **Baltic** The extravagant nobility of the pre-revolution Russian Empire took possession of the French Riviera as though it were their own northern European coastline on the Baltic Sea.

The Allées de la Liberté, Cannes.

19.5–9   **Ten years ago. . . . never coming back any more.**
Wealthy Russians visited the Riviera in winter and left
when the social season ended in April; the postpone-
ment of their annual return was caused by the outbreak
of World War I and made permanent by the Russian
Revolution.

19.6   **Orthodox church** The members of the Russian colony
belonged to the Orthodox Eastern Church of the countries that made up the Eastern Roman Empire and of
Russia and other countries evangelized from it. The
doors of the church were locked after its Russian Orthodox communicants departed from the Riviera.

19.11–12 **agates and cornelians** Types of glass marbles.

19.12   **green as green milk** An opalescent green. The term
green milk refers to milk that tastes bitter or grassy, but
that application is inappropriate here.

19.12–13 **blue as laundry water** Laundry water to which indigo
or other blueing has been added to whiten clothes.

19.15   **estaminets** Small cafés (French).

19.16   **Corniche d'Or** The Riviera coastal road between St.
Raphaël and Cannes.

19.27   **plage** Beach (French).

Book I, Chapter 4

21.5   **chicken Maryland** Chicken pieces that have been coated
with paprika-flavored flour, dipped in beaten egg, and
coated with bread crumbs before being fried. Nicole is
translating the recipe for her French cook. The second
reference to this recipe at 212.25 serves to link the
flashback in Book II to present time, June 1925.

21.11–12 **Rodinesque** Auguste Rodin (1840–1917), French
sculptor whose realistic statues departed from the classical ideal.

21.15   **cupid's bow** Magazine illustrations in the Twenties featured women with lips that resembled the curvature of
the bow and arrow used by Cupid in classic art. The

mouth is small and feminine with an upper lip narrow except for an exaggerated double curve at the center.

21.28 **grippe** Influenza.

22.7 **a garçon and a chasseur** A waiter and a porter (French).

22.10 **Tarmes** A fictional place, probably based on the village of Eze east of Antibes in the hills above the Mediterranean (see Explanatory Notes, 36.12).

22.13 **Deauville** Fashionable French resort on the English Channel.

22.18 **The New York Herald [the "Paris Herald"** The European Edition of the *New York Herald* was referred to as the *Paris Herald*. After 1924, it was owned by the *New York Herald Tribune*. The *Paris Herald* was the most successful of the three American-owned English-language newspapers published in Paris during the Twenties; the others were the Paris edition of the *Chicago Tribune* and the *Paris Times*. The 1925 circulation of the *Paris Herald* was 15,000.

Eze, the source for Tarmes.

22.21–25 **Mr. Pandely Vlasco . . . Geneveva de Momus** These names recall the guest list in *The Great Gatsby*.

23.14 **talking about Morocco** Morocco is the territory in North Africa between the Mediterranean Sea and the Atlantic Ocean, at that time divided into French and Spanish protectorates (see Explanatory Notes, 45.20).

24.9–10 **Yale prom** Formal dance at Yale University; the Junior Prom (275.16) was sponsored by the junior (third-year) class.

24.30 **Signor Campion** Campion's first name is Luis. If he is Spanish, the correct form is *Señor*, but Fitzgerald may have intended to ridicule Campion by using the Italian form *Signor*.

25.3 **the 'Book of Etiquette'** The principal guides to manners at the time were Lillian Eichler's *Book of Etiquette* (1921) and Emily Post's *Etiquette* (1922). Diver's remark ridicules Campion and Dumphry, whether or not they are actually reading an etiquette guide.

25.5 **planning to mix wit de quality** Planning to mix with the quality; i.e., to associate with the upper classes. North is ridiculing Dumphry and Campion by using lower-class pronunciation.

25.9 **Mr. and Mrs. Neverquiver** Mary North is making fun of the McKiscos and their name.

26.13 **gourmandise** Luxurious eating and drinking.

26.27 **pansy** Derogatory term for a homosexual man.

Book I, Chapter 5

28.3 **La Turbie** A village in the hills above Monaco (see Explanatory Notes, 16.15).

28.3 **old Gaumont lot** Studio formerly operated by the French Gaumont motion-picture company.

28.10 **dwarfed [dwarf** A dwarf pine is one that is much smaller than normal size.

29.14 **flats** Painted backdrops.

29.16   **brilliant pinks** White clothing was too reflective for black-and-white movie photography.

29.27   **That dress is fifteen pounds.** The dress weighs fifteen pounds and is wearing out the actress's stockings.

30.6   **cockney accent** Speech pattern of lower-class Londoners in the East End.

30.11   **the coast** California.

30.12–21 **see if you were signed . . . First National . . . Famous** The contract Rosemary signed (*Tender*, 30.13) after the release of *Daddy's Girl* was evidently for one picture, and she is again at liberty. Now (*Tender*, 30.19–21) she says that she is considering two offers. First National was a Hollywood studio that operated between 1917 and 1929. Famous Players–Lasky was formed in 1916; distributing through Paramount, it subsequently took the name Paramount Pictures.

31.3   **Connie Talmadge** Constance Talmadge (1900–1973), silent-screen comedienne.

31.20–21 **espadrilles** Canvas shoes with rope soles.

Book I, Chapter 6

33.5–6   **her hair was brighter than she** This description is echoed at 89.4–7.

33.4   **twenty-four [twenty-five** Nicole was born in mid-1900 (see Chronology.)

33.11   **Sienna** Commune in Tuscany, Italy. Also spelled "Siena."

33.18   **black and brown tulips** "Queen of the Night" is the darkest shade in tulips, a deep maroon that looks black in sunlight.

33.20   **scherzo of color** *Scherzo* is a term for a lively instrumental composition; the combining of a musical term with color is an example of Fitzgerald's use of synesthesia (the evocation of one sense in terms of another).

34.12–16 **The villa . . . garden.** A villa constructed from several houses was the Eze residence of composer Samuel Barlow (1892–1982), whose one-act opera *Mon Ami Pierrot* was the first by an American composer to be performed at the Paris Opéra-Comique (1935). The connection between Fitzgerald and Barlow is unknown (see Explanatory Notes, 36.12).

35.7 **cabinet de toilette** The bathroom (French).

35.24–25 **compromises of how many years** This phrase is repeated at 69.6.

36.7 **To resume Rosemary's point of view. . . .** Fitzgerald's signal that much of the opening section of the novel is presented through Rosemary's eyes.

36.12 **Villa Diana** Diana was the Roman goddess of the hunt and of the moon; as a huntress she accidentally killed the hunter Orion. Diana is identified with Artemis, the Greek goddess of chastity and of birth.

 The description of the Divers' villa combines the ambiance of the Murphys' "Villa America" at Cap d'Antibes with the construction of Samuel Barlow's at Eze (see Explanatory Notes, 34.12–16).

36.22–23 **Powdery Mildew or Fly Speck or Late Blight** These are actual plant diseases, but Dick Diver is joking.

The Murphys' "Villa America," Cap d'Antibes.

37.9 **'Mon Ami Pierrot'** "Au Clair de la Lune," French children's song composed by Jean-Baptiste (Giovanni Battista) Lully (1632–1689):

> In the moonlight
> My friend Pierrot
> Lend me your pen
> To write a word
> My candle is out
> The fire is out
> Open the door
> For the love of God.

39.27 **hôtel-pension** A hotel where meals are included in the rate; a boardinghouse.

39.32–33 **In the movies but not at all At them** When Alfred Dashiell, the managing editor of *Scribner's Magazine*, changed this phrase to "not of them" in the serial galleys (27 October 1933), Fitzgerald instructed him to restore "at": "There is pith in that and is exactly what I meant to say. On the whole you will find me very accurate and I much prefer that you query on the proof rather than make changes—except in the case of an obvious misspelling outside the dialogue . . ." (1 November 1933; PUL). The words *in* and *at* are lowercase in the serial.

40.11– *the seating arrangement* Unless there has been an un-
43.33 specified swapping of places among the guests in the hour and one-half at the table, the diners' seating arrangement described in the novel is impossible. On p. 40 Rosemary is between Campion and Brady; but on p. 43, Mary North is in this place, and Rosemary's position is not noted (see Peter Daughty, "The Seating Arrangement in *Tender Is The Night*," *Fitzgerald/Hemingway Annual 1979*, pp. 159–161).

Book I, Chapter 7

41.14 **musical saw** A carpenter's saw played as a musical instrument with a bow.

42.21 **Van Buren Denby** A fictional character.

43.4   **Veuve Clicquot** An expensive brand of champagne; Mrs. Abrams's consumption of wine has reddened her complexion.

43.9   **arriviste** An upstart; one who has achieved prominence or success without the proper background (French).

44.6   **Mrs. Burnett's vicious tracts** Frances Hodgson Burnett (1849–1924), Anglo-American writer of children's books, notably *Little Lord Fauntleroy* (1886), *A Little Princess* (1905), and *The Secret Garden* (1911). Fitzgerald detested the sentimentality of these works.

45.20   **the Riff** The Riff—or Rif—Mountains in northern Morocco. In 1921, the Emir Abdelkrim (Muhammad b. Abd al-Karim) led a Berber rebellion against the Spanish army and later attacked the French; he surrendered in 1926.

46.15   **"Harvard manner"** Snobbish or condescending behavior affected by students at Harvard University in Cambridge, Massachusetts.

Book I, Chapter 8

48.18   **through others blown** See epigraph.

48.20   **Iles de Lérins** Two Mediterranean islands off Cannes.

48.21   **Fourth-of-July balloon** Balloons were released as part of the celebration of the anniversary of the signing of the American Declaration of Independence on 4 July 1776.

50.17   **Isotta** Isotta Fraschini, Italian luxury car.

Book I, Chapter 9

52.9   **Aix-les-Bains** Health resort in southern France.

54.3   ***"Will you kaindlay stup tucking!"*** "Will you kindly stop talking!" Fitzgerald is transcribing upper-class English speech.

55.9   ***"Rilly, this must stup immejetely."*** "Really, this must stop immediately" (see 54.3).

55.18–19 **plagued by the nightingale** Although these are the only appearances of the word *nightingale* in the book, they connect with the Keats ode that provides the title. In Greek mythology Philomela was ravished by Tereus, the husband of her sister, Procne. Tereus cut out Philomela's tongue to prevent her from revealing the rape, but she communicated the information, by means of a tapestry, to Procne. The sisters murdered Tereus's son Itys and fed him to Tereus. The gods then changed Philomela into a swallow and Procne into a nightingale. In Roman mythology Philomela becomes a nightingale and Procne a swallow.

   In folklore, mythology, and fable the nightingale is associated with grief or unrequited love. The nightingale's song was believed to stimulate erotic impulses. The phrase "plagued by the nightingale" appeared in Marianne Moore's poem "Marriage" (1923) and provided the title for Kay Boyle's 1931 novel.

55.19 **sewing-circle** A club for women who do needlework; North is ridiculing Campion's effeminate behavior.

55.32 **coo-coo** A phonetic derivative of cuckoo; crazy.

Book I, Chapter 10

57.6 **code duello** Rules regulating duels.

57.12 **second** Someone representing one of the duellists in arranging the conditions of the duel.

57.17 **bromide** A mild sedative.

58.14–15 **delicate light of electric lamps fading** This phrase appears only in the book text; the meaning seems to be that as the morning dawns, the light in the lamps becomes relatively less bright.

59.32–33 **pot . . . forty-fives** Shoot at each other with .45 calibre pistols.

60.4 **one or the other parties** Correct usage requires "party," but Fitzgerald may have intended to represent the informality of North's speech.

60.10   **a novel of Pushkin's** Abe is actually referring to Mikhail Lermontov's 1840 novel *A Hero of Our Time* (see pp. 165–171 in the translation by Vladimir and Dmitri Nabokov [Garden City, NY: Doubleday, 1958]).

Book I, Chapter 11

61.10   **words** The idiom is "miss it for worlds," but Fitzgerald wrote "words" in MS and retained it in TS. It is possible that he intended to ridicule Campion's agitation by means of this confusion of clichés.

61.13   **no whiskers to hide in** This phrase first appears in the book text. By suggesting that a man who wears a monocle ought to have a beard, Fitzgerald is ridiculing the beardless Campion.

62.15   **Rainy** Fictional character.

62.18   **Odéon** The Théâtre de l'Odéon in Paris, the second state theater for classical and modern drama.

63.3–4   **Juan-les-Pins** Mediterranean town west of Cap d'Antibes.

65.20–23   **"Pardon, Messieurs . . . chez lui."** "Pardon, gentlemen," he panted. "Would you like to pay my fee? Naturally, it is only for medical expenses. Monsieur Barban has only a thousand-franc note and the other gentleman has left his wallet at home" (French).

65.25   **"Combien?"** "How much?" (French)

Book I, Chapter 12

67.1   **Voisin** Elegant restaurant at the corner of the Rue St. Honoré and the Rue Cambon in Paris.

68.8   **West Point** The United States Military Academy at West Point in the state of New York.

68.8–9   **that year during which no cadet can resign** Incorrect; the records of the United States Military Academy document many first-year cadet resignations.

68.25   **Corps des Pages** Young men who served at the royal court; restricted to members of the most aristocratic families in imperial Russia. After the 1917 revolution it was transplanted to Paris as an émigré social group. There were parties for les Pages Russes on 6–7 May 1925 at the Paris house of the Comtesse de Béhague.

68.27 **Mayfair party** Hollywood balls sponsored by the Mayfair Club, a movie-industry society group.

69.1 **coup de grâce** A shot or deathblow administered to a mortally wounded person (French).

69.6 **compromises of how many years** See Explanatory Notes, 35.24–25.

69.19 **Lippe-Weissenfeld** Line of German counts founded in the seventeenth century.

69.21 **President Tyler** John Tyler (1790–1862), tenth president of the United States.

70.5 **Franco-American Films** A fictional company (see Explanatory Notes, 118.28).

70.8 **Rue des Saintes Anges [Rue de Saint-Ange** This street is apparently fictional. It is spelled differently in each of three appearances in the first printing of the novel: "Rue des Saintes Anges" (70.8); "Rue des Saintes-Anges" (120.14); "Due de Saints Anges" (399.31). A correct spelling would be "Rue de Saint-Ange." The impasse (dead-end) Saint-Ange and the passage Saint-Ange are in the seventeenth arrondissement; Rue de Saintonge is near the Place de la Republique in the third arrondissement (see Explanatory Notes, 136.2–3).

At 118.28–29 Diver tells the cabdriver to take him to "the Films Par Excellence Studio—it's on a little street in Passy. Go to the Muette." This fictional studio was apparently meant to be the same as Franco-American Films because Films Par Excellence is located on the "Rue des Saintes-Anges" (120.14); but Fitzgerald wrote "Franco-American Films" and "Films Par Excellence" in MS and retained the readings in subsequent drafts. The Porte de la Muette is one of the main entrances to the Bois de Boulogne; the Passy quarter is in the sixteenth arrondissement. The Rue Michel-Ange is a principal street several blocks from the Muette.

70.9   **vestiaire** Cloakroom (French).

71.26   **chamois leather** Soft leather made from the skin of chamois, a small mountain antelope.

71.27   **Hermès** Paris shop on the Rue du Faubourg-Saint-Honoré that specializes in luxury goods. Fitzgerald's concern for details is revealed in the first TS, which reads, "jackets of Kingfisher blue and autumnal red from name"; he crossed out "name" and inserted "Hermes."

71.33   **chicle** Gum from the sapodilla, a tropical evergreen tree; chicle is the principal ingredient in chewing gum.

72.3   **Five-and-Tens** Stores in which the merchandise was priced at five cents or ten cents; Woolworth's was the largest chain of these variety stores.

72.21   **dance card** At formal dances women carried small printed cards on which men reserved certain dances.

Book I, Chapter 13

74.1–
77.13   ***the excursion to the Somme*** Fitzgerald's *Ledger* notes a June 1926 trip to "Somme." The total of casualties in the Somme battles from July to November 1916 was 419,000 British dead, 194,451 French dead, and 650,000 German dead.

74.2   **duckboard** A wooden walkway placed over a wet or muddy surface.

74.5   **Beaumont Hamel** Site of a battle during the first day of the Somme offensive, 1 July 1916, where the Newfoundlanders suffered more than 90 percent casualties in half an hour. The memorial to the Newfoundland missing lists 8,000 names.

74.6   **Thiepval** Site of a German fortress on the Somme River, taken by the 51st Highland Division in September 1916. The Memorial to the Missing at Thiepval bears the names of 73,412 men who died in 1916–1917 and have no known grave.

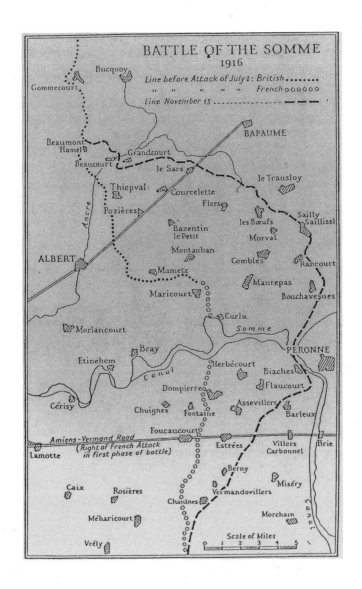

BATTLE OF THE SOMME
1916

Line before Attack of July 1: British ....
"   "   "   "   French ○○○○○○
Line November 15 ------------

75.3   **only just quit over in Turkey** The Turks had driven the Greeks out of Anatolia in 1922.

75.4   **in Morocco** Reference to the Riff (see Explanatory Notes, 45.20).

75.5   **Western Front** There were three fronts or lines of battle in Europe during World War I: the Eastern, or Russian, Front; the Western Front in France and Belgium; and the Italian Front.

75.7   **First Marne** Battle at the Marne River east of Paris where the German offensive was halted in September 1914.

75.13–14 **Crown Prince** Prince Wilhelm (1882–1951), eldest son of Kaiser Wilhelm II and heir to the German throne.

75.14   **Valence** City in southeast France on the Rhône.

75.15   **Unter den Linden** A principal boulevard in Berlin.

75.15   **mairie** Town hall (French).

75.16   **the Derby** The horse race at Epsom, England.

75.17   **General Grant . . . Petersburg** Ulysses S. Grant (1822–1885), commander of the Union armies during the Civil War and eighteenth president of the United States. He employed trenches at Petersburg, Virginia, in 1864–1865.

        Historian William Emerson states that it is incorrect to say that Grant invented trench warfare. Petersburg was a siege, and entrenchment had been an integral part of siege warfare for centuries. Trench warfare was introduced by Robert E. Lee's engineers in three campaigns previous to the Petersburg siege—the Wilderness battle, Spottsylvania Court House, and Cold Harbor.

75.20   **Lewis Carroll** Pen name of Charles Dodgson (1832–1898), English author of *Alice's Adventures in Wonderland* (1865).

75.20   **Jules Verne** French author (1828–1905) of adventure and science-fiction novels, two being *20,000 Leagues*

Ten years later (1928)

a lot of Duds, all highly explosive on the 'Chemin des Dames

Fitzgerald's annotated photo of himself during his July 1928 trip to the battlefields. The Chemin des Dames is a road from Malmaison to Craonne. The Germans occupied the area in fall 1914; it was taken by the French in November 1917, re-taken by the Germans in spring 1918, and re-taken by the French in September 1918 (*The Romantic Egoists*).

Under the Sea (1870) and *Around the World in 80 Days* (1873).

75.21   **'Undine'** Romance published in 1811 by German writer Friedrich Heinrich Karl de la Motte-Fouqué (1777–1843). The title character is a water sprite who marries a mortal.

75.22   **marraines** Godmothers (French).

75.23   **Württemberg** State, formerly a kingdom, in southwestern Germany.

75.23   **Westphalia** Province of northwestern Germany.

75.26   **D. H. Lawrence** English novelist (1885–1930) praised and vilified for his treatment of sexual drives; he was prosecuted for obscenity in connection with *Lady Chatterley's Lover* (1928).

76.4   **Ohio love** North is from Ohio; he is parodying Diver's comments about the "love battle."

76.11   **silver cord . . . golden bowl** *Ecclesiastes* 12: 6–7: "Or ever the silver cord be loosed, or the golden bowl be broken. . . . Then shall the dust return to the earth as it was: and the spirits shall return unto God who gave it."

76.15   **Newfoundland** See Explanatory Notes, 74.5.

76.15   *Beaumont Hamel inscription*

EPITAPH
BY
JOHN OXENHAM
AT
ENTRANCE TO
NEWFOUNDLAND MEMORIAL PARK
BEAUMONT HAMEL

Tread softly here! Go reverently and slow!
Yea, let your soul go down upon its knees,
And with bowed head, and heart abased, strive hard
To grasp the future gain in this sore loss!
For not one foot of this dank sod but drank
Its surfeit of the blood of gallant men,
Who, for their faith, their hope,—for Life and Liberty,
Here made the sacrifice—here gave their lives,

The Newfoundland Memorial at Beaumont Hamel.

The Thiepaval Memorial to the Missing bears the names of 73,412 British soldiers who died on the Somme in 1916-1917 and have no known graves.

And gave right willingly—for you and me.
From this vast altar-pile the souls of men
Sped up to God in countless multitudes;
On this grim cratered ridge they gave their all,
And, giving, won
The peace of Heaven and Immortality.
Our hearts go out to them in boundless gratitude;
If ours—then God's: for His vast charity
All sees, all knows, all comprehends—save bounds.
He has repaid their sacrifice:—and we——?
God help us if we fail to pay our debt
In fullest full and all unstintingly!

76.23   **Amiens** City on the Somme River, seventy-two miles north of Paris.

76.26   **six years** Six years and seven months have elapsed since World War I ended in November 1918.

77.1   **her brother's grave** The battle of the Somme was fought July–November 1916; but Americans fought on the side of the Allies before the United States entered the war in April 1917.

77.3–4   **wrong number** The registration number for locating her brother's grave.

77.22   **Gare du Nord** Railroad station in Paris for trains running to the north.

77.23   **Waterloo Station** London railroad station.

77.30   **Voilàs** *Voilà*: a frequently used French word meaning "there is" or "there are" or "there it is."

78.1–2   **"Yes, We Have No Bananas"** 1922 novelty song; music and lyrics by Frank Silver and Irving Cohn.

78.6–7   **Württembergers, Prussian Guards, Chasseurs Alpins** German and French army units.

78.7   **Manchester mill hands** Factory workers in Manchester, England.

78.8   **Old Etonians** Former students at Eton, one of the most prestigious English public (i.e., private) schools.

78.10   **mortadella** Spiced pork sausage.

78.10   **bel paese** Semi-soft Italian cheese also produced in other countries.

78.11   **Beaujolais** Light red wine from grapes grown in the Beaujolais district in central France.

Book I, Chapter 14

79.2–3   **Decorative Arts Exposition** L'Exposition Internationale des Arts Décoratifs et Industriels Modernes (the International Exhibition of Decorative and Industrial Arts) opened in Paris 18 July 1925. Known as the Art Deco Exhibition, it was intended to revive architecture and the decorative arts.

79.4   **Hôtel Roi George** No Paris hotel with this name has been identified; Fitzgerald probably based it on the Hôtel George V at 31 Avenue George-V. Since the manager of the Roi George conceals evidence in a murder, it was necessary for Fitzgerald to provide an invented hotel name.

79.13   **Suresnes** Western suburb of Paris.

80.12   **poured on the boat** Mary North is concerned that Abe will be drunk when he boards the ship for America.

81.25–26 **lymphatic glands** Masses of lymphoid tissue that secrete lymph, a fluid containing white blood cells. North is joking.

81.30   **a new score on Broadway** A new musical production at a Broadway theatre in Manhattan.

Book I, Chapter 15

86.6–7   **go into Mexico** Rosemary is conveying her willingness to give birth in Mexico or to have an abortion there should she become pregnant by Dick.

Book I, Chapter 16

89.4–7   **She . . . more beautiful than she.** See Explanatory Notes, 33.5–6.

89.9 **Rue des Saints-Pères** This street intersects with the Quai Voltaire on the Left Bank of the Seine.

89.14 **Lake Forest** Moneyed Chicago suburb.

89.23 **apache quarter** Criminal or low-life section of Paris; so called because its denizens were regarded as savages.

89.33– **Luxembourg Gardens** Extensive formal gardens on the
90.1 Left Bank.

90.15 **New Haven** Yale University is in New Haven, Connecticut. Yale men at that time referred to the university in this indirect way.

90.23 **"I have not any benenas."** See Explanatory Notes, 78.1–2.

90.32 **Tanagra** Name of a city in ancient Greece; also term identifying terra-cotta figurines of the fifth to third centuries B.C. found in the area.

91.6–8 **'itty-bitty bravekins . . . tweet?** Baby talk. Fitzgerald is ridiculing the sentimental material of Rosemary's movie.

91.14 **Duncan Phyfe** (1788–1854); American cabinet maker and furniture designer whose work was characterized by lightness and grace.

92.32 **Hartford** Connecticut city forty-two miles from New Haven.

93.6 **Lutétia** Hotel on the Left Bank.

Book I, Chapter 17

94.1–2 **Cardinal de Retz . . . Rue Monsieur** François Paul de Gondi, Cardinal de Retz (1613–1679). The Rue Monsieur—which is in the seventh arrondissement near the Boulevard des Invalides—was not opened until 1779, a century after the death of the cardinal. Fitzgerald may have meant the Rue Monsieur-le-Prince, near the Luxembourg Gardens.

Cole and Linda Porter's house at 13 Rue Monsieur featured walls covered with zebra skins and platinum

The Eiffel Tower illuminated for the 1925 Art Deco exposition.

paper; see Fitzgerald's story "The Swimmers": "Home was a fine high-ceiling apartment hewn from the palace of a Renaissance cardinal in the Rue Monsieur. . . ."

94.15 **Louisa M. Alcott** Louisa May Alcott (1832–1888), American author of *Little Women* (1868).

94.15 **Madame de Ségur** Sophie Rostopchines, Comtesse de Ségur (1799–1874), wrote *Les Mémoires d'un âne* (1860) and other books for children.

95.15 **sponges** Character types who absorb money and status through association with persons of wealth or superior social position.

95.20 **Frankenstein** Title character of a novel published by Mary Shelley in 1818. Dr. Frankenstein assembled a man who became a monster; by extension the name has been applied to anything alarmingly unnatural—in this case, the apartment and its occupants.

95.22–23 **living all in the upper registers of her throat** Speaking in a strained or unnatural manner.

95.24 **wild beating of wings** The room was filled with nervous or insecure people trying to maintain their composure. Fitzgerald compares the women to perched birds who maintain their balance by flapping their wings.

95.28 **slick [spic** *Spic* is a pejorative term for a Hispanic person (see Emendations).

96.17–27 **It was . . . the girl.** Rosemary's encounter with the lesbian was salvaged from an episode involving Francis Melarky and Wanda Breasted that Malcolm Cowley included as an appendix in "The Author's Final Version." The Francis/Wanda episode was subsequently published as "The World's Fair" in *Thirteen Great Stories*, ed. Daniel Talbot (New York: Dell, 1956).

97.1 **vis-à-vis** One face-to-face with another person (French).

97.25–26 **Place de la Concorde** Large plaza at one end of the Champs-Élysées.

100.2 **stick** Able-bodied men still carried walking sticks or canes during the Twenties.

Book I, Chapter 18

101.9 **Odyssey** The ten-year-long voyage of Odysseus (Ulysses) is recounted in Homer's *The Odyssey*; by extension the term refers to any complicated or extended itinerary.

101.17 **Shah of Persia** The king of what is now Iran.

101.25 **Teheran** The capital of Persia (Iran).

102.5–6 **Major Hengist and Mr. Horsa** Hengist (d. 488) and Horsa (d. 455) were brothers who led the first Teutonic invasion of Britain. This joke was salvaged from the manuscript of *The Great Gatsby*: "Major Hengest and his friend Mr. Horsa, two saturnine Englishmen."

102.30 **the Ritz** A luxury hotel on the Place Vendome. The Paris Ritz Hotel was opened by César Ritz in 1900.

102.31 **General Pershing** John J. Pershing (1860–1948), commander of the American Expeditionary Force in Europe during World War I.

103.7 **Goldberg cartoon** Rube Goldberg (1883–1970) was a cartoonist who drew plans for elaborate and impractical machines to accomplish ordinary acts.

103.13 **boat train** Train that connected Paris to the ocean-liner piers on the English Channel.

103.32 **Halles** Les Halles, market district in Paris; it was customary to breakfast there after a night on the town.

104.4 **Newark** There are several cities named Newark in the United States, but the reference here is to Newark, New Jersey.

104.5–6 **oil Indian named George T. Horse-Protection** Native Americans on whose land oil had been discovered were referred to as "oil Indians"; they were regarded as reckless spenders.

104.20 **Saint Sulpice** Roman Catholic Church on the Left Bank near the Luxembourg Gardens.

104.28 **Champs-Élysées** The Avenue des Champs-Élysées is the most famous Paris boulevard; it connects the Place de l'Etoile (Arc de Triomphe) with the Place de la Concorde.

Book I, Chapter 19

105.1 **Gare Saint-Lazare** Paris railroad station from which the boat trains to Le Havre and Cherbourg departed.

105.3 **Crystal Palace** Huge glass exhibition hall built in London in 1851; it influenced the use of glass in other public buildings.

105.14 **Jew-uls** Someone named Jules is being called.

105.18 **thousand-franc notes** The rate of exchange fluctuated during the Twenties, but in 1925 it was about 20 francs to the dollar.

106.17 **St. Genevieve's** The Bal de la Montagne Sainte-Geneviève was a Left Bank dance hall on the hill behind the Panthéon.

108.26 **survivant** Formerly obsolete word meaning "surviving." The latest *OED* citation is from 1677; the *OED Supplement* cites *Tender Is the Night*.

109.6–7 **sea-change** Altered by immersion in the sea. Fitzgerald is echoing Ariel's song in Shakespeare's *The Tempest* (I, ii, 398–403):
Full fathom five thy father lies;
      Of his bones are coral made;
Those are pearls that were his eyes;
      Nothing of him that doth fade
But doth suffer a sea-change
Into something rich and strange.

109.17–
110.9 ***shooting in Gare Saint-Lazare*** Maxwell Perkins suggested deleting this scene: "I thought you might conceivably cut out the shooting in the station. The purpose would be only that as soon as people get to Dick Diver their interest in the book, and their perception of its importance increases some thirty to forty percent. People do read a book differently from a serial though. . . . To be considered if at all, only when you come to the book

proof" (15 January 1934, *Dear Scott/Dear Max*, p. 190). Fitzgerald replied that he wanted to retain the scene: "It serves all sorts of subtle purposes and since I have decided that the plan of the book is best as originally conceived, the small paring away would be very little help and I think would do more harm than good" (18 January 1934, *A Life in Letters*, p. 245).

109.18   **Pullman** Railroad sleeping car produced by the Pullman Company in Illinois; the term was used by the French for a luxurious railroad car.

109.23–   **two revolver shots** In March 1927 Countess de Janze
24   (the former Alice Silverthorne of Chicago) shot Raymond Vincent de Trafford and then herself in the Gare du Nord. This event was the probable source for the shooting in *Tender Is the Night,* but Fitzgerald was in America at the time; see James Fox, *White Mischief* (New York: Random House, 1982).

     This is the second of the four shooting incidents that mark sections of the novel: duel (63–64), railroad station (109–110), hail clouds (204), ship's cannon (382).

110.3   **gendarmes** Policemen (French).

110.8   **poste de police** Police station (French).

111.19   **Diaghileff** Serge Diaghileff (1872–1929), Russian ballet impresario who directed the Ballet Russe at Monte-Carlo.

112.13–   **"Tu as vu le revolver? . . . la guerre!"** "Did you see the
16   revolver? It is very small, real pearl—a toy."

     "But sufficiently powerful! . . . Did you see his shirt? There was enough blood to believe we were at war" (French).

Book I, Chapter 20

114.10–   **Grand-Guignol** Paris theatre that presented horror
11   plays and farces.

114.11   **Russian Ballet** See Explanatory Notes, 111.19.

114.30   **wedding garment** *Matthew* 22:11: "And when the king came in to see the guests, he saw there a man which had not on a wedding garment"—that is, Collis

91

Clay lacks the manners appropriate for the Divers' friends.

114.31   **beyed** Clay's southern pronunciation of "bird."

115.15   **nutsey** Slang term meaning "attractive"; in this case, romantically appealing.

116.18   **Bones** Skull and Bones, one of the six senior societies at Yale, each of which elected fifteen men. Election to a senior society was the highest social honor at Yale. The reference to "fraternity politics" in line 11 is inaccurate: senior societies were not fraternities.

117.3   **American Club** Paris club for American residents and visitors.

117.18   **Brentano's** Bookstore on the Avenue de l'Opera that sold English-language and French books.

117.18   **Buffalo** Large lakeport city in upstate New York. Fitzgerald spent part of his boyhood in Buffalo.

117.21   **Fez** City in Morocco.

117.22   **Zürich** City at the northwest end of Lake Zürich; capital of the canton of Zürich.

117.25   **Baltimore** Principal city in Maryland, location of Johns Hopkins University.

117.31   **saw with his heels** The meaning of this phrase is unclear, but the sense seems to be that Dick Diver noticed Casasus in passing, without looking directly at him.

118.14   **pince-nez** Spectacles without temples; held on by the pressure of the nose-piece.

118.16–   **heavyweight champion** Jack Dempsey was the heavy-
17   weight champion of the world from July 1919 until September 1926.

118.28   **Films Par Excellence** Fictional movie company (see Explanatory Notes, 70.8). Fitzgerald also referred to "Films Par Excellence" in *The Beautiful and Damned* and *The Great Gatsby*.

118.29   **Passy** Residential district of Paris on the Right Bank, near the Bois de Boulogne (see Explanatory Notes, 70.8).

118.29 **Muette** The Porte de la Muette, opposite the Bois de Boulogne (see Explanatory Notes, 70.8).

119.7 **Tarkington's adolescents** Booth Tarkington (1869–1946), American novelist who wrote popular books about boys and teenagers; among the best-known of these books were *Penrod* (1914) and *Seventeen* (1916).

119.10 **1000 Chemises [100,000 Chemises** The name of the chain of stores was Au Cent Mille Chemises.

119.13 **Papeterie** Stationery shop (French).

119.13 **Pâtisserie** Pastry shop (French).

119.13 **Solde** Marked down in price (French).

119.13 **Réclame** Advertising (French).

119.14 **"Déjeuner de Soleil"** *Breakfast at Sunrise,* a movie starring Constance Talmadge, was released in October 1927, more than two years after the time of this episode.

119.15–16 **Vêtements Ecclésiastiques** Clerical apparel (French).

119.16 **Déclaration de Décès** Death notices (French).

119.16 **Pompes Funèbres** Funeral parlors (French).

119.27 **sleeve valve** A valve in an internal-combustion engine consisting of a sleeve that fits around the inside circumference of a cylinder and moves with the piston.

119.30 **Ferrara [Canossa** Canossa was the town in northern Italy where German emperor Henry IV submitted to Pope Gregory in 1077 and did public penance.

119.30–31 **sackcloth and ashes** *Daniel* 9:3: "And I set my face unto the Lord God, to seek by prayer and supplication, with fasting, and sackcloth and ashes." Wearing coarse begrimed garments covered with ashes was an act of penance.

Book I, Chapter 21

120.25 **Tad** Cartoonist Thomas Aloysius Dorgan (1877–1929) signed his work "Tad."

121.5 **San Antone** Colloquialism for San Antonio, Texas.

121.7   **Eighty-fourth Division** There was no AEF 84th Division in France; but there was an 84th Infantry Brigade. It is impossible to determine whether this incorrect detail is Fitzgerald's error or the news vendor's invention.

121.28 **Sunny 'Times'** The Sunday edition of *The New York Times.*

122.9   **bought a lead disk** Purchased a metal slug or token in order to use the public phone.

122.11 **Cheyne-Stokes** A breathing pattern characterized by rhythmical waxing and waning of the depth of respiration, associated with cardiac asthma and chronic heart disease; it was identified by physicians John Cheyne (1777–1836) and William Stokes (1804–1878).

122.21 **Bois** The Bois de Boulogne, a large Paris park.

122.30 **Otard** A brand of cognac or grape brandy.

122.30– **Rhum St. James** Dark, aromatic Martinique rum.
31

122.31 **Marie Brizard** Brand of French liqueur.

122.31 **Punch Orangéade** This drink was not bottled; it was a specialty of the Ritz bar—mixed to order from white Martinique rum, orange juice, Curaçao, and soda water.

122.31– **André Fernet Blanco [Fernet-Branca** Italian bitters
32   used as an aperitif and recommended for upset stomachs and hangovers.

122.32 **Cherry Rocher** A brand of cherry brandy.

122.32 **Armagnac** Brandy made from grapes grown in the Bas-Armagnac and Tenareze regions of France.

123.8   **"And two-for-tea"** "Tea for Two," 1924 song; music by Vincent Youmans, lyrics by Irving Caesar.

124.12 **Boucher** Probably a reference to an exhibition of paintings by French rococo artist François Boucher (1703–1770); but possibly a misspelled reference to American painter Louis Bouché (1896–1969), who studied in Paris.

124.26   **Fouquet's** Champs-Élysées restaurant that had an American bar.

Book I, Chapter 22

125.6   **"Entrez!"** "Enter!" (French).

125.8   **sergent de ville** Policeman who walks a regular beat (French).

125.10   **"—he is here?"** The policeman speaks English imperfectly.

125.22   **carte d'identité** Identity card carried by French citizens and foreigners.

126.22   **"Meestair Crawshow, un nègre."** "Mr. Crawshaw, a Negro." Fitzgerald is reproducing the pronunciation of the French hotel employee.

127.1   **Rue de Rivoli** Right-Bank street that parallels the Tuilleries Gardens; location of shops selling luxury items.

127.25–   **Teput Dome** North's mispronunciation. In 1922 Secre-
26   tary of the Interior Albert B. Falls illegally leased U.S. Navy oil reserves at Teapot Dome, Wyoming, for commercial use. This event, a major scandal of the Harding administration, involved figures within and outside of the government.

127.27–   **shandel-scandal . . . kaa** Abe North is drunk; "kaa" is
28   his mispronunciation of "can't".

128.17   **Montmartre** Right-Bank district where there were night-clubs and cabarets. At 139.11 the location of the dispute is given as Montparnasse, which is on the Left Bank.

128.18–   **Negro from Copenhagen** North is referring to Jules Pe-
19   terson, who is identified as from Stockholm at 139.2 and 140.7, 24. It is impossible to determine whether the inconsistency resulted from Fitzgerald's carelessness or was intended to indicate North's alcoholic condition.

128.22   **"Why you back in Paris?"** Diver is speaking abruptly in anger.

128.23   **Évreux** Cathedral city fifty-five miles west-northwest of Paris.

128.24   **St. Sulpice** North is drunk; but he means that he returned to Paris in order to compare the architecture of the Évreux cathedral with the church of St. Sulpice.

128.26   **baroque** Seventeenth-century art style characterized by elaborate ornamentation in architecture.

128.26   **St. Germain** The church of St. Germain-des-Prés on the Left Bank.

129.23–   **play close to the line** To live or work under pressure, to
24   take risks. The expression probably derives from sports.

129.28   **Fernand** French cubist painter Fernand Léger (1881–1955).

130.11   **padded waiters** The meaning is that the waiters work noiselessly.

130.27   **gold-star muzzers** The Gold Star Mothers were American women whose sons had died in World War I.

131.4   **Mosby** John Singleton Mosby (1833–1916), leader of Confederate Partisan Rangers during the American Civil War.

Book I, Chapter 23

132.1   **Ritz bar** In the Paris Ritz Hotel, an expensive bar for male patrons.

132.10   **concessionnaire** Paul rents the bar concession from the hotel—that is, he pays for the privilege of operating the bar. The celebrated head barman at the Ritz from 1921 to 1947 was Frank Meier; but he was an employee of the hotel.

132.16   **motor** Automobile.

132.17   **Boulevard des Capucines** This street is three blocks from the Ritz. Paul regards it as improper to be seen arriving at work in an expensive car.

132.21   **"Why din you?"** "Why didn't you?" Paul speaks English with a French accent.

The Ritz Bar, Paris (Agence France-Presse).

132.23   **'Liberty'** American weekly mass-circulation magazine; in 1927 *Liberty* made an offer for rights to Fitzgerald's novel-in-progress.

133.4   **'France'** Vessel in the French Line (CGT); not the *Ile de France*, which made its maiden voyage in 1927.

133.10   **Cherbourg** The British-owned Cunard Line docked at Cherbourg. The French Line docked at Le Havre. North had presumably booked passage on a Cunard vessel because his luggage went to Cherbourg.

133.22   **bag from bag** Loose-fitting trousers with wide legs worn by collegians were known as bags.

133.33   **stingers** Cocktails combining brandy and crème de menthe.

133.33–   **martinis** Cocktails combining gin with a smaller quan-
134.1   tity of dry vermouth.

134.4   **". . . vera-much."** ". . . very much."

134.10   **Briglith** A nonsense word. Possibly North's alcoholic rendering of "brillig." In Lewis Carroll's *Through the Looking Glass:* Humpty Dumpty explains that "brillig" means four o'clock in the afternoon.

134.25   **Peterson** An African American named W. S. Gilbert manufactured shoe polish in Stockholm before World War I; see John Hanson Mitchell, *Living at the End of Time* (Boston: Houghton Mifflin, 1990), pp. 157–160. No connection has been found between Gilbert and Fitzgerald.

135.3   **"I can't allow it."** France did not practice strict segregation, but blacks were not served in establishments catering to wealthy tourists.

135.5   **Rue Cambon** Street that connects the Rue de Rivoli with the Boulevard de la Madeleine.

Book I, Chapter 24

136.2–3   **seventh arrondissement** Paris is divided into twenty arrondissements, or wards; the seventh arrondissement,

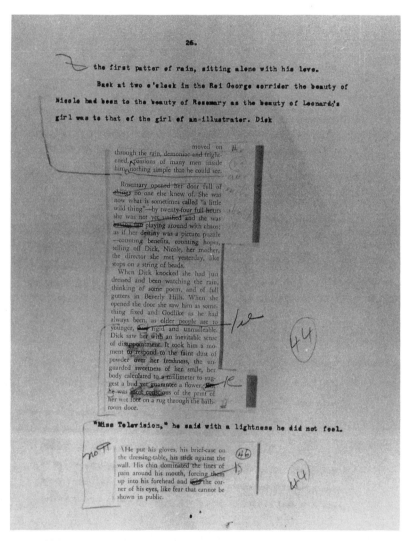

the first patter of rain, sitting alone with his love.

Back at two o'clock in the Rei George corridor the beauty of Nicole had been to the beauty of Rosemary as the beauty of Leonardo's girl was to that of the girl of an illustrater. Dick

moved on JL through the rain, demoniac and frightened, passions of many men inside him, nothing simple that he could see.

Rosemary opened her door full of things no one else knew of. She was now what is sometimes called "a little wild thing"—by twenty-four full hours she was not yet unified and she was playing around with chaos; as if her destiny was a picture puzzle —counting benefits, counting hopes, telling off Dick, Nicole, her mother, the director she met yesterday, like stops on a string of beads.

When Dick knocked she had just dressed and been watching the rain, thinking of some poem, and of full gutters in Beverly Hills. When she opened the door she saw him as something fixed and Godlike as he had always been, as older people are to younger, rigid and unmalleable. Dick saw her with an inevitable sense of disappointment. It took him a moment to respond to the faint dust of powder over her freshness, the unguarded sweetness of her smile, her body calculated to a millimeter to suggest a bud yet guarantee a flower. he was most conscious of the print of her wet foot on a rug through the bathroom door.

"Miss Television," he said with a lightness he did not feel.

He put his gloves, his brief-case on the dressing-table, his stick against the wall. His chin dominated the lines of pain around his mouth, forcing them up into his forehead and the corner of his eyes, like fear that cannot be shown in public.

Fitzgerald inserted the reference to television in the revised galleys for the second serial installment (Princeton University Library).

where government buildings and schools are located, is on the Left Bank.

136.10 **Crillon** Luxury hotel on the Right Bank.

136.11 **two fingers** An inch and a half of straight gin in a bar glass.

136.14– **dark outside . . . four-o'clock night . . . falling** The
16 time of the action is July; the early darkness indicates the impending rainstorm.

137.6 **Leonardo's girl** A portrait by Leonardo da Vinci (1452–1519), probably the Mona Lisa.

137.20 **Beverly Hills** Residential area in Los Angeles favored by people in the motion-picture industry.

137.28 **Television** The year is 1925; this reference is not anachronistic, although Fitzgerald inserted the words in the 1934 serial galleys. Articles about television appeared in the *New York Times* during 1924 and 1925. The first license for a television station (W2XBS) was issued to RCA in 1928.

138.6–7 **her face getting big as it came up to him** Repeated at 204.9–10.

139.8–9 **heels the Republican Party in the border states** Ambitious African Americans joined the Republican Party in the states between the deep South and the North— e.g., Maryland. At that time the Democratic Party depended upon the Southern vote (the Solid South), where African Americans were disenfranchised.

139.10– **It appeared . . . scene.** According to Morley Cal-
25 laghan's *That Summer in Paris* (New York: Coward-McCann, 1963), the Abe North/Freeman/Peterson material was based on Fitzgerald's experience: "Last night he had been in a nightclub, he said. His wallet had been stolen. He had accused a Negro, the wrong Negro, and the police had come; there had been a humiliating scene, then long hours of police interrogation as he tried to undo his false accusation yet prove his wallet had actually been stolen. The accused man and his friends had turned ugly" (p. 191).

139.11 **Montparnasse** The bohemian district of Paris on the Left Bank of the Seine (see Explanatory Notes, 128.17).

139.29 **Latin Quarter** The university district of Paris on the Left Bank, so called because in former times the students spoke Latin. It is separated from Montparnasse by the Luxembourg Gardens.

140.3 **friendly Indian** Fitzgerald is describing Peterson's situation in terms of the plot of a Western story or movie (See Explanatory Notes, 145.25).

140.11 **Versailles** Suburb twelve miles southwest of Paris; location of the palace of Louis XIV.

141.7 **the Chambord** Luxury hotel on the Avenue des Champs-Élysées.

141.8 **Majestic** Luxury hotel on the Avenue Kléber near the Etoile.

141.26 **Senegalese** Senegal was a French colony in Africa; North's reference is intended as humor.

142.1 **anagrams** A game in which words are built by adding to and transposing the letters of other words.

142.13 **George the Third** King of England (1738–1820) at the time of the American Revolution. North is facetiously alluding to Abraham Lincoln's response to reports of Ulysses S. Grant's drinking; Lincoln proposed sending Grant's brand of whiskey to the other Union generals. other Union generals.

Book I, Chapter 25

145.7 **couverture** Bedspread (French).

145.25 **hostile Indian** Fitzgerald is emphasizing the melodrama of North's predicament by continuing the cowboys-and-Indians metaphor (see Explanatory Notes, 140.3).

145.30 **the Arbuckle case** In 1921–1922 movie comedian Fatty Arbuckle was tried in connection with a rape-death; although he was found not guilty, his career was destroyed.

146.8 **McBeth** Possibly a reference to the murder of Duncan in Shakespeare's *Macbeth* and Lady Macbeth's attempt to wash her bloody hands. Fitzgerald wrote "M^cready" and "M^{ac}ready" in MS and revised to "McBeth" in the first TS. William C. Macready was performing Macbeth the night of the Astor Place Riot between the admirers of Macready and the admirers of Edwin Forrest in 1849. The hotel manager's name was spelled "MacBeth" at 217.23 of the first printing.

147.27   **All Fools Day** April first, a day when it is customary to play jokes or perpetrate hoaxes.

147.27–   **Zürichsee** Lake Zürich.
28

147.31   **domino** a loose cloak worn with a small mask to a masquerade.

Book II, Chapter 1

151.2   **twenty-six [twenty-seven** Diver was born in April 1889 (see Chronology).

151.10   **local board** Diver's draft board in America.

151.13   **Gorizia** Scene of World War I battle on the Austrian-Italian front.

151.14   **the Somme and the Aisne** French rivers that were sites of World War I battles in which terrible casualty rates were sustained (see Explanatory Notes, 74.1–77.13).

151.17   **Berne and Geneva** Cities in Switzerland.

152.1–2   **Constance and Neuchâtel** Lake Constance is on the German-Austrian-Swiss border; the Lake of Neuchâtel is the largest lake within Switzerland.

152.9   **sister republic** Switzerland.

152.12–   **Oxford Rhodes Scholar from Connecticut in 1914**
13   Each year thirty-two American college seniors or graduate students are selected to attend Oxford University, normally for two years. A candidate may apply from his home state or from the state of his college. The scholarship was funded by Cecil Rhodes, who made a great fortune in South Africa. Since Oxford did not have a

medical school before 1939, Diver could not have studied medicine as a Rhodes Scholar; but he could have taken pre-clinical courses.

Diver graduated from Yale in 1911, studied medicine at Johns Hopkins for three years, attended Oxford during 1914–1915, and then returned to Johns Hopkins.

152.13 **a final year at Johns Hopkins** The Johns Hopkins School of Medicine in Baltimore, Maryland. Dick Diver received his M.D. in 1916. He could have received training in psychiatry or clinical psychology; the 1915–1916 Johns Hopkins catalogue lists seven courses in the Psychiatry Department.

152.16 **Freud** Sigmund Freud (1856–1939), Austrian physician, founder of psychoanalysis.

152.18– **Damenstiff Strasse [Damenstiftgasse** This street name
19 no longer exists in Vienna; "Damenstiftgasse" means Convent Street.

153.10 **flying rings** Rings at the end of hanging ropes, for acrobatic exercises.

153.11 **Danube** River that flows through Vienna.

153.18 **quarterbacks in New Haven [quarterbacks at New Haven** The quarterbacks who played for Yale; the quarterback is the player in American football who calls the signals and throws passes (see Emendations).

153.31 **Thackeray's "The Rose and the Ring"** *The Rose and the Ring; or, The History of Prince Giglio and Prince Bulbo: A Fireside Pantomime for Great and Small Children* (1855) by William Makepeace Thackeray (1811–1863). The Fairy Blackstick says of Princess Rosalba: "the best thing I can wish her is a *little misfortune.*"

154.1 **locker-room** Place where people—usually athletes—change clothing and leave clothing or equipment in locked cabinets.

154.1–2 **Tap Day** At the end of junior year the Yale senior societies selected members in a public ceremony known as Tap Day because the chosen students were tapped on

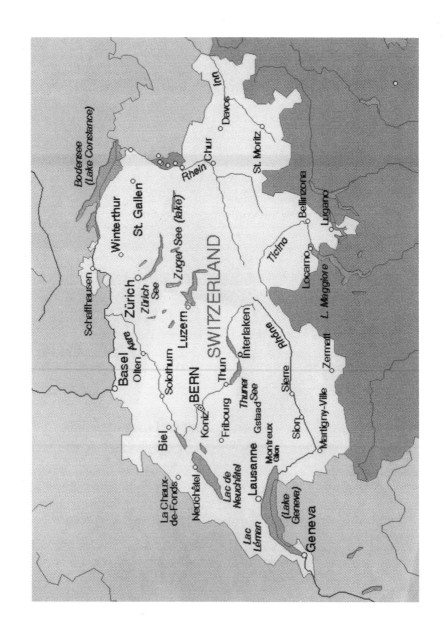

the shoulder; see Bones (Explanatory Notes, 116.18) and Elihu (Explanatory Notes, 154.3).

154.3   **Elihu** One of the Yale senior societies.

154.9   **swallowed my pin** Members of certain Yale senior societies were required always to wear the society pin. It was supposedly held in the mouth while bathing.

154.13   **Goethe** Johann Wolfgang von Goethe (1749–1832), German poet, dramatist, and philosopher.

154.14   **Jung** Carl Gustav Jung (1875–1961), Swiss psychiatrist, founder of the Jungian School of psychiatry.

154.25   **Achilles's heels** Only the heel of the Greek warrior Achilles was vulnerable to injury.

154.26   **centipede** A many-segmented arthropod, each segment having a pair of legs.

154.32   **Bar-sur-Aube** Town in northeastern France.

155.5–6   **Grant . . . Galena** Before the Civil War Ulysses S. Grant, who would become commander of the Union Army and president of the United States, worked in his family's Galena, Illinois, general store; at this point in his life he was regarded as a failure (see 408.9).

Book II, Chapter 2

156.2   **Albishorn** Mountain south of Zurich.

156.13   **Salzburg** City in Austria renowned as the birthplace of Mozart and for its music festivals.

156.16   **cervical [cortex** *Cervical* is an adjective meaning "related to the neck or cervix". The correct word is *cortex*, the outer layer of the cerebrum and cerebellum.

156.19   **gigantic Christ** A copy of *Christus Consolator* by Danish sculptor Bertel Thorwaldsen (1770–1844) is in the entrance hall of Johns Hopkins Hospital, Baltimore, Maryland.

157.2   **pathologist [psychopathologist** Franz Gregorovious is a psychopathologist, a doctor who deals with the causes and nature of mental illness—not a pathologist who examines changes in diseased tissues.

157.3   **Vaudois** Someone from the Swiss canton of Vaud, of which Lausanne is the capital.

157.4   **tram** Trolley, a passenger car that runs on rails by means of electrical power from overhead wires.

157.5   **Cagliostro** Count Alessandro di Cagliostro (1743–1795), Italian con-man.

157.7   **Kraepelin** Emil Kraepelin (1856–1926), German psychiatrist who classified mental diseases under the categories of manic-depressive and dementia praecox.

157.18 **shell-shocks** During World War I it was thought that soldiers developed a condition of nervous collapse as the result of exposure to prolonged artillery barrages.

158.13 **Krenzegg [Kreuzegg** The Kreuzegg is a mountain twenty miles east-southeast of Zurich, between Wald and Wattwil at the east end of the Obersee.

158.26 **transference** A redirection of feelings toward a new person.

159.30–31 **"Daddy-Long-Legs"** Jean Webster's 1912 juvenile novel about orphanage life.

159.31 **"Molly-Make-Believe"** Eleanor Hallowell Abbott's 1910 novel about an epistolary love affair.

160.1   **Armistice** World War I ended on 11 November 1918.

160.8   **Mon Capitaine** My captain (French).

160.10 **Je m'en fiche** I don't care (French).

160.17 **sissies** Effeminate males.

161.17–19 **"plus petite et moins entendue"** "Smaller and less significant" (French). Nicole has apparently seized upon the expression as an offer of reassurance.

161.25 **Michigan Boulevard** A principal thoroughfare in Chicago along Lake Michigan.

162.7   **twin six . . . not if I were a million girls.** The twin six was a twelve-cylinder automobile engine introduced by Packard in 1915. Nicole has free-associated the phrase with a diagnosis of multiple personality.

162.15 **Tout à vous** Always yours (French).

163.27–
28 **"Play in Your Own Backyard"** Possibly a reference to the 1928 popular song "Back in Your Own Back Yard," music and lyrics by Al Jolson, Billy Rose, and Dave Deyer; if so, it is anachronistic.

164.12–
13 **asphodel and edelweiss** a member of the lily family and a white flower that grows in the high alps.

164.29 **"The Switchboard"** Telephone switchboards had apertures into which cylindrical plugs were inserted.

Book II, Chapter 3

166.3 **Lausanne** City in Switzerland on Lake Léman (Lake of Geneva).

166.6 **sixteen [seventeen** Nicole was born in mid-1900 (see Chronology).

166.11 **un homme très chic** A dapper man (French).

166.16 **Göttingen** German university.

167.7 **eleven [fourteen** See *Tender*, 89.10–11: "when I was twelve Mother and Baby and I once spent a winter there" (see Chronology).

168.21 **pretty gone on her at that.** Romantically attracted to Nicole; infatuated.

168.25 **fellow and docent** A fellow, often a graduate student, receives a stipend from a university in return for research or teaching duties. A docent is a university teacher or lecturer, not necessarily on the permanent staff. A fellow or docent is usually a graduate student.

168.32–
169.1 **Armour, Palmer, Field, Crane, Warren, Swift, and McCormick** The Armour and Swift fortunes were made in meatpacking; the Palmer fortune in land; the Field fortune in retail merchandising; the Crane fortune in valves and plumbing fixtures; and the McCormick fortune in farm machinery.

169.13 **submarine blockade** During World War I Germany maintained an Atlantic submarine blockade of Europe.

170.8   **"une folie"** A reckless or extravagant act (French).

170.9   **Vevey** City on Lake Léman between Lausanne and Montreux.

170.12   **Tuileries Guard** The Swiss unit that defended the Tuileries Palace and the French royal family against the Paris mob in August 1792 and was slaughtered almost to a man.

Book II, Chapter 4

172.8–9   **so-called social cures** Patients who are discharged from a sanitarium but who remain emotionally fragile.

174.20–21 **psychologist** Dr. Diver is a psychiatrist (182.14), having completed the medical specialization. People who have made a study of psychology—a category that includes psychiatrists—are psychologists.

174.27   **Grossmünster** Cathedral in Zurich erected between the eleventh and thirteenth centuries.

174.28   **Lavater** Johann Kaspar Lavater (1741–1801), Swiss theologian, poet, and physiognomist.

174.30   **Heinrich Pestalozzi** Johann Heinrich Pestalozzi (1746–1827), Swiss educator who worked with poor children.

174.30   **Alfred Escher** Escher (d. 1882) was a statesman, not a medical doctor.

174.31   **Zwingli** Huldreich Zwingli (1484–1531), Swiss Roman Catholic priest who became a leading figure in the Protestant Reformation.

175.9   **Clinic on Interlacken [clinic at Interlaken** Interlaken is a Swiss town between the Lake of Thun and the Lake of Brienz; it is not a lake.

Book II, Chapter 5

177.4   **gladiola bed** A member of the iris family, a gladiolus is a tall, stiff plant with sword-shaped leaves and summer-blooming flowers. At this point it may be too early in the year for the gladiola to be blooming.

177.20   **"Muy bella,"** "Very beautiful" (Spanish).

178.7   **Como** Northern Italian lake famous for its beauty.

178.10   **Suppé's** By Franz von Suppé (1820–1895), composer of the "Light Cavalry Overture."

178.17   **Buenas noches** Good night (Spanish).

178.26   **'Hindustan'** 1918 song; music and lyrics by Oliver G. Wallace and Harold Weeks.

178.27–
28   **'Why Do They Call Them Babies?'** 1918 song by Jack Egan.

178.28   **'I'm Glad I Can Make You Cry'** 1918 song by Charles R. McCarron and Carey Morgan.

179.7   **'Wait Till the Cows Come Home'** 1917 song; music by Ivan Caryll, lyrics by Anne Caldwell.

179.8   **'Good Bye, Alexander'** Patriotic 1918 song; music by Henry Creamer and J. Turner Layton.

179.22   **Lothario** A seducer of women, from the character so named in Nicholas Rowe's play *The Fair Penitent* (1703).

179.23–
24   **so sorry, dear** Phrase from "I'm Sorry, Dear," 1931 song; music and lyrics by Anson Weeks, Harry Tobias, and Johnnie Scott. The reference is anachronistic; Fitzgerald may have been thinking of "I'm Sorry I Made You Cry," a 1918 song by N. J. Clesi.

179.24   **meet each other in a taxi, honey** Reference to "The Darktown Strutters' Ball" (1917), music and lyrics by Shelton Brooks: "I'll be down to get you in a taxi, honey. . . ."

179.25   **preferences in smiles** Reference to "Smiles" (1918); music by Lee G. Roberts, lyrics by Will Callaghan: "There are smiles that make you happy. . . ."

179.26–
27   **nobody knew and nobody seemed to care** "Nobody Knows (and Nobody Seems to Care)," 1919 song by Irving Berlin.

179.28–
29   **left the other crying, only to feel blue, to feel sad** Reference to "After You've Gone" (1918); music by Turner Layton, lyrics by Henry Creamer: "After you've

gone,—and left me crying. . . . you'll feel blue,—
You'll feel sad,—"

179.31   **Valais [Swiss** The first printing reads "Valais," a Swiss
canton of which Sion is the capital; but Valais is a long
way from the Zurichsee, on which Dohmler's clinic is
located at 157.2 (see 194.30, where Valais is referred
to correctly).

      When Ernest Hemingway read the "final version"
of *Tender Is the Night,* he informed Malcolm Cowley:
"Also you can't see a Valais night at a clinic described
as a short way out of Zurich" (10 November 1951;
Bruccoli, *Fitzgerald and Hemingway: A Dangerous Friendship* [New York: Carroll & Graf, 1994], p. 225).
(See Emendations).

180.1   **Lay a silver dollar. . . .** From "Silver Dollar," copyrighted in 1939 by Jack Palmer and Charlie Van Ness
but popular at least as early as the Twenties.

180.24   **'So Long, Letty'** 1916 song; music and lyrics by Earl
Carroll.

Book II, Chapter 6

181.22–
23
    of sacrificial ambrosia, of worshipping myrtle In my-
thology, ambrosia is the food of the gods, conferring
immortality; myrtle is an evergreen shrub emblematic
of love and held sacred to Venus.

182.15   **St. Hilda's** St. Hilda's Hall, a women's society at Oxford University; later St. Hilda's College.

182.21–
22
    'Deep Thoughts for the Layman' Gregorovious is
warning Diver against trivializing his ideas.

183.10–
11
    "Du lieber Gott! . . . Glas Bier." "Dear God! Please
bring Dick another glass of beer." (German).

184.4   **morning [afternoon** Dick ate lunch with Franz Gregorovious on pp. 182–183.

Book II, Chapter 7

186.18 **twenty-four [twenty-three** Baby was born in mid-1896 (see Chronology).

187.17 **Burberry** Raincoat made by the Burberry firm in England.

188.23 **debutante** An upper-class American girl who has been presented to society as eligible for matrimony.

190.5-11 **"Bonjour. . . Monsieur."** "Good day, Doctor."
"Good day, sir."
"The weather is fine."
"Yes, marvelous."
"Are you staying here?"
"No, only visiting."
"Good. Well, goodbye, sir." (French)

Book II, Chapter 8

192.5–6 **absent himself from felicity** *Hamlet*, V, 2, line 308: "Absent thee from felicity a while". It is possible that Diver understands the ironic "felicity" of union with Nicole to be fatal to his career; more likely Fitzgerald has forgotten that Hamlet's dying speech enjoins Horatio from suicide.

192.9 **Rolls** A Rolls-Royce, an English luxury automobile.

192.15–
16 **goblins on the Grossmünster** Gargoyles on the cathedral (see Explanatory Notes, 174.27).

192.25 **Nice to Coblenz** From southern France to Germany.

193.16 **Montreux** Small city on the shore of Lake Léman.

193.17 **Jugenhorn [Dent du Jaman** There is no Jugenhorn mountain in Switzerland. The Dent du Jaman and the Rochers de Naye are mountain peaks visible from Montreux. The Rochers de Naye is mentioned at 205.12 (see Emendations).

193.22 **trained-bands [train-bands** Companies of citizen soldiers.

111

Approach to Montreux: the Dent du Jaman and the Rochers de Naye.

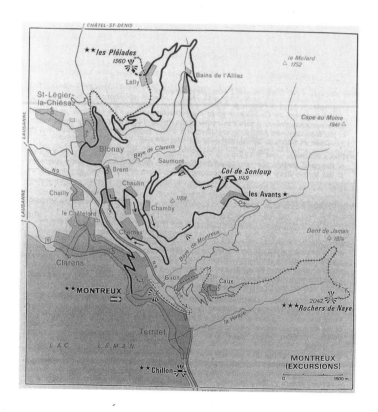

Glion et la Dent du Midi

Glion - Caux et les Rochers de Naye.

113

193.26   **June [July** Diver returned to Zurich in "the first week of summer" (181.24–25), which would be the week following June 21: "weeks" (192.1) elapse before his encounter with Nicole on the Glion funicular (see Chronology).

194.1   **Glion funicular** Glion is a mountain resort reached by cable car (funicular) from the Territet section of Montreux.

194.4   **La Tour-de-Peilz** Town on Lake Léman between Vevey and Montreux.

194.20   **Two years ago** The time is 1919. Germany would not have been selling cables during the war.

194.27   **confrère** Colleague (French).

194.28   **undulati** Fitzgerald invented a pseudo-Latin term referring to those who are in motion.

194.30   **Vaud, Valais, Swiss Savoy** Vaud and Valais are Swiss cantons; Swiss Savoy refers to the region that includes the Dents du Midi.

194.31   **cyclorama** A circular pictorial presentation or the curved wall of a stage set.

194.33   **the Rhône** River that flows into Lake Léman from the Alps and then into France.

195.3   **Kursal** The casino at Montreux.

195.4   **Chillon** Castle on a small island in Lake Léman; setting for Lord Byron's poem "The Prisoner of Chillon."

195.4   **island palace of Salagnon** The Ile de Salagnon in Lake Léman near Clarens, now part of Montreux; there is a chateau—not a palace—on this small island.

195.8–9   *Défense de cueillir les fleurs.* Picking flowers is prohibited (French).

195.11   **Dorothy Perkins roses** Scentless, double, bright pink flowers that bloom early in summer; possibly intended as Fitzgerald's private greeting to Maxwell Perkins.

195.28–29   **Irene Castle** Dancer (1893–1969) who with her husband Vernon (1887–1918) formed an enormously successful dance team before World War I and originated the Castle Walk. She was credited with starting the bobbed-hair fashion.

196.8   **Caux** Mountain resort above Montreux.

196.28   **narcissus** Spring-blooming bulbous plant with fragrant white or yellow cup-shaped flowers; species include the jonquil and the daffodil. In Greek mythology Narcissus was a youth who fell in love with his own reflection and was changed into the flower.

197.8   **donkey-engine** A small locomotive.

197.19   **twenty-five [twenty-three** It is June 1919, and Baby was born in mid-1896 (see Chronology).

Book II, Chapter 9

198.8   **transformations** False hair, especially as worn by a woman.

199.23   **'Vanity Fair'** American magazine (1913–1936) of sophisticated life and fashion. The name was revived for a later magazine.

199.24   **schizoid** Predisposed to schizophrenia.

199.33   **Byron** George Noel Gordon, Lord Byron (1788–1824), English poet and romantic figure (see Chillon, Explanatory Notes, 195.4).

200.1   **Guards** The troops assigned to the British sovereign: the Household Cavalry and the Brigade of Guards. These were the most fashionable regiments.

200.8   **"Poor Butterfly"** Popular song introduced in 1916; music by Raymond Hubbell, lyrics by John Golden. It includes the words *the moments pass into hours.*

200.20   **North Side . . . South Side** North and south of Madison Street.

202.24   **Chicagoese** Tough language or slang associated with Chicago.

202.24   **"Bull!"** Euphemism for *bullshit:* verbose insincerity.

202.34   **intellectual stockyards** Diver is comparing the University of Chicago to the pens where livestock are assembled for the Chicago slaughterhouses.

204.9–10 **her face getting big every time she came close** Repeated from 138.6–7.

204.13 **cannons were shooting** The object was to prevent a hailstorm from destroying the crops.

204.27 **Strauss waltz** Dance music by Viennese composer Johann Strauss (1825–1899).

205.12 **Rochers de Naye** Mountains near Montreux (see Explanatory Notes, 193.17).

206.16 **"gone coon"** "Gone": doomed to destruction; "coon": shortened form of raccoon. The expression possibly alludes to the high incidence of rabies among raccoons.

Book II, Chapter 10

208.2–3 **Mad Anthony Wayne** (1745–1796); American Revolutionary War general, nicknamed "Mad" because of his recklessness.

208.9–10 **Marshall Field** (1834–1906); Chicago department-store millionaire (see Explanatory Notes, 168.32).

208.13–14 **American ducal family** A family whose great wealth and influence have persisted beyond the founding generation.

209.15 **roly-poly** A weighted rocking doll that returns to an upright position.

209.16–17 **"Je m'en fiche de tout."** "I don't care at all" (French).

209.18 **blue baby** An infant born with a heart defect that causes imperfectly oxygenated blood.

209.23 **camérière** Obsolete term for chambermaid (French).

209.25 **Orvieto** City in central Italy.

209.29 **Capri** Island resort in the Bay of Naples.

209.30 **Blue Grotto** The Blue Grotto (La Grotta Azzurra), a cavern on the north shore of Capri, is famous for its interior blue light.

210.19–
20   **blue obscurity** Echo of "Harvardiana," Harvard University football song: "Poor Eli's [Yale's] hopes we are dashing / Into blue obscurity."

210.20   **Pallas Athena** One of the titles of Athena, the patron goddess of Athens; a daughter of Zeus, she was goddess of wisdom, the arts, and justified warfare.

210.21–
22   **waters lapping in the public toilets** Nicole is referring to the movement of the water in shipboard toilet bowls.

210.24   **Woolloomooloo Bay** The bay is at Sydney, Australia; but it is unlikely that the Divers had traveled to Australia. Fitzgerald may have thought that Woolloomooloo sounded as though it were in North Africa.

210.25   **Biskra** City in Algiers, North Africa, at the edge of the Atlas mountains.

210.29   **Ouled Naïl** Algerian tribe whose young women perform erotic dances. The name is variously transliterated "Walad Nail" or "Ouled-Nail" or "Uled-Nayl." The Ouled Naïls are described in "Show Mr. and Mrs. F. to Number—," a 1934 article bylined F. Scott and Zelda Fitzgerald but mostly her own work:

> The Ouled Naïls were very brown and clean-cut girls, impersonal as they turned themselves into fitting instruments for sex by the ritual of their dance, jangling their gold to the tune of savage fidelities hid in the distant hills.

211.7   **Timgad** Ruined Algerian city founded in A.D. 100 by Trajan.

211.28–
29   **Affaires Étrangères** The French ministry of foreign affairs (Ministère des Affaires Étrangères).

211.32   **Mistinguett** Jeanne Bourgeois (1875?–1956); French singer and dancer who starred in Paris at the Folies-Bergère, the Casino de Paris, and the Moulin Rouge.

211.33   **Picasso** Pablo Picasso (1881–1973), Spanish cubist painter; he was a friend of the Murphys and visited them at Cap d'Antibes.

211.33   **"Pas sur la Bouche"** Title song for 1925 show by Maurice Yvain, a popular French composer of musical comedies.

212.30   **very fashionable for July [very fashionable for June** This reference to Rosemary completes the flashback and links Book II, Chapter 10, with Book I, Chapter 1; see 4.8: "one June morning" (see Chronology).

Book II, Chapter 11

213.4   **mistral** A cold northerly wind in the Mediterranean provinces of France.

213.5   **Esterel** Mountain region on the Mediterranean coast of France near Cannes.

213.10   **service stripe** Military uniforms include sleeve stripes signifying years of service.

213.12   **Havre** Le Havre, French port on the English Channel.

213.24   **la Napoule** A sea-bathing resort eight kilometers (about five miles) from Cannes.

215.10–
11   **the Nice Carnival Song** Rosemary is associated with this song at 18.11–12 (see Explanatory Notes, 18.11–12).

215.14   **belladonna** A poisonous plant from which the drug atropine is extracted.

215.15   **mandragora** A Mediterranean herb also known as mandrake; the root of the plant was used as a soporific drug.

215.23–
24   **perceptibly by Captain Doctor Hoyt,** Sired by Hoyt; *by* is a term from animal breeding.

216.19–
20   **fiftieth German edition** It is most unlikely that a translation of a medical monograph would require fifty editions.

217.9   **Bon Ami** A cleaning powder.

217.16   **luminol** A sedative.

217.23–
24   **three Chinese monkeys** The monkeys—one covering its eyes, another its mouth, the other its ears—repre-

sented "see no evil, speak no evil, hear no evil"; that is, McBeth was to keep the secret of the circumstances of Freeman's murder.

217.28   **wagon-lit** Railroad sleeping car (French).

217.30   **ceinture** Inner-circle or outer-circle railway for a French city.

218.12   **Paris-Lyons-Méditerranée** Luxury train that ran between Paris and the Riviera; known as the PLM.

218.19   **the Luxembourg** The Luxembourg Gardens (see Explanatory Notes, 89.33–90.1).

220.5   **poussée** Thrust or outbreak (French).

Book II, Chapter 12

221.8   **Bartholomew Tailor** A fictional character.

221.11   **Ciro's menagerie** The sort of people who frequented Ciro's, a fashionable Paris restaurant-nightclub on the Rue Danou. Ciro's had branches in Deauville, Monte-Carlo, and London.

222.1   **a suck** A social hanger-on, someone living by attempting to please people of wealth or superior social position.

222.6   **Ward McAllister** (1827–1895); New York society leader who reportedly drew up a list of the four hundred most prominent people in New York City society.

222.16   **"Just picture you . . ."** From "Tea for Two" (see Explanatory Notes, 123.8).

222.26   **three thousand a year** Diver's income earned by the money inherited from his mother; 3 percent interest on $100,000 earns $3,000.

222.28   **cellar charges** The cost of the wine and other alcoholic beverages purchased for the household.

224.2   **Syndicat d'Initiative** Local organization for the encouragement of tourism.

Book II, Chapter 13

225.5   **Gstaad** Ski resort in the Swiss Alps, near Montreux.

225.6   **"Don't Bring Lulu"** 1925 song; music by Ray Henderson, lyrics by Billy Rose and Lew Brown.

225.7   **the Charleston** Prototypical dance of the Twenties, allegedly originating in Charleston, South Carolina. The 1923 song "Charleston" was written by Cecil Mack and James P. Johnson.

225.8   *Sturmtruppen* German for storm troopers—soldiers trained for attack. The reference here is to a vanguard of stylish vacationers.

225.9   **St. Moritz** Fashionable ski resort in eastern Switzerland.

226.6   **scarcely down from Cambridge** A recent graduate of Cambridge University.

226.19   **bob-run** Bobsled trail.

226.20   **telemark** A crouching turn on skis.

226.21   **kvass** A fruit- or mint-flavored liqueur.

226.24– 28   **ickle durls. . . . 'Ickle durl, oo is de pwettiest sing.'** Baby talk: i.e., "little girls" and "Little girl, you is the prettiest thing."

228.15– 16   **fondue . . . Welsh rarebit** Fondue is a spiced cheese dish served at boiling point; Welsh rarebit (Welsh rabbit) consists of seasoned melted cheese served over toast.

229.6   **Zugersee** Lake in Switzerland near Lucerne.

229.28   **the professor** Gregorovious is presumably referring to Dr. Dohmler; but see 183.32–33: "Six months later . . . when he saw Dohmler dead. . . ."

230.20   **Privatdozent** Unsalaried university lecturer (German) (see Explanatory Notes, 168.25).

230.28   **Croesus** King of Lydia (c. 560–546 B.C.) whose wealth became proverbial.

231.13   **Jung . . . Bleuler . . . Forel . . . Adler** Karl Jung (1875–1961), Swiss psychiatrist responsible for the concept of the "collective unconscious." Eugen Bleuler (1857–1939), Swiss psychiatrist who examined Zelda Fitzgerald. Oscar Forel (b. 1891), Swiss psychiatrist who treated Zelda Fitzgerald at his Les Rives de Prangins clinic at Nyon. Alfred Adler (1870–1937), Austrian psychiatrist, founder of the school of individual psychology.

231.30   **gashouse** Place where gas for household appliances and illumination is produced.

232.14   **Saanen** Unfashionable winter sport resort near Gstaad.

232.19   **football cleats** Shoes worn by American-football players.

232.31   **"mental hygiene"** The once-popular concept of a healthy mind.

233.1   **Amazons** Legendary women warriors.

233.3   **Humpty Dumpty** The personified broken egg of the nursery rhyme: "All the King's horses, / And all the King's men, / Couldn't put Humpty together again."

235.12   **Wiener waltzes** Viennese waltzes.

Book II, Chapter 14

236.5   **"Love of Three Oranges"** [**"Love for Three Oranges"** 1921 opera by Russian composer Sergey Prokofiev (1891–1955).

236.18;   **this past year and a half on the Zugersee. . . . For**
238.3–4   **eighteen months now he had lived at the clinic** The time is summer 1927 (see Chronology).

238.14   **truck farm** A farm devoted to the growing of vegetables (also called "truck") for the retail market.

238.15   **ergo-therapy** Treatment of neurasthenia based on the principle that effort leads to cure; the aim was to enable the patient to relate to the environment by performing certain tasks. The term is not a misprint for *ego-therapy*.

240.1   **Edwardians** British society during the reign (1901–1910) of King Edward VII (1841–1910).

240.10–
11
from the Étoile to the Place de la Concorde The length of the Avenue des Champs-Élysées from the Arc de Triomphe to the end of the Jardin des Tuileries.

240.18
whoopee cures Clinics with low medical standards that catered to treating alcoholics and drug addicts.

240.24
nervous eczema Zelda Fitzgerald was diagnosed with this skin condition after her collapse in 1930.

240.25
as imprisoned in the Iron Maiden Vertical body-shaped, hinged, spike-lined instrument of torture and death.

241.28
Pyrrhic victory A victory achieved at ruinously great cost, like that of King Pyrrhus of Epirus over the Romans at Asculum in 279 B.C.

243.2
sarcophagus of her figure Fitzgerald is describing the bandaged woman as resembling a stone coffin.

243.24
the Caucasus Mountainous area in southern Russia between the Black Sea and the Caspian Sea.

243.27
paresis Late stage of syphilis characterized by locomotor ataxia and madness.

Book II, Chapter 15

245.23
Renault Popular small French car.

246.4
Zug City fifteen miles south of Zurich.

246.5
Ägeri Fair Traditional pre–Ash Wednesday carnival in the area of the Ägerisee, Zug Canton. However, Fitzgerald's descriptions of the temperature (245.27–28) and the characters' clothing (247.5–6) make it clear that this episode occurs in the summer.

246.18
Punch-and-Judy show A traditional puppet show of long-enduring popularity, in which Punch, a grotesque, hook-nosed figure, beats his wife, Judy, to death.

246.29
guignol Punch-and-Judy show (French).

247.3
hootchy-kootchy show A carnival sideshow featuring supposedly erotic dancing girls.

247.14–
16   **"Est-ce que je peux laisser . . . je vous donnerai dix francs."** "May I leave the children with you for a few minutes? It is very urgent—I will give you ten francs" (French).

247.18–
19   **"Alors—restez avec cette gentille dame."** "Stay with this nice lady" (French).

247.24   **buvette** Refreshment bar in a public place.

247.27–
28   **"La septième fille . . . entrez, Monsieur——"** "The seventh daughter of a seventh daughter born on the banks of the Nile—come in, sir" (French).

247.29   **plaisance [pleasance** A pleasance is a space laid out with trees and walks; *plaisance* means "pleasure" in French.

247.30   **Ferris wheel** Amusement park ride, in which patrons seated on open benches are carried aloft with each revolution of a vertically rotating wheel. This ride was invented by G. W. G. Ferris (1859–1896).

248.4–5   **"Regardez-moi ça!" ¶"Regarde donc cette Anglaise!"** "Look at that!" ¶"Look at that English woman!" (French).

248.23   **Bock** A strong Bavarian beer (German).

249.3   **Svengali** The sinister, brilliant, manipulative hypnotist in George DuMaurier's novel *Trilby* (1894).

249.13   **corium** Sensitive vascular layer beneath the epidermis.

250.8–9   **"Merci . . . petits."** "Thank you, sir. Ah, you are too generous. It was a pleasure, sir, madam. Goodbye, my little ones" (French).

250.21   **schizophrène** Someone afflicted with schizophrenia.

251.31   **'La voiture Divare est cassée.'** 'The Divers' car is broken' (French). Diver pronounces his surname as a Frenchman would.

252.29   **Cognac** French brandy distilled from grapes grown in the Cognac region.

Book II, Chapter 16

254.5   **the elder Forel** Auguste Forel (1848–1931), Swiss psychiatrist and entomologist; father of psychiatrist Oscar Forel.

254.6   **dementia praecox** Literally, "precocious insanity," a form of insanity usually occurring or beginning at puberty.

254.11   **Schwartz** Unidentified; probably a fictional character.

254.22   **Rotarian** Member of the Rotary Club, an American businessmen's service organization.

254.29   **Vorarlberg Alps** Mountainous region in western Austria.

255.10–   **the "Century," the "Motion Picture," "L'Illustra-**
11   **tion," and the "Fliegende Blätter"** American, French, and German magazines.

255.16   **Crucified, Died, and was Buried** Fitzgerald's use of the Roman Catholic text of the "Apostles' Creed" reflects his upbringing; but Diver, as the son of a Protestant clergyman, would have known the *Book of Common Prayer* text: "crucified, dead, and buried."

255.25   **Savona** Italian province and seaport on the Gulf of Genoa.

255.26   **illuminated missal** Prayer book with paintings in bright colors, often utilizing gold leaf.

Book II, Chapter 17

256.2   **Marienplatz** The principal square in Munich, facing the Rathaus.

256.13   **Prince Chillicheff** A fictional character.

257.25   **Beale Street** In Memphis, Tennessee; a principal street in the black section, inspiration for W. C. Handy's "Beale Street Blues" (1917).

257.30   **Pilsudski** Józef Pilsudski (1867–1935), Polish marshal and statesman, dictator of Poland during the Twenties.

258.10   **Red Guards** Communist soldiers.

258.16 **Marxian** The correct noun is *Marxist:* an advocate of the socialist economic and political theories of Karl Marx (1818–1883).

258.16–17 **St. Mark's** Boys' preparatory school in Southborough, Mass. In a working draft Abe North is identified as a St. Mark's alumnus.

258.30 **Innsbruck** Resort town in the Austrian Tirol province, situated in a valley of the Stubai Alps.

259.1 **Packard** American luxury car.

259.7 **drawn in a blind contract [drawn into a blind contract** Committed to a course of action without sufficient information (see Emendations).

259.10 **unscrewed two blooded wire-hairs** The leashes of the pedigreed wire-haired terriers had become wound around the table leg to which they had been tied.

259.11 **departed [stood ready to depart** In the first edition McKibben leaves the café at this point but then speaks at 260.9. The serial reads "stood ready to depart."

259.16 **speakeasy** An American bar, restaurant, or nightclub selling liquor between 1919 and 1933, when the sale of alcohol for consumption was prohibited by Constitutional amendment. These establishments were called "speakeasies" because admission required a spoken password or reference ("Joe sent me").

260.1 **Racquet Club** The Racquet and Tennis Club is a private club in New York on Park Avenue between Fifty-second and Fifty-third Streets. The circumstances of North's death may have been suggested by the 1928 death of Cornelius R. Winant, Princeton '18, who died at the New York Princeton Club after having been beaten in a speakeasy. Fitzgerald was a member of the classes of 1917 and 1918: see Bruccoli, "Bennett Cerf's Fan Letter on *Tender Is the Night:* A Source for Abe North's Death," *Fitzgerald/Hemingway Annual 1979*, pp. 229–230; see also Winant, *A Soldier's Monument* (Privately Printed, 1929).

260.7   **Harvard Club** Private club for Harvard alumni in New York on West Forty-fourth Street.

260.23   **stock-broking** Trading in stocks and other securities.

Book II, Chapter 18

262.2–3   **Emperor Maximilian** Statue of Maximilian I (1459–1519), ruler of the Holy Roman Empire from 1493 to 1519.

262.4   **Jesuit novices** Young men who are being trained for the priesthood by the Roman Catholic Society of Jesus, known as the Jesuits.

262.7   **Erbsensuppe** Pea soup (German).

262.7   **Würstchen** Small sausage (German).

262.8   **helles [steins** Dick had four mugs of light-colored Pilsener beer. *Helles* (light ale) describes the beer, not the size of the glass; Fitzgerald meant *steins*. He may have confused the German *Halbes* (a one-half litre) with *Helles*.

262.9   **"Kaiserschmarren."** A raisin pancake cut into strips (German/Austrian).

263.6   **gigolo** A man paid to provide escort or sexual services for a woman.

263.8–9   **settlement in the continental style** In certain European societies the bridegroom receives a sum of money or property from his wife's family—a dowry.

263.12–   **He loitered . . . easy?** This account of Diver's interest
264.26   in the woman at Innsbruck was reduced from a longer account in the serial (see Appendix C: Material Deleted between Magazine and Book Publication).

263.13   **October [January** More time is required between Nicole's summer collapse and Dick's arrival at Innsbruck, but the "cool" weather does not describe winter in Austria.

263.31   **scapegrace drummers** Traveling salesmen (drummers), having a reputation as casual seducers, were often treated with automatic disdain by respectable women.

264.5–6 **Birkkarspitze** The highest peak (9,019 feet) in the Karwendel range, north of Innsbruck.

265.16 **formally his father's curate** See 207.17–18; in 1919 Diver states, "My father is a clergyman, now retired."

266.16 **it [the income** Dick is receiving only the interest on his mother's money, not the principal.

266.18 **the Gilded Age** Post–Civil War period in America, a time of rampant financial speculation.

Book II, Chapter 19

267.8 **Westmoreland County** In Virginia on the western shore of the Chesapeake Bay.

267.10 **Chesapeake Bay** Inlet of the Atlantic Ocean separating Virginia and the mainland of Maryland from the peninsula that includes Delaware and the Maryland "Eastern Shore."

267.11 **buckboards** Small, open, horse-drawn wagons.

267.14–23 **Next day . . . fathers.** This material was adapted from an unfinished essay, "The Death of My Father"; see *Princeton University Library Chronicle*, 12 (Summer 1951), 187–189. Edward Fitzgerald died in January 1931.

268.7 **Andorra** Small principality, having a population of about 20,000, in the Pyrenees between France and Spain.

269.10 **captain's table** The most important passengers on an ocean liner were invited to dine with the captain.

269.13 **couturières** Designers of custom-tailored women's garments, or the establishments where such garments are sold.

269.15 **Boise** Capital city of Idaho.

269.20 **Gibraltar** Some trans-Atlantic passenger ships on the Mediterranean route stopped at Gibraltar.

269.20–31 **Naples . . . Cassino and Frosinone** Diver disembarked at Naples and traveled to Rome by train, passing through Cassino and Frosinone.

269.33   **Hotel Quirinale** Luxury hotel on the Via Nazionale in Rome.

270.4–5   **Mediterranean crossing** The transatlantic route from New York to the European ports on the Mediterranean Sea.

270.11   **black-seed oil** Probably oil of black mustard seed, used as a gastric and intestinal stimulant and as an emetic, especially for horses and cattle.

270.11   **hoops [hoofs** Varnish was applied to horses' hoofs to provide an elegant appearance (see Emendations).

270.17   **"The Grandeur That Was Rome"** Probably based on *Ben-Hur,* an American movie that was being made in Rome during 1924 while the Fitzgeralds were there. The title derives from Edgar Allan Poe's poem "To Helen" (1845): "To the glory that was Greece, / And the grandeur that was Rome."

270.31   **Via Nazionale** Wide, modern street that begins at the Rome railroad station.

270.32   **portières** Curtains across a doorway.

271.1   **"Corriere della Sera"** Evening newspaper published in Milan.

271.1–3   **"una novella di Sainclair Lewis . . . citta Americana." ["un romanzo di Sainclair Lewis . . . città Americana."** "a novel by Sinclair Lewis, 'Wall Street,' in which the author analyzes the social life in a small American city" (Italian). The misspelling "Sainclair" and the incorrect reference to *Main Street* (1920) were intended by Fitzgerald.

271.7,14   **four [three** Diver and Rosemary first met in June 1925, and the Rome meeting takes place in March 1928 (see Chronology).

271.15   **thirty-four [thirty-six** See Explanatory Notes, 271.7, 14.

271.16   **twenty-two [twenty-one** See Explanatory Notes, 271.7, 14.

271.16   **thirty-eight [thirty-nine** See Explanatory Notes, 271.7, 14.

272.6–7   **". . . tied up in bags! And how!"** American slang: ". . . sexually attracted to her! Very much so!"

Book II, Chapter 20

274.13   **Edna Ferber** Popular American novelist (1887–1968) who wrote historical fiction; *Show Boat* was published in 1926.

275.24   **". . . those things are rhythmic"** Rosemary is in the fertile period of her menstrual cycle and means to avoid pregnancy.

275.31   **"That would be poetic justice . . . you"** Rosemary remembers that she offered herself to Diver three years before with a disregard for the risk of pregnancy.

276.8   **six hundred and forty** Rosemary's joke constitutes a refusal to answer the question. Some readers have taken this figure literally.

276.12   **twenty-two [twenty-one** Rosemary was born in July 1907 (see Chronology).

276.13   **nineteen twenty-eight** This is the latest year stipulated in the novel.

276.20   **Pincio** The northern slopes of Rome are known as the Pincian Hill, site of the Borghese Gardens.

277.10   **Porta San Sebastiano** One of the gateways to Rome.

277.11   **Appian Way** Ancient road from Rome across the Campagna or countryside.

277.11   **the Forum** From the beginnings of the city, the public square where Romans met to conduct trade and government; it was later called the Roman Forum to distinguish it from the Imperial Forum. Fitzgerald may have meant the Coliseum, the amphitheatre where gladiatorial combat and fights between men and beasts were held.

277.16   **Nicotera** A fictional character.

277.17   **hopeful Valentinos** The success of Rudolph Valentino (1895–1926) as a silent-screen Latin lover prompted other actors to emulate him.

277.31   **on the hop** Taking drugs.

278.20   **Castello dei Cesari** Restaurant on the Via di Santa Prisca, with a view of the Palatine Hill.

Book II, Chapter 21

279.4   **Excelsior** Luxury hotel on the Via Vittório Véneto.

279.16   **black band** At that time men wore black bands on their coat sleeves to indicate that they were in mourning.

280.13   **dove of a house** An attractive dwelling.

280.13   **Talbot Square** A small square near Paddington Station. In the 1920s it was an upper-middle-class address with five- and six-story private residences.

280.18   **Michael Arlen** (1895–1956); Armenian-born English novelist, author of *The Green Hat* (1924), a hugely popular novel featuring a tragically misunderstood heroine of legendary promiscuity.

281.9   **Ulpia** Restaurant near the Piazza di Venézia.

281.11   **"Suona Fanfara Mia"** No song with this title—which translates as "Play, Oh My Band"—has been identified. "Chitarra Romana" includes the line, "Suona, suona mia chitarra . . . (Play, play my guitar)." However, this song by E. di Liozzaro and C. Bruno was not copyrighted in Italy until 1936.

281.29   **Lord Paley** Fictional character.

283.4   *trattoria* Restaurant (Italian).

284.13   **Victorian** Referring to sexual prudery associated with the British reign (1837–1901) of Queen Victoria (1819–1901).

285.9   **adagio** A musical term meaning slowly and gracefully.

286.4   **Livorno** Also known as Leghorn, seaport 160 miles northwest of Rome.

286.19 **Black Death** Bubonic plague, which ravaged fourteenth-century Europe.

Book II, Chapter 22

Chapters 22–23 **Fitzgerald and Italy** Corresponding with his agent about a companion piece to his humorous articles "How to Live on $36,000 a Year" (*Saturday Evening Post*, 5 April 1924) and "How to Live on Practically Nothing a Year" (*Saturday Evening Post*, 20 September 1924), Fitzgerald wrote, "I hate Italy and the Italiens so violently that I can't bring myself to write about them. . . ."(letter received 23 January 1925; *As Ever, Scott Fitz——*, p. 73). Lacking the optimism and good nature of the earlier pieces, the article proved unsellable in 1925. "The High Cost of Macaroni" (*Interim*, 4 [1954]) includes a humorous account of Fitzgerald's 1924 brawl with cabdrivers in Rome.

287.2 **frail** Slang term for a young woman. Fitzgerald apparently used the word to mean a woman of easy virtue.

287.6 **Dick was always vividly conscious of his surroundings** See 288.19–21: "he was scarcely conscious of places . . . until they had been invested with color by tangible events." Fitzgerald here distinguishes between "places," as geographic entities, and "surroundings," as an individual's immediate environs.

287.18–19 **Princess Orsini** Fictional character.

288.15–16 **American Express** Office of the American Express Company that provides banking and other services for travelers.

288.17 **Spanish Steps** Flight of 137 steps in front of the church of the Trinità dei Monti; known as the Scala di Spagna, they lead into the Piazza di Spagna.

288.28 **Bomboniera** Italian for candy box; this cabaret has not been identified.

290.5   **Italian mousseux** Mousseux is a sparkling French wine. "Italian mousseux" is an imprecise reference to spumante (see Explanatory Notes, 291.6).

290.10   **fifty lire** The rate of exchange was about 20 lire to the dollar in 1928.

290.25   **a quick trick or else I don't know bridge** Clay's play on words, using the word *trick* to mean both a sexual encounter and the collected round of cards in the game of bridge, constitutes a boast of experience with women.

291.6   **spumante** An Italian sparkling wine (see Explanatory Notes, 290.5). Fitzgerald meant that Diver ordered a second bottle of sparkling wine, probably spumante.

291.12   **Birmingham** That the office is in Alabama may reinforce Clay's contempt for the job; more likely, Fitzgerald forgot that Clay is a Georgian (90.14).

291.31–   **remarkable . . . she had disappeared** Diver may have
33   experienced an alcoholic blackout; it is almost dawn when he leaves the Bomboniera (292.20).

292.3   **Su'nly** Diver's alcoholic pronunciation of *suddenly*.

292.9   **Colonna** Noble Roman family who achieved wealth and power by the eleventh century. Influential in the church, they produced many cardinals. The Colonnesi were rivals of the equally powerful Orsini family.

292.9   **Gaetani** The Gaetani, or Caetani, were a medieval Italian clan that, according to legend, descended from the dukes and consuls of Gaeta. Claiming four cardinals and taking prominent roles in the political and military activities of Pisa, the Pisan branch flowered in the twelfth and thirteenth centuries.

292.10   **Yenci [lenci** Panno lenci are felt dolls manufactured in Italy.

292.18–   **Rome beating** Phyllis Shafmeister, a member of the
305.33   Foreign Service, wrote Arthur Mizener:

> . . . Fitzgerald was leaving a night club in Rome one night and wanted a taxi to the Hotel Excel-

sior. The "after-12" taxi rates were exorbitant and Mr. Fitzgerald, in a fit of pique, got into a fight with the taxi driver on this account. The night club detective arrived on the scene and in the ensuing commotion, Fitzgerald was carted off to jail and quite brutally manhandled. His nose was broken (and as Mr. Bornstein stated, "he was a vain and good-looking man"), his face was cut badly but the greatest injury was to his vanity.

In the morning, Zelda arrived at the Embassy in a hysterical state and the young Vice-Consul Bornstein was delegated to the aid of the prisoner. He remembered that he went to the jail and diplomatically told the judge that this was a famous American author, the notoriety concerned might injure the reputation of the court, etc., etc., and ended his freedom plea by saying, "I think the man has been punished enough."

The judge then dismissed the charges and Fitzgerald immediately turned on his detective apprehender of the night before and saying, "I told you I was innocent," socked him in the nose (4 January 1952, Princeton University Library).

292.19   **campagna** The countryside.

292.24   **"Quanto a Hotel Quirinale?"** "How much to take me to the Hotel Quirinale?" (Italian). The correct form is "Quanto per andare all' Hotel Quirinale?"—but Diver does not speak Italian (294.12).

292.25   **"Cento lire."** The cabdriver wants one hundred lire, but Diver offers thirty and then thirty-five.

292.29   **"Trente-cinque lire e mancia,"** "Thirty-five lire and a tip" (Italian). The correct form is "Trentacinque lire più la mancia."

293.12   **"wan huner lire,"** Phonetic spelling of "one hundred lire."

293.16   **The passionate impatience of the week . . .** Diver has been in Rome three days.

294.1   **carabinieri** Members of the Italian national police force.

294.11   **"Spick Italiano?"** "Do you speak Italian?"

294.15– **"Alors . . . . Quirinale."** "Well. Listen. Go to the
27   Quirinale. You dope. Listen: you are drunk. Pay what
         the driver asks. Do you understand?"
         "No, I don't want to."
         "*What?*"
         "I will pay forty lire. That is more than enough."
         "Listen. . . . You are drunk. You have hit the
         driver. Like this, like that. . . . You are lucky that I
         am releasing you. Pay what he says—one hundred lire.
         Go to the Quirinale" (French).

294.21   **lires** The correct word is *lire.*

295.22   **"Due centi lire!"** "Two hundred lire!" An Italian would
         say "Duecento."

Book II, Chapter 23

296.2   **Marion Crawford** F. Marion Crawford (1854–1909),
         American author of romantic novels, some of which
         were set in Italy.

296.5   **harlequin hats** The wide-brimmed, high-crowned hats
         that were part of the carabinieri uniform resemble the
         hats worn by characters in comedy or pantomime.

296.6   **mains'ls coming about** The mainsail of a sailboat
         swings across the beam when the vessel reverses direc-
         tion (comes about).

296.7   **guards officer** Probably a reference to the Corazzieri,
         the guards at the royal palace in Rome; not the British
         Brigade of Guards.

297.20   **Wops** Derogatory slang term for Italians.

298.3   **"Non capisco l'inglese."** "I don't understand English"
         (Italian).

298.9   **"Bene. *Bay-nay! Bene!*"** "All right. *All right!* [phonetic
         spelling] *All right!*" (Italian).

299.1   **Hime** The butler speaks with a cockney accent: i.e.,
         "I'm."

299.8   **Groton voice** Groton is a preparatory school in Massa-
         chusetts; the students spoke with a distinctive upper-
         class accent at that time.

299.22	**mustache bandage** A device for training a mustache while a man sleeps.
300.13	**Eastern seaboard** The states on the Atlantic coast, usually referring to the Northeast.
300.33	**Consul** An official residing in a foreign country who protects the commercial interests of his country and its citizens.
301.18	***semper dritte, dextra and sinestra*** Either Baby's mispronunciations or Fitzgerald's misspellings: "sempre dritto" ("always right"), "destra" ("right hand"), "sinistra" ("left").
301.22	**Piazza di Spagna** Spanish Plaza (see Explanatory Notes, 288.17).
302.3	**musta** Must have.
304.7	**Aryan** Accurately, a descendant of the prehistoric people who spoke Indo-European languages; but generally used to mean someone of Nordic stock. Fitzgerald's use of the term is innocent of the malignant racism that would accrue in the 1930s and 1940s in consequence of Nazi doctrine.
305.29	**Frascati** Hill town ten miles southeast of Rome.

Book III, Chapter 1

309.28	**cable [telegram** Cables are trans-oceanic messages.
310.4	**Norma Talmadge** (1897–1957); silent movie actress, sister of actress Constance Talmadge.
312.13	**hare and tortoise** Aesop fable about a footrace; the victorious tortoise metaphorically demonstrates the superiority of persistent plodding to natural facility weakened by overconfidence.

Book III, Chapter 2

314.3	**Wassermanns** The Wassermann is a blood-serum test for syphilis, developed by August von Wassermann (1866–1925).
314.31;	**Pardo y Cuidad Real [Pardo Ciudad Real** Fitzgerald's

315.3; name for this character is impossible as a Spanish name;
319.20; but "Pardo Ciudad Real" is possible.
320.19

315.5–6 **Hôtel des Trois Mondes** Literally, hotel of the three worlds—an invented name.

315.9 **Harrow** Prestigious English school.

315.9–10 **King's College, Cambridge** One of the best known of the colleges that form Cambridge University in England.

315.15 **cantharides** An aphrodisiac known as Spanish Fly.

317.3 **forties** Although Dick Diver is not yet forty in May 1928, he foresees the decade ahead as a time of increased personality fragmentation.

317.15 **swam into his ken** An echo of Keats's "On First Looking into Chapman's Homer" (1816): "When a new planet swims into his ken"—i.e., comes into his line of vision.

317.30 **no laggard with his pick and spade** The meaning of the phrase is that Dumphry is capable of intrusive behavior.

318.28 **Genevois** Person from Geneva.

318.32 **only fifty** That Devereux Warren was eighteen at the birth of his daughter Baby, who cannot be younger than thirty-two, is surprising.

319.15 **around the lake** In the vicinity of Lake Léman.

319.15 **Herbrugge** Fictional character.

320.17 **Charles [Devereux** At 166.3 Warren's first name is Devereux. Charles Warren, a young Baltimore writer Fitzgerald befriended while writing *Tender Is the Night*, claimed that Fitzgerald changed the character's name as a mark of friendship. More likely, Fitzgerald forgot Devereux Warren's first name, which appears only twice in the novel. "Charles" was emended to "Devereux" in the third printing of 1934.

320.21 **mediatized principalities** A state that has been annexed to another state.

320.22 **barbital** An addictive hypnotic drug.

320.27   *persona gratis* [*persona grata* Welcome person (Latin).

322.27   **passed the remnant of the buck** To "pass the buck" means to shift responsibility to someone else.

323.2   **flat cars** Open railroad cars for transporting goods. Fitzgerald meant passenger cars.

323.6–7   **The New York Herald** [the "Paris Herald" See Explanatory Notes, 22.18.

323.11   **"Comment?"** "What?" (French)

323.20–21   **took up his bed and walked** Matthew 9:6: "But that ye may know that the Son of a Man hath power on earth to forgive sins, (then saith he to the sick of the palsy,) Arise, take up thy bed, and go unto thine house."

324.13   **highball** Drink consisting of an alcoholic beverage (usually whiskey) and water or club soda, served in a tall, stemless glass.

325.5   **"The Wedding of the Painted Doll"** Popular song of 1929; lyrics by Arthur Freed, music by Nacio Herb Brown.

Book III, Chapter 3

327.18   **bad cess** Anglo-Irish expression meaning bad luck.

328.25   **Mount Everest** Highest mountain in the world, in the Himalayas between Nepal and Tibet.

329.21   **vin-du-pays** The local wine (French).

Book III, Chapter 4

331.2–3   **rented again for the summer** The summer of 1928 (see Chronology).

331.11   **eleven and nine** [**eight and six** Lanier was born in 1920, Topsy in 1922 (see Chronology).

332.11   **Pomeranians** A breed of small, long-haired dogs.

332.13   **nine** [**six** See Explanatory Notes, 331.11, and Chronology.

332.29–   **visit to the Minghettis** Fitzgerald did not delete this ep-
341.11   isode in his marked copy, but it is identified for deletion
in his "Analysis of *Tender*" (see Introduction: "The Author's Final Version").

332.29   **Boyen [Bozen** Bozen (Bolzano) in the South Tirol was
ceded to Italy in 1919 (see Emendations).

333.2   **Sealyhams** Breed of terrier developed in Wales.

333.2   **Pekinese** Breed of small Chinese dogs.

333.9   **a chest of servants' trunks** Fitzgerald wrote "servants
trunks" in MS, which he emended to "a chest of servants' trunks" in second TS. This emended phrase is
puzzling; Fitzgerald seems to have meant a trunk containing drawers.

333.30   **a papal title** An honorary title granted by the Pope; but
if Hindu by birth, Hosain has presumably undergone
a formality of conversion to Roman Catholicism (see
Explanatory Notes, 334.1).

333.33   **Pullman south of Mason-Dixon** During the period of ra-
cial segregation in America the so-called Jim Crow laws
prevented black passengers from using railroad sleeping
cars in the South (below the Mason-Dixon Line).

334.1   **Kabyle-Berber-Sabaean-Hindu** This combination of
terms for ethnic groups, religion, and language refers to
peoples from coastal Algeria through North Africa to
Iraq and into central/north India. The Kabyle are one
of the three principal groups of Berbers; they are non-
nomadic and occupy the Tiziuzu region of coastal Algeria. Berber is the name give by modern ethnologists to
the North African stock of aboriginal races. Sabaean
designates an adherent of a religious sect mentioned in
three passages of the Koran. Hindu refers to the principal religion of India.

334.7   **majordomo** Chief steward of a large household.

334.10   **salaamed** Bowed in obeisance.

334.19   **swank** Ostentatious luxury.

334.22   **Buddha** A god in the Buddhist religion.

334.22 **Bolshevik** The communist faction led by Lenin that emerged victorious after the 1917 Russian Revolution.

334.23 **Stalin** Joseph Stalin (1879–1953), Soviet dictator from 1924 to his death.

334.27 **royal bus** There is no royal bus; Nicole is making a joke about Mary's newly acquired wealth and prominence.

335.28 **smoke** Pejorative term for a black.

336.10 **beaters** Servants who rouse game for a shooting party.

Book III, Chapter 5

342.10 **tripos [trident** A trident is a three-pronged spear; it was used by gladiators.

342.13 **Chablis Moutonne** Chablis is a dry white wine; wines from the Moutonne vineyard are designated Chablis Grand Cru Moutonne.

343.5 **bastide** Country house (French); a reference to Diver's work house.

343.14– **Commune** There were three French revolutionary
15 groups known as communes: La Commune de Paris was the assembly that took responsibility for Paris after the fall of the Bastille in 1789; it was succeeded by the extremist Commune Insurrectional in 1792; La Commune was a council that seized power in Paris in 1871.

344.7 **Saland [Salaud** A term of abuse: filthy beast (French).

344.12– **"Au revoir, Madame! Bonne chance!"** "Goodbye,
13 madam! Good luck!" (French).

345.12 **the law of diminishing returns** Diver means that Nicole's symptoms have diminished as a result of his dedication to her cure. Fitzgerald apparently misused the idiom; it refers to the need for ever-increasing efforts to maintain ever-diminishing benefits. Diver may be expressing his conviction that he is wasting his time on Nicole's care, but he does not intend that she understand him.

345.22 **T. F. Golding** A fictional character.

345.23   **Nicean Bay** The Bay of Nice.

345.31   **already summer dusk [already dusk** This is the evening following Diver's altercation with the cook, which takes place in April. See *Tender*, 342.3.

345.32   **"Margin"** The yacht is named for the stock-market procedure of buying stocks by partial payment—usually a speculative method.

346.7   **companionway [ladder** A companionway is a flight of steps connecting one deck of a vessel with another.

346.12–   **I'm yours . . .** Unidentified song.
13

346.29–   **laundered chests** Starched dress shirts.
30

347.3   **Antoninian bench** Reference to the art of the Antonine period (Roman emperor Antoninus Pius, 86–161). A triclinium, a couch on which Romans dined, was associated with feasts.

347.17   **Five [Four** Four years have elapsed since the opening of the novel in June 1925 (see Chronology).

347.23–   **"Mais pour nous autres héros . . . il faut faire les**
25   **grandes compositions."** "However, for us heroes," he said, "we need time, Nicole. We cannot perform small acts of heroism; we must participate in the major events" (French) (see Emendations).

347.27   **"Parlez français avec moi, Nicole."** "Speak French to me, Nicole." (French)

348.6–7   **Corps d'Afrique du Nord [la Légion Étrangère** Barban is referring to the unit known as the French Foreign Legion, which is la Légion Étrangère—not the Corps d'Afrique du Nord, the first-edition reading. Ronald Colman starred in the 1926 production of P. C. Wren's *Beau Geste*, the best-known novel about the French Foreign Legion. Colman also appeared in another Foreign Legion movie, *Condemned* (1930).

348.31   **cat of the stripe** A member of a social class or group.

348.32   ***chemin-de-fer*** Card game known as twenty-one or blackjack in English.

348.33　　*mille Swiss* One thousand Swiss francs; the 1929 rate of exchange was five francs to the dollar.

349.10　　**John Held's flat-chested flappers** Held (1889–1958), the most popular illustrator of the Twenties, drew boyishly slim young women known as flappers. Flappers were liberated young American women of the time; but the term originated in England during World War I to designate women deprived of suitors by military service.

349.23　　**Lady Sibly-Biers [Lady Caroline** Lady Caroline Sibly-Biers is partly based on Bijou O'Conor, an Englishwoman Fitzgerald allegedly had an affair with in Switzerland in 1930; see *Bijou O'Conor Remembers F. Scott Fitzgerald* (London: Audio Arts, 1975). Bijou O'Conor also provided the model for Lady Capps-Karr in "The Hotel Child" (*Saturday Evening Post*, 31 January 1931; see Emendations.)

349.27　　**Sepoys** Indian mercenaries in the British army in Bengal who mutinied in 1857–58.

349.28　　**green hat** Reference to the self-destructive heroine of Michael Arlen's 1924 novel *The Green Hat* (see Explanatory Notes, 280.18).

350.4　　**a chep's a chep** A chap is a chap; Fitzgerald represents Lady Caroline's upper-class English accent.

350.9　　**"Danny Deever"** Rudyard Kipling's poem, collected in *Barrack–Room Ballads* (1892), about a military execution: "An' they're hangin' Danny Deever in the mornin'." The poem is traditionally recited with a lugubrious intonation.

350.13–　　*There was a young lady from hell, . . . from*
19　　*hell*—— This song lyric was presumably written by Fitzgerald.

350.24–　　**"Quelle enfanterie . . . Racine!" ["Quelle enfantil-**
26　　**lage! . . . Racine!"** "What childish behavior! . . . He sounds like he's reciting Racine!" (French). Jean Baptiste Racine (1639–1699) was a French tragic dramatist (see Emendations).

351.20　　**untipped the capped barbs** Removed the coverings

from the arrow points. Fitzgerald appears to have scrambled this expression: he meant that Dick had removed the coverings from the arrow points of his irony.

351.28   **Malay game** Unidentified.

352.32   **poule** Whore (French).

353.15–   **good stocks. . . . All goes well.** This remark supports
16   the claim that the time is before the October 1929 stock-market crash.

353.16   **it** The pronoun-noun disagreement is probably deliberate. Fitzgerald explained to Dashiell: "Tommy is supposed to speak with a faint foreignness indicated only at intervals" (6 February 1934; Princeton University Library).

353.17   **Dick's getting rich** There is no previous mention of Dick's investments.

353.19   **afterdeck** Deck area at the stern of a vessel.

354.13   **brains addled a l'anglaise** Diver is referring to Lady Caroline in menu terms; i.e., brains muddled in the English fashion.

Book III, Chapter 6

355.14   **café au lait** Coffee with heated milk (French).

356.7   **Georgia pine** Georgia pine, known as long-leaf pine, is a hard pine, but pine is a soft wood.

356.8   **lignum vitæ** Technically a South American subtropical plant, but the term is used in Australia and New Zealand for eucalyptus and acacia.

357.17   **Niçois and Provençal** The French dialects of Nice and Provence.

Book III, Chapter 7

362.27   **Chinese Wall** The Great Wall of China, a high wall that extends 1,500 miles from Kansu Province to the Gulf of Chihli; for Nicole it symbolizes a monument of protective exclusion.

362.33   **couturiers** Designers of custom-tailored men's garments, or the establishments where such garments are made and sold.

363.1   **Dites donc!** Hey! (French).

363.19   **pajamas** At that time beach pajamas were worn over bathing suits as protection against the sun.

363.24   **five [four** Rosemary first arrived on the Riviera in June 1925, and it is now summer 1929 (see Chronology).

363.30   **trout nook [trout hook** Fitzgerald meant the hook on a shiny metal fishing lure known as a spoon (see Emendations).

364.5,14   **five [four; 364.8 Five [Four** See Explanatory Notes, 363.24, and Chronology.

364.30   **aquaplane** A board towed by a motorboat; riding aquaplanes was popular before water skis were introduced.

365.1   **Last summer [The summer before last** See *Tender*, 366.26–27.

367.1   **Baby Gar** Make of motorboat manufactured in the Twenties by speedboat builder and driver Garfield Arthur "Gar" Wood (1880–1971).

367.26   **"Château"** The character's nickname; the word means "mansion" in French.

369.31   **Anita Loos** (1893–1981); American author of *"Gentlemen Prefer Blondes"* (1925), a comic novel about a shrewd chorus girl.

369.31–
32   **faits accomplis** Completed matters or actions (French).

370.15   **Balkan-like** The Balkan states include Serbia, Croatia, and Montenegro; although they had been combined with part of Austria-Hungary to form the Republic of Yugoslavia in 1918, they remained symbols of ineffectual and contentious statehood.

370.30   **Chargés d'Affaires** French title for diplomats who substitute for ambassadors or ministers.

371.22   **comédiennes** Actresses who perform non-tragic parts.

371.27–
372.8   **"The danger. . . . character again."** Critics have attempted to apply Diver's analysis of acting to the meaning of the novel, but his observations are muddled. Fitzgerald intended them as another example of Diver's attempts to impress Rosemary.

373.30   **Schubert** Franz Peter Schubert (1797–1828), Austrian composer.

374.1   **Thank y' father-r** "Thank Your Father," 1930 song; music by Ray Henderson, lyrics by B. G. DeSylva and Lew Brown:

> Thank your father,
> Thank your mother!
> Thank 'em both for meeting up with one another!

374.9   **Moorish roof** Reference to a style of architecture introduced into Europe by the Moors in the Middle Ages.

Book III, Chapter 8

375.16   **Chanel Sixteen [Chanel Nineteen** Chanel Number Five is the best-known perfume made by the firm, and the proofreader tried to emend the reading. Fitzgerald informed *Scribner's Magazine* editor Alfred Dashiell on 6 February 1934: "Also he [the proofreader] seemed completely upset by Chanel 16 and should ask his wife" (Princeton University Library). There has never been a Chanel Sixteen, the reading of the first printing; Fitzgerald probably meant Chanel Nineteen, described by the firm as: "Forever young. . . . Intensely female. . . . Contemporary. Brilliant. Witty. . . . Outspoken. Supremely confident and completely independent."

376.20–
21   **landings . . . bears in the hall** Fitzgerald's metaphor evokes the anxieties of a child's solitary climb upstairs to bed.

377.1   **white-duck** A stiff cloth used for summer clothing.

377.15–
16   **white crook's eyes** Possibly a description of the white-ringed irises of someone with wide-open eyes.

379.14   **mad puritan** A deranged practitioner of a strict morality.

379.33 **police blanks** It was necessary for guests at French hotels to register with the local police.

380.6 **Puck** Mischievous sprite and agent of disorder; he appears as a character in Shakespeare's A *Midsummer-Night's Dream*.

380.27– *departure of American sailors* On 6 February 1934 Fitzgerald wrote to Glenway Wescott: "About six years
383.33 when I was doping out my novel *Tender Is the Night* . . . somebody told me about the departure of an American battleship from Villefranche with the attendant *poules*, etc. I built an episode of my book around it and spoke of it to several people. A year or so later a letter came from Ernest Hemingway [September or October 1928] telling me that you had used it for a background in a short story ['The Sailor,' *Good–bye Wisconsin* (1928)]. His advice was that I should read it and thus avoid any duplication, but my instinct was to the contrary, and I waited until I had written my own scene before I read *Goodbye to Wisconsin*. There are, unavoidably, certain resemblances, but I think that I will let it stand" (*The Letters of F. Scott Fitzgerald*, p. 507).

380.28– **Oh, way down South . . .** Parody of "Dixie," the Confederate anthem in the American Civil War.
30

381.14 **Languedoc** Coastal region in southern France between the Rhone Valley and the Pyrenees.

381.27– **Cézannes and Picassos** Paintings by French post-impressionist Paul Cézanne (1839–1906) and by Pablo Picasso (see Explanatory Notes, 211.33).
28

382.6 **Korniloff** Lavr Georgyevich Korniloff (1870–1918), Cossack general who opposed the Russian Revolution.

382.15 **Dulschmit** The name of one of the brawling sailors.

382.15 **you son** Short form for *son of a bitch*.

383.5 **pass-outs** Those who were rendered unconscious by alcohol.

383.18 **Kwee** Phonetic spelling for "Can we?"

145

383.25   **gen'al alivery** General delivery; mail to be picked up at the post office by the addressee.

383.28   **step-ins** Brief panties.

383.31–   **Oh, say can you see . . . the Star-Spangled Banner**
33   The American national anthem, celebrating the symbolic endurance of the national flag in the Battle of Fort McHenry in 1814, was written by Francis Scott Key; Fitzgerald was his namesake and second cousin three times removed.

384.2   **Beaulieu** Riviera town east of St. Jean-Cap-Ferrat.

384.5   **Menton** The most eastward city on the French Riviera.

384.9–10 **Damascus . . . Mongolian plain** Damascus is the capitol of present-day Syria; under Genghis Khan (1167–1227) the Mongol Empire extended from China to the Danube River.

384.12   **yielding up of swords** Ceremony of surrender.

Book III, Chapter 9

386.11   **Avignon** City in southeast France, seat of the papacy from 1309 to 1377; when the papal see was returned to Rome in 1378, rival popes established themselves in Avignon (1378–1417).

387.8   **"Nicole, comment vas-tu?"** "Nicole, how are you doing?" (French).

389.22   **top dog** The person in control.

Book III, Chapter 10

391.1–   *Cannes police station episode* When Perkins asked Fitzgerald to cut this episode in the serial, he responded:
396.17

> Isn't there any mechanical means by which you can arrange to include the 1400 words of the arrest in Cannes? The more I think of it the more I think that it is absolutely necessary for the unity of the book and the effectiveness of the finale to show Dick in the dignified and responsible aspect

toward the world and his neighbors that was implied so strongly in the first half of the book. It is all very well to say that this can be remedied in book publication but it has transpired that at least two dozen important writers and newspaper men are reading the book in the serial and will form their impressions from that. . . .

If I do not hold these two characters to the end of the book it might as well never have been written. It is legitimate to ruin Dick but it is by no means legitimate to make him an ineffectual. In the proof I am pointing up the fact that his intention dominated all this last part but it is not enough and the foreshortening without the use of this scene, which was a part of the book structure from the first, does not contain enough of him for the reader to reconstruct his whole personality as viewed as a unit throughout—and the reason for this is my attempt to tell the last part entirely through Nicole's eyes. I was even going to have her in on the Cannes episode but decided against it because of the necessity of seeing Dick alone (5 February 1934; *A Life in Letters*, p. 246.).

Fitzgerald wired Perkins twice on the fifth. First in a night letter received the next day:

> FEEL CANNES JAIL SCENE SHOULD GO INTO SERIAL OPINIONS INDICATE SAME OTHERWISE DICKS CHARACTER WEAKENS AND NOVEL FORSHOTENS TOWARD END IT IS NEEDED AND WAS WRITTEN TO BOLSTER HIM UP IN INEVITABLE UNDIGNIFIED CUCKOLD SITUATION STOP PLEASE PERMIT WILL TREAT TACTFULLY WIRE (1:28 a.m.)

(*Correspondence of F. Scott Fitzgerald*, p. 329).
Then in a straight wire:

> FEEL DOWNRIGHT ESSENTIAL FOR READER TO GET GLIMPSE OF DICK THROUGH IMPERSONAL EYES NOT TOMMYS AND NICOLES TO SUSTAIN HIM AT THE END OTHERWISE FINAL TRIAL OFF INSPIRES SCORN INSTEAD OF PATHOS CANT REPEAT MISTAKE OF BEAUTIFUL

> DAMNED STOP SCENE IS FOURTEEN HUN-
> DRED WORDS BUT CANT YOU ARRANGE IT
> SOMEHOW (1:29 p.m.)

(*Correspondence*, p. 329).

391.4   **"Oui, oui . . . mais à qui est-ce-que je parle? . . . Oui . . ."** "Yes, yes . . . but to whom am I speaking? . . . Yes" (French).

391.19   **Ophelia** In Shakespeare's *Hamlet*, a young woman who, beset by conflicting loyalties after Hamlet's affection is withdrawn, becomes deranged and drowns herself.

392.1–2 **'pas de mortes—pas d'automobiles'** 'Not death—not automobiles' (French).

392.7   **Alpes-Maritimes** The department, or administrative district, of France that encompasses the Riviera and adjoining areas.

392.18   **Alsatian coma** Gausse, a heavy sleeper, is a native of the French region of Alsace.

393.7   **fifty stripes of the cat** Fifty lashes with the cat-o'-nine-tails, a whip formerly used in the British navy.

394.25   **John D. Rockefeller Mellon** Diver has combined the names of two American financiers, John D. Rockefeller (1839–1937) and Andrew Mellon (1855–1937), in order to impress the French police officer.

394.28   **Lord Henry Ford** Diver ennobles American automobile manufacturer Henry Ford (1863–1947).

394.29   **Renault and Citroën companies** French automobile manufacturers.

395.3   **Prince of Wales** The future King Edward VIII of England was a glamorous figure during the Twenties.

395.3   **Duke of Buckingham** Dick Diver has invented a royal prince as a bluff. There was no Duke of Buckingham in the late 1920s.

395.21   **landaulet** An automobile having a convertible top for the back seat; the front (chauffeur's) seat is either roofed or open.

396.10   **leg-irons** Metal bands encircling each ankle and connected by chain; used to restrain prisoners.

Book III, Chapter 11

397.7   **Carlton Hotel** Luxury hotel in Cannes.

397.14   **coiffeuse** Female hairdresser (French).

398.13   **citron pressé** Lemon juice.

398.14   **demi** A half-pint of beer.

398.15   **Blackenwite with siphon** Diver is ordering scotch and soda. He is pronouncing Black and White, a brand of whiskey, as the recognizable single word used by French waiters.

398.16–
17   **"Il n'y a plus de Blackenwite. Nous n'avons que le Johnny Walkair"** "There is no more Black and White. We have only Johnny Walker."

398.18   **"Ça va."** "O.K."

398.19   **She's—not—wired** Unidentified; possibly Fitzgerald's lyric.

398.31–
32   **"Donnez mois du gin et du siphon."** "Bring me gin and a bottle of carbonated water."

399.20   **"Cessez cela! Allez ouste!"** "Stop this! Get out of here!" (French).

399.28   **Tour de France** The major European bicycle road race. In 1929 it arrived in Cannes on 15 July.

399.29   **"allez-vous-en"** "Go away" (French).

399.31   **five [four** Diver had previously encountered the newsvendor in July 1925.

400.4   **"Elle doit avoir plus avec moi qu' avec vous."** "She will have more with me than with you" (French).

400.9   **"L'amour de famille,"** "Domestic love" (French).

400.22   **harlequinade** Comedy or pantomime featuring the character Harlequin in costume of variegated colors.

401.21   **"I never did go in for making love to dry loins," said Dick.** When Fitzgerald was attempting to persuade Bennett Cerf to publish a revised text of *Tender Is the Night*

149

in the Modern Library, he wrote: "There is not more than one complete sentence that I want to eliminate, one that has offended many people and that I admit is out of Dick's character: 'I never did go in for making love to dry loins.' It is a strong line but definitely offensive" (13 April 1936; *A Life in Letters*, p. 306). Fitzgerald did not delete the sentence in his marked copy.

Book III, Chapter 12

402.7 **Fräulein** The children's German governess; a presumably French governess was identified as Mademoiselle at 245.24, 246.4, and 369.27. Lucienne, who was unable to change the bathwater at the Minghetti house (336), is the Divers' maidservant, not their attendant governess, who has a maid of her own (332.32).

403.1 **Sardinia** Italian island in the Mediterranean.

403.10 **A & P [AP** The Associated Press, an American news syndicate (see Emendations).

403.29 **six years** Nicole is referring to the years of their marriage before Diver encountered Rosemary.

404.5 **Hapsburg** The German royal house to which the Austrian rulers belonged.

404.18 **anisette** Liqueur flavored with aniseed.

404.28 **Doctor Eliot's classics** Charles W. Eliot (1834–1926), president of Harvard, editor of the fifty-five-volume set of *Harvard Classics*, known as the "Five-Foot Shelf."

405.23 **against the sky** There may be a perspective problem here; Diver is looking down at the beach from the terrace.

405.28 **bit** Unsuspectingly accepted the conversational baited hook.

Book III, Chapter 13

407.6– **Buffalo . . . Hornell** Cities or towns in upstate New
408.10 York. Diver's moves are meant to convey the impres-

sion of his downward progress from small town to smaller town. In 1930 Buffalo had a population of more than half a million; Batavia had 17,375; Lockport had 23,160; Geneva had 16,053; and Hornell had 16,250. Therefore the census figures do not jibe with Fitzgerald's intention. Batavia was not "a little town," and Hornell was not "a very small town."

408.3–10 **last letter . . . . latest note** Fitzgerald is distinguishing between a letter and a note, indicating that Dick is no longer maintaining a full correspondence.

408.7 **Finger Lakes** Five long, narrow lakes in upstate New York. Geneva is at the head of Seneca Lake.

408.9 **career . . . like Grant's in Galena** See Explanatory Notes, 155.5–6. This reference reinforces the connection between Diver and Grant as representative American figures.

Editorial Rationale

Tender Is the Night is protected by American copyright until 2009. The Editorial Rationale and Emendations sections provided here are required for an eventual critical edition that corrects the damaging errors in existing texts and thereby fosters a reevaluation of the novel.

The base text[1] for this projected edition is the first printing of the first edition of *Tender Is the Night* (New York: Charles Scribner's Sons, 1934). The pre-book typed drafts do not provide a final setting copy for the novel because they are all work in progress.[2] Fitzgerald rewrote and revised through every stage of production, including final galleys and book galleys. His latest corrected book galleys would be the best base text for a critical edition of *Tender*, but only a few of Fitzgerald's marked book galleys survive. See "Introduction: Editing and Publication."

For the reasons adduced in the Introduction, Fitzgerald's marked copy of the book has been rejected as base text. His revisions related to restructuring the novel have not been incorporated here; but particular substantive corrections or punctuation alterations have been accepted. See Appendix B.

The editorial rationale for this edition is to establish the text that could have been published in 1934 if Fitzgerald had had ample time for proof revision and if Scribners had been able to give the book details the thorough checking required for factual and chronological accuracy. The editor of this edition has done what Maxwell Perkins and his staff should have done in 1934. The obvious limitation on this endeavor is that the present editor cannot check queries with Fitzgerald this side of paradise; therefore certain cruces can be noted but not emended. Thus: did Fitzgerald intend *asthma* or *miasma* (113.5); did he intend *palpable* or *palatable* (306.18)? Although the extent of the Emendations list (eighty-two word alterations—exclusive of spellings and foreign terms) suggests that the emendations policy here is promiscuous, substantive emendations have been made only where Fitzgerald's intentions are sufficiently clear from documentary evidence (MS, TS, proof) or where verifiable factual errors require correction.

Fitzgerald was a social realist who used details meaningfully but often got them wrong. The reader who knows the things Fitzgerald wrote about and understands how the meanings of fiction are conveyed through real details is distracted by individual errors. A certain concentration of errors damages the reader's capacity to trust the author and the work.

There are editors who hold that their duty is to protect a text from corrections because authorial blunders become integral to the meaning of the work. The operation of this mystical process has not been explicated. The timid and convenient position of the preservationists does not differentiate between intentional functional errors, which do not require correction (e.g., Abe North's drunken speech), and unintentional errors, which require correction (e.g., incorrect geography and contradictory chronology in Fitzgerald's narrative).[3]

Apparently Perkins—who has been described by Charles Scribner, Jr. as "totally useless when it came to copy editing or correcting a text"—was not concerned with factual errors.[4] Whether he prevented the other Scribners editors from interfering with Fitzgerald's work has not been established. Fidelity to the errors and inattentions of Perkins or other editors does not constitute protection of Fitzgerald's art.

It is not an act of piety to cherish authorial blunders that damage the work and confuse good readers. Fredson Bowers has provided the proper response to preservationists: ". . . I take it that the business of an editor is to edit. If he is unprepared to take the risks of backing his own judgments, he should peddle another line of goods."[5] Yet the introduction of substantive emendations into the text of a classic work of literature triggers protests from civilians, amateurs, and indecisive editors: "How dare you rewrite

Fitzgerald!" Emendation of non-functional errors is not rewriting. Emendation of non-functional errors is not collaboration. Emendation is the recovery of what the author wrote or what he expected to have corrected by his editors. In this edition emendation of factual errors is limited to simple substitution: thus, at 193.17 the nonexistent Jugenhorn mountain is replaced by the actual Dent du Jaman. Alterations that would require rewriting a phrase or a sentence have not been made in the text; they are identified as *stet* entries in the Emendations list.

The champions of uncorrected errors claim that it is sufficient for an editor to call attention to the errors by means of an editorial—or non-editorial—apparatus in order for the readers to decide what to do. But the texts of so-called "definitive editions" are republished without apparatus, thereby making it impossible for readers to decide anything about emendations, whether or not incorporated in the texts. The issue comes to this: Is a text that retains unidentified authorial errors preferable to a text with unidentified emendations? It is difficult to justify the work necessitated by scholarly editing unless the resulting text is closer to the author's intentions and expectations than the best unedited text.

The editorial procedures for substantives (the words themselves) is clear; but establishing editorial policy for Fitzgerald's accidentals (punctuation, spelling, capitalization, typographic styling) is troublesome.[6] It is more difficult to emend his punctuation than it is to correct factual errors. The options are to retain Fitzgerald's idiosyncratic or incorrect punctuation to the extent that it can be recovered from the pre-book documents, or to retain the inconsistent or incorrect Scribners punctuation from the first printing,[7] or to attempt to impose corrections and consistency on the text while retaining the characteristics of Fitzgerald's practice. This projected edition adopts the third option.

As discussed in the "Editorial Principles and Procedures" for the Cambridge University Press editions of *The Great Gatsby* and *The Love of the Last Tycoon: A Western*, Fitzgerald punctuated by ear—not by the rules.[8] His habits and preferences can be determined from the manuscripts and revised typescripts.

Comma usage:

a) Fitzgerald usually omitted a comma between adjectives;

b) he customarily omitted a comma before the conjunction connecting two independent clauses;

c) he almost always omitted a comma before *and* or *or* in a three- element combination;

d) he habitually omitted a comma after a short introductory phrase;

e) he used a comma before the name of the character in direct address more often than not, but no system is evident;

f) he inconsistently omitted the first or the second of paired commas with parenthetical phrases;

g) but he occasionally inserted a superfluous comma in long sentences.

Fitzgerald rationed colons and semicolons—preferring to link sentence units with dashes. He distinguished between short dashes and long dashes, using the long dash to indicate interrupted speech or a broken sentence. He resisted hyphens in word division as well as in compound adjectives. He rejected italic type for titles.

The ability to determine Fitzgerald's manuscript punctuation habits does not justify a policy of blanket restoration.

Fitzgerald expected his editors to do the necessary to render his writing publishable. He understood the consequences of factual or mechanical errors, instructing Alfred Dashiell to have the serial proofs checked for errors in French and German: "There is a certain sort of critic, who when he is over his head, takes refuge in schoolmarm quibbling, and another type of reader who is legitimately annoyed by inaccuracy."[9]

The present edition endeavors to preserve the characteristics of his style on a case-by-case basis. Fitzgerald's manuscript practice has been emended in two categories: 1) Incorrect or distracting punctuation—see split speech and comma splices below—and 2) departures from the conventions of typography and printing—such as the placement of punctuation with quotation marks. But Fitzgerald's idiosyncratic punctuation has been retained when it seems to be functional—for example, the unnecessary comma at 303.16. Fitzgerald treated rhetorical questions as declarative sentences: ". . . Isn't it funny and lonely being together, Dick." He ended this sentence with a period in the MS, which was retained in the TSS. The serial replaces the period with a question mark; but the period is restored at book 209.6—presumably by Fitzgerald. Incorrect or distracting pointing has been emended when it cannot be defended as deliberate or functional. Fitzgerald's unconventional punctuation of split speech has been corrected because it serves no discernible purpose for style or sense: for example, 21.26; 38.6; 45.30. Comma splices have been retained in characters' speech but emended in Fitzgerald's narrative—see 59.19–20.

This edition emends some 450 accidentals. The policy for the accidentals in *Tender Is the Night* must be flexible, with ad hoc exceptions. An editor cannot take the easy way and accept all the punctuation in the first printing on the basis that Fitzgerald had the opportunity to alter it in proof. Only parts of eleven marked book galleys survive, but a complete set would not eliminate definite errors (such as misplaced apostrophes) or obviate Fitzgerald's reliance on Scribners editing. In general, he accepted house styling, except when it conflicted with certain strong preferences. For example, Fitzgerald restricted italic type to indicating emphasis, instructing Perkins:

> Confirming our conversation on the phone this morning, I wish you could get some word to the printers that they should not interfere with my use of italics. If I had made a mess of a type face, that would be another matter. I know exactly what I am doing, and I want to use italics for *emphasis,* and not waste them on the newspaper convention laid down by Mr. Munsey in 1858. Of course, always you have been damned nice in having your printers follow my specifications, but in this case, and under the very pressing conditions under which we are working, it worries me that the book galleys came back with exactly the same queries that the magazine galleys had. Could you tip them the wink some way so that they would please follow my copy exactly as they used to, as this is my last chance at the book? Whoever has been in charge of it must be very patient because I know at the ninth revision that the very sight of any part of it fills me with nausea. However, I have to go on in this particular case while they don't, and so are liable to get careless.[10]

The house styling of the 1934 text is incomplete and inconsistent. The Scribners editors did not know that they were working on a masterpiece. Even if they had recognized that *Tender Is the Night* would become a classic, the conditions and deadlines of publishing made it impossible for them to perform their work properly. That kind of editing is the responsibility of a scholar-editor after a work has achieved the permanent stature that mandates such an investment of time, money, and research.

Notes

1. The base text is the form of the work that the editor emends, normally the latest version the author saw through the press.
2. See *Tender Is the Night,* 5 vols.; Part 4 of *F. Scott Fitzgerald Manuscripts,* ed. Bruccoli. New York & London: Garland, 1991.
3. Bruccoli, "Getting It Right: The Publishing Process and the Correction of Factual Errors—With Reference to *The Great Gatsby,*" *The Library Chronicle of the University of Texas at Austin,* 21, nos. 3/4 (1991), 41–59. Revised and separately published, Columbia, S.C., 1994.
4. *In the Company of Writers: A Life in Publishing* (New York: Scribners, 1991), p. 44.
5. "Scholarship and Editing," *The Papers of the Bibliographical Society of America,* 70 (Second quarter 1976), 161–168.
6. The terms *substantive* and *accidental,* introduced by W. W. Greg ("The Rationale of Copy-Text," *Studies in Bibliography,* 3 [1950–1951], 19–36; reprinted in *The Collected Papers of Sir Walter Greg,* ed. J. C. Maxwell [Oxford: Clarendon Press, 1966]), have generated misunderstanding. Accidentals do not result from accidents; they are deliberate, although they may not be authorial in printed texts.
7. If the Scribners editorial department relied on a particular style manual, it has not been identified. The undated eight-page pamphlet *To the Author* provides instruction about correcting galley proofs (Bruccoli Collection, Thomas Cooper Library, University of South Carolina).
8. *The Great Gatsby,* ed. Bruccoli. Cambridge & c: Cambridge University Press, 1991; *The Love of the Last Tycoon: A Western,* ed. Bruccoli. Cambridge & c: Cambridge University Press, 1993.

9. 2 February 1934. *Correspondence of F. Scott Fitzgerald*, ed. Bruccoli and Margaret M. Duggan (New York: Random House, 1980), p. 328.

10. 4 March 1934. *F. Scott Fitzgerald: A Life in Letters*, ed. Bruccoli, with the assistance of Judith S. Baughman (New York: Scribners, 1994), p. 248.

Emendations

The serious reader can prepare an accurate text of *Tender Is the Night* by entering these emendations in the 1934 text. The first reading is the emended reading in this edited text; the left-pointing bracket ( ]) is following by the rejected reading in the 1934 first printing (the base text). The notation *stet* identifies a reading that has not been emended although emendation is possible; all *stet* entries are accompanied by textual notes or are cross-referenced to explanatory notes. Carets indicate omitted punctuation mark; the wavy rule signifies that the word is unchanged. The letter C following an emendation indicates that Malcolm Cowley introduced this reading in his 1951 "Author's Final Version." Asterisks on the page/line references identify emended readings that have explanatory notes.

The form of this editorial apparatus represents a departure from conventional treatment. Instead of citing the pre-base-text variants by means of symbols, this edition briefly describes the variants—see diagram of drafts. All the MS, TS, and proof documents* cited in these notes are facsimiled in *Tender Is the Night*, 5 vols.; Part 4 of *F. Scott Fitzgerald Manuscripts*, ed. Bruccoli (New York & London: Garland, 1991). The editor has long believed that editorial apparatus consisting of a thicket of symbols intimidates and discourages all but a few zealots. This apparatus represents an attempt to make textual scholarship more usable.

---

* Both the Emendations list and the Explanatory Notes use the standard abbreviations: MS (manuscript—a document in Fitzgerald's hand); TS (secretarial typescript—Fitzgerald did not type); and RTS (revised typescript—a typescript revised in Fitzgerald's hand).

The following words have been silently regularized in accordance with Fitzgerald's MS usage:

anyone] any one

One-word spelling for pronoun usage is invariable in MS.

everyone] every one

Invariable in MS.

goodbye] good-by

The "bye" spelling is invariable in MS; it is impossible to be certain whether Fitzgerald wrote two words or one word in every case, but "goodbye" is his clear preference.

Monte-Carlo] Monte ∧ Carlo

Rue] *stet*

Although "rue" is now the standard French form, "Rue" is acceptable in English-language publications, and it was Fitzgerald's invariable usage.

someone] some one

It is impossible to be certain in every case whether Fitzgerald wrote one word or two words, but "someone" is his MS preference for adverbial use.

sometimes] some times

It is impossible to be certain in every case whether Fitzgerald wrote one word or two words, but "sometimes" is his clear MS preference.

today] to-day

Invariable in MS.

tomorrow] to-morrow

Invariable in MS.

tonight] to-night

Invariable in MS. Scribners practice in 1934 was to hyphenate "to-day," "to-morrow," and "to-night;" but A Manual of Style, Seventh Edition (Chicago: University of Chicago Press, [1920]) and Eighth Edition (1937), stipulates that they are to be printed as one word. The hyphenated forms were used in England at that time, and it is possible that the Scribners proofreaders were under the influence of a British style guide, such as F. Howard Collins's *Authors' & Printers' Dictionary*, Sixth Edition (London: Humphrey Milford, 1928).

(599)

I don't think I've helped you. I've only
bolstered your self-confidence a little
and you had plenty of that in the beginning."
Nicole stood up suddenly.
"I'm going to bed."
"I am too. Goodbye Francisco."
Goodbye all you unfortunates, good
bye Hotel of Three Worlds, Goodbye
Lausanne, Farwell, Goodbye goodbye.

Space here →

~~Goodbye ...~~
~~Spring became ...~~
The total affect of this incident upon
Nicole did not show for several days; the
~~was~~ restless unhappiness that she wore in
the interval ~~until~~ week off his guard but
at the time of menopause the reaction

Manuscript page showing Fitzgerald's spellings of "goodbye" (Princeton
University Library).

161

*Epigraph line 1 ∧ *Already*] "∼

Epigraph line 1 *night. . . .*] ∼ ∧ . . .

Epigraph line 2 ∧ ∧ ∧ *But*] . . . ∼

Epigraph line 4 *ways.*∧] ∼ ."

*3.14 alp] Alp

4.10   hotel] C; Hotel

*6.13;   354.7 Golfe-Juan] ∼ ∧ ∼

9.9   *know*,"] ∼"

*12.6   Antheil] C; Anthiel

**12.8   'Ulysses'] ∧ ∼ ∧

13.5   'Ulysses,' "] ∧ ∼ , ∧ "

*17.11–   the Pont du Gard at Nîmes] The ∼ ∼ ∼ ∼ Arles
12

*17.12   amphitheatre] Ampitheatre

*18.9   Allées] Alliés See Emendations, 213.2.

*18.12–   "Le Temps"] ∧ ∼ ∼ ∧
13

*18.13   "The Saturday Evening Post"] ∧ ∼ ∼ ∼ ∼ ∧

*18.14   citronnade] citronade

18.25   hotel] Hotel

*18.30   czar] C; Czar

*19.1   Buddhas'] C; Buddha's

*19.6   church] Church

19.16   hotel] C; Hotel

20.19   were] *stet* Cowley corrected *were* to *was*, but the use of
          were is common.

21.26   swimming."] C; ∼ ,"

*22.18   the "Paris Herald."] ∧ The New York Herald. ∧

23.28   other—she] ∼ , ∼ Fitzgerald wrote paired dashes in
          MS and retained them through serial. The comma was
          substituted for the dash after *other* in the book text.

24.23	uninterested] C; disinterested The sense requires *uninterested*; but Fitzgerald wrote *disinterestedly* in MS and revised to *disinterested* in first TS.
*24.30	Signor Campion] *stet*
*25.3	'Book of Etiquette'] ∧ ~ ~ ~ ∧
*28.10	dwarf] dwarfed
29.8	of a stage] ~ ∧ ~ Fitzgerald wrote "wall of a studio" in the Melarky MS, which became "wall of a stage" in TS and was retained through the serial. The book reading is presumably a compositorial oversight.
*33.4	twenty-five] ~ -four
*36.23	Speck ∧] ~ , This comma first appears in book text.
37.13	∧ Au] " ~
37.20	Dieu. ∧] ~ ."
38.6	heels. "In] ~ , "in
38.11	think——"] ~ —"
38.11	game.] ~ ,
42.8	Divers'] Diver's
*43.4	Clicquot] Cliquot
43.18	madonna] Madonna
45.24	communist] Communist
45.25	socialist] Socialist
45.25	McKisco.] ~ ,
45.30	excuses."] ~ ,"
46.7	world ∧ and,] ~ , ~ ∧ Fitzgerald misplaced this comma in all drafts.
*48.20	Iles de Lérins] C; Isles des Lerins
49.32	too-obvious] ~ ∧ ~
52.7	education ∧] ~ , The comma after *education* first appears in book text.
54.7	thing——"] ~ —"
54.22	her,] ~ . Fitzgerald's comma after *her* in MS and TS was altered to a period in the serial text.

55.13   moved another bench] *stet* Thus in MS, first TS, and serial.

59.8   temper——"] ~ —"

59.19–20 years, we] *stet* Thus in MS. The comma splice presumably represents McKisco's strained speech.

*60.4   parties] *stet*

*60.10   Pushkin's] *stet*

*61.10   words] *stet*

62.11   Speers's] Speer's

*63.3–4;   Juan-les-Pins] ~ ∧ ~ ∧ ~
223.30;
354.8

65.25   doctor,] ~ .

*67.1   Voisin] Voisins

68.16   chair. . . .] ~ ∧ . . .

69.19   count] Count

69.24   other,] ~ ∧ Fitzgerald emended this sentence in first TS by employing paired commas; but the comma after *other* was not retained in serial setting copy.

*70.8   Rue de Saint-Ange] ~ des Saintes ∧ Anges

*71.27   Hermès] Hermes

*75.5   Western ∧ Front] western-front

*75.7   First Marne] first ~

*75.21   'Undine,'] ∧ ~ , ∧

*75.23   Württemberg] C; Wurtemburg

75.29   high-explosive] ~ ∧ ~

*77.23   Waterloo Station] ~ station

*78.6   Württembergers] C; Wurtemburgers

*78.8   Old Etonians] C; old ~

*78.10   mortadella] mortadel

*79.2   Arts] C; Art

*79.4   Hôtel Roi George] C; Hotel ~ ~

79.16	ambition ∧] ~ , Fitzgerald inserted this superfluous comma in the first TS, and it was retained thereafter.
83.7	you——"] ~ —"
83.18	him,] ~ ; In the MS a semicolon connects two independent clauses. In the first TS Fitzgerald emended the construction to an independent clause followed by a participial phrase; his alteration of the semicolon to a comma was not clear, and the semicolon was retained in subsequent stages.
84.6	so——"] ~ —"
85.3	he] He
85.4	proximity—] ~ ,
85.21– 22	show me, I'm] *stet* Thus in MS. The comma splice may have been intended to represent Rosemary's passionate speech.
85.29	Mother] mother
86.1	Mother] mother
86.22	simply——"] ~ —"
88.4	fall] *stet* The Yale Junior and Senior Proms were held in February during the Twenties, but the internal chronology of the novel requires "fall" here.
88.5	Paris, was] ~ ∧ ~ Since the rest of the sentence is carefully punctuated, this comma has been supplied.
89.10	Mother] mother
90.3	before. When] ~ — ~ Fitzgerald rewrote this paragraph between serial and book; the dash construction originates in the book text.
90.20	"Daddy's Girl"] ∧ *Daddy's Girl* ∧
*90.32	Tanagra] tanagra
91.10	evitable;] ~ , A semicolon is required to link two independent clauses.
91.26	"Daddy's Girl"] ∧ *Daddy's Girl* ∧
91.32	large.] ~ ,

*93.6   Lutétia] Lutetia

93.10   "But——"] " ~ —"

95.2   esoteric;] ~ , The sentence first appears in book text; a semicolon is required to link two independent clauses.

*95.28   spic] slick The first TS has *spick* inserted in holograph. This word is retained in the serial setting copy and the serial. The alteration to *slick* in the book text is probably nonauthorial. The word is spelled "spic" in MS appearances for 285.3 and 335.26.

96.6   all——"] ~ —"

97.5   hotel] Hôtel

97.9   Mr.——"] ~ —"

102.5   whom Abe addressed conscientiously] *stet* The phrase first appears in the book text; Fitzgerald may have meant *punctiliously*.

*102.5   Hengist] C; Hengest

102.11   technic] *stet* The use of this word with the meaning of *technique* is acceptable. Fitzgerald wrote *technique* in MS and retained it through the serial setting copy; *technic* first appears in the serial.

*104.20   Saint ∧ Sulpice] Saint-Sulpice

*104.28; Champs-Élysées] C; ~ ∧ ~
136.15;
137.2

*105.1   Saint-Lazare] C; ~ ∧ ~

105.9   beach] Beach

106.9   on world cruise] *stet* Fitzgerald wrote "on the world cruise of the Adriatic" in MS and revised it to "on the world cruise of the Paris" in the first and second TSS. The serial text reads "on world cruise."

*106.17   Genevieve's——"] ~ —"

*108.26   survivant] *stet*

109.31   yards] years Fitzgerald wrote *yards* in the MS, which is retained in the first and second TSS and serial text. The reading *years* is almost certainly a printer's error.

111.21   décor] C; decor

111.30   accustomed] *stet* The sense here seems to require *unaccustomed,* but Fitzgerald wrote *accustomed* in MS and retained it in all subsequent drafts.

113.5   asthma] *stet* Fitzgerald may have intended *miasma,* but he wrote *asthma* in MS and retained it in subsequent drafts.

113.26   unmodulated. "We] ~ , "we

*114.   Grand-Guignol] ~ ∧ ~
10–11

117.5   friend] friends The sense requires a singular noun.

117.22   Zürich] Zurich All appearances.

*117.31   saw with his heels] *stet* Thus in MS, first and second TSS, and serial.

*119.10, 100,000 Chemises] C; 1000 chemises
12

*119.30   Canossa] Ferrara

120.6   purposes;] *stet* Fitzgerald inserted the incorrect semicolon in the revised second TS to break up a long sentence; it was retained thereafter.

120.14   Rue de Saint-Ange] ~ des Saintes-Anges

121.11   a while] awhile

121.11   through?"] ~ ." The question mark appears in every draft until the book text.

*121.28   'Times'] ∧ ~ ∧

*122.31   Marie Brizard] C; ~ Brizzard

*122.31   Punch Orangéade] ~ Orangeade

*122.   ∧ Fernet-Branca] André ~ -Blanco
31–32

*122.   Cherry Rocher] C; ~ Rochet
31–32

123.8   ∧ And] " ~

123.11   Alow-own. ∧] ~ ˌ ~ ."

125.4   she had awakened by] *stet* Fitzgerald wrote "what had awakened her" in MS and revised to "she had awakened by" in first TS, which was retained in second TS and serial.

*125.8   sergent ∧ de ∧ ville] ~ ، ~ ، ~

127.20   who,] ~ ∧ The comma appears in all drafts beginning with the revised first TS but was omitted from the book text.

*127. 25–26   Teput Dome] teput dome

127.29   a——"] ~ —"

128.20   there——"] ~ —"

*128.23   Évreux] C; Evreux

128.26   baroque] Baroque

129.26– 27   conservatism] conversation The second TS has Fitzgerald's holograph insertion: "Nicole clung to her conservatism." The word *conservatism* is retained in the serial setting copy, the serial galleys, and the serial. The reading *conversation* in the book text is a typo.

*131.4   Mosby] C; Moseby

*132.10   concessionnaire] concessionaire

*132.23   'Liberty'] ∧ ~ ∧

*133.4   'France'] ∧ ~ ∧

133.4–5   this name] *stet* The first and second TS and serial read "his name." In the lost book proof Fitzgerald may have revised "his name" to "this name" to characterize Paul's speech.

133.8   'France.' "] ∧ ~ . ∧ "

134.31   here——"] ~ —"

*136.2–3   arrondissement] C; arrondisement

*136.16   falling] failing Fitzgerald wrote *falling* in MS and retained it in first and second TSS. The word *failing*, which first appears in the serial text, is probably a compositorial blunder.

137.18– 19   and been watching] *stet* Fitzgerald wrote "she had been watching the rain" in MS and revised the clause to "she had just dressed and been watching the rain" in first

TS. The revised reading is retained in second TS and serial.

137.21 godlike] C; Godlike

*139.8–9 Party in the border states] party ~ ~ ~ States

*139.29 Latin Quarter] ~ quarter

141.17 watch man] *stet* Fitzgerald wrote "watch a man" in RTS, but the *a* was marked for deletion in proof.

*142.13 George the Third] C; ~ ~ third

144.16 still-unfastened] ~ ∧ ~

145.32 unexceptionably] unexceptionally Fitzgerald wrote *unexceptionally* in MS and retained it in all subsequent drafts; but the sense requires *unexceptionably*.

147.27– Zürichsee] Zurichsee All appearances.
28

*151.2 twenty-seven] ~ -six

151.3 bachelorhood.] ~ ∧

*152. Damenstiftgasse] C; Damenstiff Strasse
18–19

*153.18 at New Haven] in ~ ~ Fitzgerald made this correction in his copy.

153.27 criterion] C; criteria The sense requires a singular noun.

*153.31 "The Rose and the Ring,"] ∧ ~ ~ ~ ~ ~ , ∧

154.17 yourself. Once] ~ —once Fitzgerald made this emendation in his marked copy.

*154.25 Achilles's] Achilles'

154.28 people—] ~ ; An unidentified hand altered Fitzgerald's dash to a semicolon in the serial setting copy.

154.29 falsely ∧] ~ , This comma first appeared in serial setting copy. An unidentified hand deleted and then restored it in serial galleys, and it was retained in the serial and the book.

*156.16 cortex] C; cervical

157.1 Gregorovious] *stet* The usual spelling for this German-Swiss name is "Gregorovius" (see 227.23).

*157.2   psychopathologist] pathologist

*157.7   Kraepelin] Krapaelin

158.5   privates] private soldiers Fitzgerald made this correction in his marked copy.

*158.13   Kreuzegg] Krenzegg In first TS Fitzgerald altered *Jugenhorn* to *Kreuzegg*, which was typed as *Krenzegg* in second TS and retained thereafter.

159.10   menacing ∧] ~ , Fitzgerald inserted this unnecessary comma in the second TS.

159.13   one] they Fitzgerald made this correction in his marked copy.

159.20   room. Push] ~ ; push Fitzgerald made this emendation in his marked copy.

*160.1   Armistice] armistice

160.3   thence] *stet* Fitzgerald wrote *there* in RTS and retained it in subsequent TSS, but he altered it to *thence* in serial galleys.

161.31   on] in Fitzgerald wrote "harping constantly on the" in MS and retained it through the serial; the book reading "in" may be a printer's error.

162.21   farcical] farcicle There are no other spelling errors in Nicole's letters; this misspelling, which was usual for Fitzgerald, was almost certainly an unintentional error here. There is no MS corresponding to this appearance, but in the MSS for other appearances of the word Fitzgerald spelled it "farcicle" at 211.6 and 248.17 (the latter of which he corrected to *farcical*).

163.10   train nurse] *stet* There is no MS for this passage; the first TS and all subsequent stages read "train nurse."

164.3   life. . . .] C; ~ ∧ . . .

164.4   clouds. . . .] C; ~ ∧ . . .

164.5   war. . . .] C; ~ ∧ . . .

164.8   me. . . .] C; ~ ∧ . . .

164.13   edelweiss. . . .] C; ~ ∧ . . .

*166.6   seventeen] sixteen

*167.7   fourteen] eleven

168.21   that."] that. ∧

169.6   down——"] ~ —"

170.31   Personality.] ~ ,

171.9–10 God ∧ damned] ~ -/ ~ Fitzgerald's MS preference was to spell this expletive as two words with a capital G (see 297.31 and 305.7).

173.11   phantasy] phantom Fitzgerald wrote *phantasy* in MS and retained it in TSS and serial; *phantom* is probably a printer's error.

*174.27; Grossmünster] Gross-Münster
192.16

*175.9   clinic at Interlaken] Clinic on Interlacken

175.33   watch ∧] ~ , When Fitzgerald revised this sentence in the second TS, he retained the unnecessary comma.

*178.10 Suppé's] C; Suppe's

*179.8   Good ∧ Bye] ~ -by

*179.31 Swiss] Valais In MS and first TS Fitzgerald wrote *Swiss*, which he emended to *Valois* in second TS and retained through serial. *Valais* first appeared in book.

180.1   ∧ Lay] " ~

180.4   round—∧] ~ —"

180.12   down. . . .] ~ ∧ . . .

180.17   complementary] complimentary The sense requires *complementary*.

180.29   There! ∧ "] ~ !,"

181.26   service] Service

182.4   theme] *stet* Fitzgerald may have meant *plan*, but he wrote *theme* in MS and retained it in TSS and serial.

*183.11 Glas ∧ Bier] C; ~ -. ~

*184.4   afternoon] morning

186.2   do—] ~ , The comma splice first appears in a typed insert for the revised serial galleys.

*186.18. twenty-three] ~ -four

171

*187.17   Burberry] burberry

188.2–3   forthcoming. ∧] ~ ."

190.19   Well——"] ~ —"

191.3   alpine] Alpine

192.12   who] whom Fitzgerald inserted *whom* in the first TS; the serial corrects the word to *who*, but the book restores *whom*.

193.10   (twice) -*Kraepelin*] C; -*Krapælin*

193.15–   German.* *space break* ¶Going] ~ .* *no space break*¶ ~
16   The space break was marked by Fitzgerald in the first and second TSS and in the serial setting copy. The break appears in the revised serial galleys and in the serial. The loss of the space break in the book text certainly resulted from a printer's error. Fitzgerald restored the space break in his marked copy of the book.

*193.17   Dent du Jaman] Jugenhorn

*193.22   train-bands] trained- ~ The correct term is *train-bands*.

*193.26   July] June

193.29   Versuch,] ~ ∧

193.31   (twice) -Kraepelin] C; -Krapaelin

193.31   sie] C; siz

193.34   Meinung,] ~ ∧

*194.4   Tour-de-Peilz] ~ ∧ ~ ∧ Pelz

194.7   slid down port] *stet* In the second TS Fitzgerald revised "slid into port" to "slid down port."

*194.20   Two years ago] *stet*

*194.27   confrère] confrere

195.33   di] de The character is an Italian.

196.5   dignified——"] ~ —"

*197.19   twenty-three] ~ -five

*199.24   schizoid] schizzoid

*200.1   Guards ∧] C; guards'

201.2   doctor——] ~ —

202.14   you——"] ~ —"

202.22   nurse——"] ~ —"

203.25–   how he could do with me] *stet* Fitzgerald wrote
26   this phrase in MS and retained it in all subsequent
          drafts.

205.4   whomever] whoever Correct usage requires *whomever*.

205.18   ∧ I'm] " ~

205.20   happened. ∧] ~ ."

207.3   ill-advised] ~ ∧ ~

207.3   said.] ~ ,

208.1   Rhodes Scholar] ~ scholar

208.1   governor] Governor

208.26   Sister] sister

208.33   supposed ∧] ~ . The mark after *supposed* is a printing-
          plate flaw that resembles a period.

*209.23   camérière] camerière

*209.30   Grotto] C; Grotte Fitzgerald wrote *Grotte* in MS and
          retained it in subsequent drafts. His spelling may have
          reflected the pronunciation of the Italian *La Grotta Az-
          zurra.*

210.4   ∧ Oh] " ~

210.7   me—— ∧] ~ ——"

*210.20   Athena] Athene

*211.   Affaires Étrangères] C; *Affaires Etrangères*
28–29

*211.32   Mistinguett] Mistinguet

*211.33   "Pas sur la Bouche"] ∧ *Pas sur la Bouche* ∧

*212.30   June] July

213.2;   Allées] Alliées See Emendations, 18.9.
215.6;
349.21;
398.9

213.16   hands. ∧] ~ ."

215.14   caffeine] caffein

173

216.7   high stool] highstool Fitzgerald wrote this phrase as two words in MS and all subsequent stages; *highstool* in the book text is a printer's error.

216.17   "A Psychology for Psychiatrists."] ∧ *A Psychology for Psychiatrists.* ∧

216.25   lived,] *stet* Fitzgerald inserted this unnecessary comma in second TS and retained it thereafter.

217.23   McBeth] C; MacBeth See 146.8, 11, 21, 24, 28.

218.25   anywhere——"] ~ —"

220.2   hotel] Hotel

*220.5   poussée] pousse

*221.11   menagerie] C; Menagerie

222.16   ∧ Just] " ~

222.18   me—— ∧] ~ ——"

223.28   hotel] C; Hôtel

223.29   casino] C; Casino

227.23   Gregorovious] Gregorovius The name is spelled "Gregorovious" in all other appearances.

227.24   half ∧ hour] ~ - ~

230.11   have] C; haven't The sense requires Franz to have examined the books. Fitzgerald wrote *have* in MS, which was retained in first and second TSS. The serial alters the reading to *haven't.*

*230.20   Privatdozent] Privat docent

232.17   without,] *stet* The superfluous comma has been retained as written by Fitzgerald because he seems to have wanted a pause in the rhythm of the sentence at this point.

*233.3   Humpty ∧ Dumpty] C; ~ - ~

235.11   season] Season

235.18   good bye! ∧] good-by!"

*236.5   Love for] C; ~ of

237.7   Nothing] *stet* Fitzgerald wrote *nothing* in MS and retained it through serial; the personification *Nothing* appears only in the book.

239.30   uninstructed] instructed The second TS has *instructed* inserted in holograph, which is retained in serial; but the sense requires *uninstructed.*

239.31   filigree] filagree

*240.25   as imprisoned in the Iron Maiden.] *stet* Fitzgerald revised "like a turtle beneath a shell" to "imprisoned in the iron maiden" in the second TS; the serial reads "as imprisoned in the Iron Maiden."

242.7   here——"] ~ —"

243.14   with ∧ nail] C; ~ a ~ Correct usage requires that *scissors* be treated as a plural form.

245.1   manic] maniac In the setting copy for the serial Fitzgerald altered *manic depressive* to *manic.* The book reading *maniac* is almost certainly a typographical error.

*246.5   Ägeri] Agiri

*247.29   pleasance] plaisance

*247.30   Ferris wheel] ferris ~

248.1   the crowd, a crowd] *stet* This construction first appears in the serial setting copy.

*248.23   Bock] bock

249.20   apposite] *stet* Fitzgerald wrote this word in MS and retained it through all subsequent drafts.

*250.21   schizophrène] schizophrêne

252.20   Émile's] C; Emile's

252.30   Émile] C; Emile

253.18   persuasive] *stet* A holograph insertion on the second TS, this word was retained through all stages. Fitzgerald may have meant *pervasive.*

254.7   patients'] patient's

255.8   usurp] *stet* The meaning requires *reclaim,* but Fitzgerald wrote *usurp* in MS and retained it in all subsequent drafts.

*255.   the "Century," the "Motion Picture," "L'Illustration,"
10–11   and the "Fliegende Blätter,"] The ∧ ~ , ∧ The ∧ ~ ~ , ∧ ∧ ~ , ∧ ~ ~ ∧ ~ ~ , ∧

256.13   a battered] C; A ~

256.20–   Munich anyhow?] *stet* Formal punctuation requires a
21   comma after *Munich*, but Fitzgerald omitted it in MS
           and all subsequent drafts.

257.7   or feel his] nor ~ their Fitzgerald wrote "he did not
           like any man much nor feel the presence of other men"
           in MS; he revised the phrase to "he did not like any
           man much nor feel their presence" in the second TS.

257.   prince] Prince
27, 32

258.2   tour] Tour

*258.16   Marxian] *stet*

258.22   papier-mâché] ~ ∧ ~

*259.7   drawn into] ~ in Correct usage required *into*.

*259.11   stood ready to depart] departed

259.31   the "Herald"] The ∧ ~ ∧

*262.7   Erbsensuppe] erbsen-suppe

*262.7   Würstschen] C; würstschen

*262.8   steins] helles

*262.9   "Kaiserschmarren."] "kaiser-schmarren."

262.27   Zurichsee] Zürichsee

*263.8   continental] Continental

*263.13   January] October

265.5   ∧ YOUR FATHER DIED PEACEFULLY TONIGHT HOLMES
           ∧] "Your father died peacefully tonight. HOLMES."

*266.16   the income] C; it

*266.18   Gilded Age] gilded age

268.17   the ship's] its The pronoun cannot refer to *harbor*.

269.26   that , ∧ falling . . . plot ∧ and . . . women ∧
           thought] ~ , and ~ . . . ~ , ~ . . . ~ , ~ This
           sentence was revised by Fitzgerald in the second TS:
           "He pretended they were this and that and falling in
           with his own plot, drinking too much to keep up the

illusion—and all this time the women thinking only that this was a windfall from heaven—riding along with them all night and even kissing one of the sisters on the platform of the train. . . .”

*269.33;   Quirinale] Quirinal
287.1;
292.24;
293.3,   5,
11;
294.15,
27;
306.21

*270.11   black-seed oil] Black-~ ~

*270.11   hoofs] C; hoops The sense requires *hoofs*. The word *hoops* first appears in the book text and is probably a printer's error.

270.17   Was] was

*271.1   “Corriere della Sera”] ∧ ~ ~ ~ ∧

*271.1–3 “un romanzo di Sainclair Lewis, 'Wall Street,' nel quale l'autore . . . città Americana.”] “una novella ~ ~ ~ ∧ '~ ~ ∧ 'nella ~ autore . . . citta ~ .”

*271.7,   three] four
14

*271.15   thirty-six] ~ -four

*271.16   twenty-one] ~ -two

*271.16   thirty-nine] ~ -eight

274.2   'Daddy's Girl'] ∧ ~ ~ ∧

274.17   now. . . .”] C; ~ ∧ . . .”

274.21   heaven. . . .] C; ~ ∧ . . .

276.11   psychology?”] ~ ?'

*276.12   twenty-one] ~ -two

*277.11,   Forum] forum
12

277.13   props;] stet This semicolon appears in MS and is retained in every subsequent stage.

277.32   answer,] ~ ⋀

*278.20   Castello dei Cesari] Castelli ~ Cæsari

279.6   from] to Idiomatic usage requires *from.*

282.6   Englishmen] Englismen

282.29   ⋀ ——Only the very big ones, Baby. ⋀] "— ~ ~ ~
          ~ ~ , ~. " This sentence is Dick Diver's thought,
          not his speech. The quotation marks first appear in
          the book text, probably the result of a proofreader's
          error.

285.3   jealousy—] ~ , Fitzgerald inserted this dash in the re-
          vised second TS, but a comma appears in serial and
          book texts.

288.16   Nazionale] C; Nationale

*288.28; Bomboniera] Bonbonieri
289.20;
293.7

*290.5   mousseux] mousseaux

*292.10   lenci] Yenci

*292.19   campagna] Campagna

*294.16, soûl] C; saoûl
23

295.12   down ⋀] ~ , Fitzgerald employed the comma in the
          revised second TS; it was omitted in the serial but re-
          stored in the book text.

295.19   ghastly] *stet* The word is *aghast* in the first and second
          TSS and serial.

*296.7   guards ⋀] guards'

*297.20   Wops!"] ~ ! ⋀

297.31   God damn] goddamn

*298.3   l'inglese."] inglese."

*301.18   *semper dritte, dextra* and *sinestra*] *stet*

*301.22   Piazza di Spagna] C; Piazzo d'Espagna

302.2   himself,] ~ ⋀

303.16   continent,] *stet* The superfluous comma has been re-
          tained as written by Fitzgerald because he seems to have

wanted a pause in the rhythm of the sentence at this
point.

304.8   forgives,] ~ ∧

304.8   life;] ~ ,

305.7   God damn] god ~

306.18   palpable] *stet* Fitzgerald may have intended *palatable*
(agreeable), but *palpable* (tangible) first appears in the
TS for the Melarky version and continues through the
Diver TSS, serial, and book.

*309.28   telegram] C; cable

311.4   children——"] ~ —"

311.26   clinic] C; Clinic

*314.3   Wassermanns] Wassermans

314.15   Chilean] C; Chilian

*314.31;   Pardo ∧ Ciudad Real] ~ y Cuidad ~
315.3;
319.20;
320.19

316.1   Francisco.] ~ ,

316.7, 25; Chile] C; Chili
319.22

317.21   collect] *stet* In the serial setting copy Fitzgerald revised
"trying to put the name of the man together" to "trying
to collect the man's name." Emendation to *recollect* is
not required.

*318.28   Genevois] Génevois

319.15   best-known medicine men] *stet* Fitzgerald wrote "one
of the best internal medicine man" in MS, which was
typed as "one of the best internal medicine men" in the
first TS. The holograph insertion *known* was made in
the second TS but retyped as "one of the best known
medicine men" in the serial setting copy.

319.24   Paris——"] ~ —"

*320.17   Devereux] Charles

*320.22   barbital] barbitol

*320.27 *grata*] *gratis*

323.6–7 the "Paris Herald"] The ∧ New York Herald ∧ See Explanatory Notes, 22.18.

323.33 thousand-dollar] ~ ∧ ~

324.7 Father] father

*325.5 "The Wedding of the Painted Doll."] ∧ ~ ~ ~ ~ ~ ~ . ∧

*327.18 ∧ cess] C; ' ~

329.26 pair. "Lladislau] ~ . ∧ ~ Dick Diver's speech resumes after *pair.*

*331.11 eight and six] eleven ~ nine

332.4 regimen] C; regimentation The sense here requires *regimen*; *regimentation* first appears in the serial setting copy and is retained in the retyped serial galley insert.

332.12 Father] father

*332.13 six] nine

*332.29 Bozen] Boyen In the first TS Fitzgerald inserted *Offengotten*, which was altered to *Boyen* in a typed revision for the serial galleys.

*339.9 a chest of servants' trunks] *stet*

*333.33 Pullman] pullman

*334.1 Kabyle-] C; Kyble-

335.26 'spic'] ∧ ~ ∧

336.27–28 of itself] ~ herself Fitzgerald inserted "of herself" in the first TS and retained it in subsequent drafts. It is unlikely that he was using incorrect pronoun reference to characterize Lanier.

337.11 La] El Mary Minghetti's title is Italian, not Spanish.

337.27 Western] western

340.5 saying——"] ~ —"

340.22 "blunder,"] ∧ ~ , ∧

*342.10 trident] tripos

*343.5 bastide] Bastide

*343.14– Commune] commune
15

343.18   you——"] ~ —"

*344.7   Salaud] Saland The correction was made in the fourth printing (1951).

345.7   him, ∧ which] ~ , about ~ In the second RTS Fitzgerald revised "in his mind toward some conclusion and that Nicole could only snatch at" to "inside him toward which she could only guess at." The serial reads "inside him which she could only guess at."

345.23   bay] C; Bay

*345.31   already ∧ dusk] ~ summer ~

*345.32   "Margin"] ∧ ~ ∧

346.6   'Margin'!"] ∧ ~ ∧ !"

*346.7   ladder] companionway

347.3   down] own The word *own*, which first appears in the book text, is clearly a typographical error for *down*.

347.5   Negroes] negroes

*347.17   Four] Five

*347.   nous autres héros . . . il ∧ faut . . . d'héroïsme] ~
23–25   ∧ ~ . . . ~ nous ~ . . . d'héroisme Barban's French presumably is fluent.

347.32   all——"] ~ —"

*348.6–7 la Légion Étrangère] Corps d'Afrique du Nord

349.16   "Margin"] ∧ ~ ∧

*349.23   Lady Caroline] C; ~ Sibly-Biers The form Lady Caroline is appropriate for the daughter of a duke, marquess, or earl. Lady Sibly-Biers is appropriate for the wife of a knight, baronet, or other titled gentleman ranking from baron through marquess. Since the character is referred to as Lady Caroline at 349.30; 350.27; 351.4; 353.30; 392.22; 393.1; 393.8–9; 393.20; 393.28; 395.20;

181

395.26; 396.2; and 396.6 in the novel, Lady Sibly-Biers should be emended.

350.13   ∧ There] "There

350.19   hell—— ∧] hell—"

*350.   "Quelle enfantillage!"] C; " ~ enfanterie!" The correct
24–26   French word for *childishness* is *enfantillage*.

*353.16   it] *stet*

*353.19   afterdeck] after deck

*354.13   brains addled à l'anglaise] Brains ~ a l'Anglaise

355.14   waking] *stet* Fitzgerald inserted "waiting for café au lait" in the second TS, but the serial reads "waking for café au lait."

357.4   death ∧] ~ , The superfluous comma first appears in serial text.

*357.17   Niçois] C; Niçoise

360.4–6   DEARS WILL BE AT GAUSSES TOMORROW UNFORTU-NATELY WITHOUT MOTHER AM COUNTING ON SEEING YOU ROSEMARY] Dears will be at Gausses to-morrow unfortunately without mother am counting on seeing you. ROSEMARY.

361.14   hopeful ∧ —] ~ ,— The comma-dash combination first appears in book text.

361.20   personified] *stet* Fitzgerald may have meant *indicated, symptomized,* or *expressed.*

362.3–5   guess . . . or] ~ . . . nor Fitzgerald inserted this ho-lograph wording in the second RTS: "She could not guess . . . nor." He revised this passage to "she couldn't guess . . nor" in serial setting copy—which he retained in serial and book.

*362.33   couturiers—] ~ ,

*363.24   four] five

*363.30   hook] nook The word *nook,* clearly a printer's error for *hook,* appears only in the book.

*364.5,   four] five
14

*364.8 Four] Five

364.15 some,] ~ ∧

*365.1 The summer before last] Last summer

368.17 her] Her

368.18 direction—] ~ ∧

368.33 Abrams's] Abram's

*369.31 Loos] Loos'

*369. faits accomplis] Faits Accomplis
31–32

370.12 boat ∧ —] ~ ,— The comma-dash combination first appears in book text.

372.20 Michel] Michelle The chauffeur would have been male; Michelle is the feminine form of the name.

372.28 changed ∧ —] ~ ,— The comma-dash combination first appears in book text.

*374.1 ∧ Thank] " ~

374.3 another—— ∧] ~ ——"

374.7 ∧ —Thank] " — ~

374.8 tight—— ∧] ~ —— "

*375.16 Nineteen] Sixteen

378.8 eyes, did] ~ ∧ ~

378.16 certain——"] ~ —"

380.10 animal, she] ~ ∧ ~

380.15 highlights] high lights

*380.28 ∧ Oh,] " ~ ,

380.30 away——∧] ~ ——"

382.23 place] palace Fitzgerald wrote *place* in MS and retained it in TSS and serial. The alteration to *palace* was almost certainly the result of a typographical error.

383.4 voices;] ~ ,

383.4 denials,] ~ ;

383.33– Banner. *space break* ¶They] ~ . *end of page*¶ ~ The
384.1 space break indicating a time shift is marked in MS and

183

retained in the first and second TSS and serial. The break was lost in the book page makeup.

*384.5   Menton] Mentone

387.21   to——"] ~ —"

389.31– receptacles] receptables Fitzgerald wrote *receptacles* in
32   MS, which was retained in TSS and serial. The alteration to *receptables* resulted from a printer's error.

*391.4   Oui. . . ."] ~ ∧ . . ."

391.28   Sibly-Biers] Sibley-Biers

*392.7   Alpes-Maritimes] ~ ∧ ~

392.10   However,] ~ ∧

394.17,   cartes d'identité] Cartes d'Identité
21,
395.17

394.23   countess] Countess

394.30   However,] ~ ∧

396.12   casino,] Casino,

*397.7   Carlton] Carleton

398.11   Under the arching trees, central in summer,] *stet* The meaning of "central in summer" is unclear; but it presumably indicates that the branches of the trees on either side meet overhead, forming a summer canopy. The phrase does not appear in MS or extant TS. MS reads "under the arch of palms." Dashiell queried "central in summer" in the serial galleys (1 March 1934); Fitzgerald's response is unknown.

*398.19   ∧ She's] "She's

398.21   it—— ∧] it——"

*398.31– Donnez mois du gin et du siphon] *stet* The correct
32   French is *Donnez-mois du gin et un siphon.*

399.4   five years] *stet* Barban's desire for Nicole likely predated the 1925 opening of the novel.

399.16–   the "Herald" and of the "Times"] The ∧ ~ ∧ ~ ~
17   The ∧ ~ ∧

*399.20   ouste] C; Ouste

399.29   en,"] *stet* The comma is battered in the plate and appears as a period.

399.31   Rue de Saint-Ange] Due ~ Saints ∧ Anges

*399.31   four] five

400.31   dupes] *stet* This word refers to people who are easily imposed on; the context indicates that Fitzgerald meant *victims.*

400.34   half-cut] ~ -washed See *Tender,* 398.4.

401.11   principle] principal Correct usage requires *principle.*

*401.21   "I never did go in for making love to dry loins,"] *stet*

403.5   beach] C; Beach

*403.10   AP] C; A & P For AP, the Associated Press, Fitzgerald wrote "A & P"—which is a chain of supermarkets. Dashiell queried this reading in the serial galleys: "It is true, I believe, that there is an Atlantic & Pacific Picture concern, but I am afraid the grocery chain has the call on the initials in the minds of most of the people" (1 March 1934). Fitzgerald's response is unknown.

404.29   not——"] ~ —"

404.30   "Even] "even

407.16   public-health] ~ ∧ ~

408.7   section] C; Section

Time Scheme

The clear understanding of the chronology of events and the passage of time[1] in *Tender Is the Night* is essential to the reader's proper response to the novel. The effectiveness of the 1925–1917–1925 flashback has generated debate; but the structural flaw in *Tender* is the blurred time scheme from summer 1925 to summer 1929. Reviewers who challenged the credibility of Dick Diver's dive were in part reacting to inadequate or contradictory time signals in the novel. The progress of Dr. Diver's decline from brilliantly promising psychiatrist to alcoholic failure is difficult to trace because the reader is not always certain when an episode is occurring. How much time elapses between the Gstaad trip at Christmas 1925 and the next chapter at the clinic? *Nineteen or twenty months.* How much time elapses between Nicole's breakdown at the fair and Diver's arrival in Rome? *About eight months.* How much time elapses between the Divers' departure from the clinic and their return to the Villa Diana? *About nine months.* Does Diver depart from the Riviera in 1929 or 1930? *In 1929.* What is the time span of the novel from Book I, Chapter 1, to Book III, Chapter 12? *Four years: summer 1925–summer 1929.*

The key time signals are at 236.18 ("this past year and a half on the Zugersee") and 238.3–4 ("For eighteen months now he had lived at the clinic"). Eighteen months after Christmas 1925 in the previous chapter places the time of Book II, Chapter 14, in summer 1927, allowing a month or two for the Divers' move to Switzerland. This calculation fits the 1928 date (276.13) that Fitzgerald stipulates in the Rome chapters.

The chronology difficulties can be attributed to the conditions of writing, editing, and publication. Fitzgerald was revising or rewriting the serial and book texts at the same time; the production schedules made it impossible for Scribners to give *Tender* the scrupulous line editing it required—even if the publisher had been prepared to invest the time.

The chronology in the first edition is unworkable, but Fitzgerald meant it to be accurate. He prepared preliminary character chronologies (see Introduction)—though they have internal contradictions and he did not strictly adhere to them. It is improper for an editor to insert dates or other time signals into the text of *Tender*, but a critical edition must emend the misleading time references that are in the first edition.

The editor of *Tender* has two choices: to retain the years that Fitzgerald stipulates (1925 and 1928) in the first edition, emending the intervening elapsed time, or to emend the year 1928 to 1929 in the Rome sequence. The former option requires that Diver's departure from the Riviera in Book III, Chapter 12, take place in summer 1929; the latter option extends the time span to summer 1930. There is more involved in this decision than arithmetic. Whether Diver's departure occurs before or after the October 1929 stock-market crash shapes the concluding moods of the novel. If, as the editor of this text contends, the final Riviera episodes take place before the crash, there is the dramatic irony of impending catastrophe—a sense that the rich who have corrupted Diver and his Riviera protectorate are unknowingly living on borrowed time. A postcrash ending conveys the irony that the rich are still rich but that Diver has been ruined by them.

The compelling reason for preferring the precrash ending is that the crash is not mentioned in the novel. The financial data in the closing chapters are all related to the boom: aboard the *Margin* Barban states that he has "good stocks in the hands of friends who are holding it for me. All goes well"; and Nicole replies that "Dick's getting rich" (353.15–17). The assertion that Fitzgerald was indifferent to the crash is unconvincing. He had written brilliantly about the effects of the crash on American expatriates in "Babylon Revisited" (published in February 1931). The inaccurate age tables for Diver and Nicole both stipulate that the story ends in July 1929.

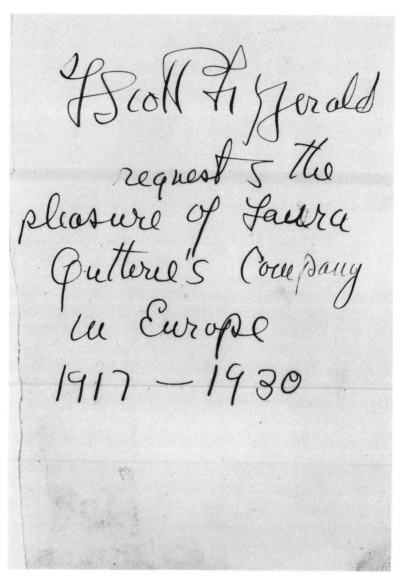

Inscription removed from a copy of *Tender Is the Night* (Bruccoli Collection, University of South Carolina).

The only piece of documentary evidence supporting the post-crash ending is an inscription in a copy of the novel: "F Scott Fitzgerald requests the pleasure of Laura Guthrie's Company in Europe 1917–1930."[2] This inscription was written in 1936 or 1937. Malcolm Cowley, who supported the 1925–1930 time span, claimed that 1930 "was the year when, in spite of the crash, there were more rich Americans in Europe than ever before and when the summer season on the Riviera was the biggest and maddest."[3] He was not in France at that time. Cowley argues that "the chronology of the novel requires thirty months, not eighteen, between the Christmas holidays at Gstaad and Dick's working at the clinic. One can assume that the Divers spent another year on the Riviera while the clinic was being remodelled, and then eighteen months on the Zugersee."[4] This assumption creates a hole in the novel.

The chronology for this critical edition of *Tender Is the Night* provides an emended time scheme for the 1925, 1917–1925, 1925–1929 structure.

Notes

1. The concentration of time words in the novel reinforces the theme of mutability or deterioration in the novel: *year(s)*, 135; *month(s)*, 34; *weeks*, 36; *day(s)*, 104; *hours(s)*, 64; *minute(s)*, 72.
2. Bruccoli, "Inscribed TITN," *Fitzgerald Newsletter* (Washington, D.C.: NCR Microcard Editions, 1969), 202. See also *F. Scott Fitzgerald: Inscriptions* (Columbia, S.C., 1988), Item 27.
3. *The Author's Final Version*, p. 355.
4. P. 352.

Chronology

The *Tender Is the Night* readings cited in this chronology are from the emended text.

April 1889	Birth of Richard Diver.
Mid-1896	Birth of Baby Warren. At Christmas 1925 she is "almost thirty" (*Tender*, 226.5).
Mid-1900	Birth of Nicole Warren. In June 1929 she is described as a "woman of twenty-nine" (*Tender*, 376.7, 14, 20).
July 1907	Birth of Rosemary Hoyt. In July 1925 she celebrates her birthday with the Divers and the Norths: "yesterday was my birthday—I was eighteen" (*Tender*, 81.1–2).
Fall 1907	Diver enters Yale; he is about eighteen and one-half years old.
Spring 1911	Diver graduates from Yale.
Fall 1911	Diver enters Johns Hopkins School of Medicine.
1914	"Nicole's mother died when she was fourteen" (see Explanatory Notes, 167.7).
1914–15	Diver attends Oxford University: "he was an Oxford Rhodes Scholar from Connecticut in 1914" (see Explanatory Notes, 152.12–13).
1915–16	Diver completes medical school: "He returned home for a final year at Johns Hopkins, and took his degree" (see Explanatory Notes, 152.13).

1916–early 1917	Diver is in Vienna, where he writes pamphlets and studies at the university: "In 1916 he managed to get to Vienna" (*Tender*, 152.14); "At the beginning of 1917 . . ." (*Tender*, 152.32–154.25).
Early 1917	Following an incestuous episode, Nicole Warren shows signs of mental illness: " 'About eight months ago, or maybe it was six months ago or maybe ten' " (*Tender*, 167.26–27). She is not yet seventeen years old.
Spring 1917	Diver goes to Zurich, where he studies at the university: "In the spring of 1917, when Doctor Richard Diver first arrived in Zurich, he was twenty-seven" (see Explanatory Notes, 151.2).
Late 1917	"About a year and a half before" (*Tender*, 166.1) Diver's second visit to the clinic in April 1919, Devereux Warren brings Nicole to Dr. Dohmler's clinic in Zurich; she is "a girl of seventeen" (see Explanatory Notes, 166.6).
1918	Diver receives post-MD degree from the University of Zurich and is commissioned in the American army: "After he took his degree, he received his orders to join a neurological unit forming in Bar-sur-Aube" (*Tender*, 154.30–32).
1918	At Dohmler's clinic Diver meets Nicole Warren for the first time: " 'I only saw her one time. . . . It was the first time I put on my uniform' " (*Tender*, 158.1–4).
Spring 1919	Diver is discharged from the army and returns to Zurich: "He returned to Zurich in the spring of 1919 discharged" (*Tender*, 155.3).
April 1919	Diver sees Nicole for the second time at Dohmler's clinic: "It was a damp April day" (*Tender*, 156.1).
May 1919	Dick lunches with Nicole in a Zurich restaurant: "It was May when he next found her" (*Tender*, 181.1).
June 1919	"The first week of summer found Dick reestablished in Zurich" (*Tender*, 181.24–25).
July 1919	Diver bicycles from Zurich to Montreux: " 'By August, if not in July?' " (see Emendations,

193.26); he encounters Nicole on the Glion funicular (*Tender*, 195.22–23).

July 1919

Diver escorts Nicole back to the clinic and commits himself to taking care of her: "he knew her problem was one they had together for good now" (*Tender*, 206.31–32).

September 1919

The marriage is agreed upon and may take place the same month: "In Zurich in September Doctor Diver had tea with Baby Warren" (*Tender*, 207.1–2).

Fall 1919

Marriage and honeymoon: "How do you do, lawyer. We're going to Como tomorrow for a week and then back to Zurich" (*Tender*, 208.24–25).

1920

Birth of Lanier: "—I'm afraid of falling, I'm so heavy and clumsy—" (*Tender*, 209.14).

1920–21

After birth of Lanier, Nicole has relapse: "We travelled a lot that year" (*Tender*, 210.24); "But I was gone again by that time. . . . That was why he took me travelling" (*Tender*, 210.32–211.1).

1922

Following the birth of Topsy in 1922, Nicole has a more serious relapse: "after my second child, my little girl, Topsy, was born everything got dark again" (*Tender*, 211.1–3).

1923

Rosemary Hoyt is hired by a film producer "when she blossomed out at sixteen" (*Tender*, 52.7–8).

January–June 1925

Rosemary contracts pneumonia and convalesces while traveling in Europe with her mother: " '—we landed in Sicily in March. . . . I got pneumonia making a picture last January' " (*Tender*, 21.22–24).

June 1925

Rosemary arrives on the Riviera beach where she first meets the Divers: "one June morning in 1925" (*Tender*, 4.8–9); "very fashionable for June" (see Explanatory Notes, 212.30).

July 1925

Rosemary celebrates her eighteenth birthday in Paris. Diver is thirty-six: "Eighteen might look at thirty-six through a rising mist of adolescence" (see Explanatory Notes, 271.15).

August 1925

Diver tries to resume work after his return from Paris to the Riviera: "Doctor Richard Diver and

Mrs. Elsie Speers sat in the Café des Allées in August" (*Tender*, 213.1–2).

August 1925

The Divers have been married almost six years; Dick tries unsuccessfully to conceal from Nicole his growing sense of estrangement: "this pretense became more arduous in this effortless immobility, in which he was inevitably subject to microscopic examination" (*Tender*, 223.18–20).

December 1925

Franz Gregorovious joins Diver in Gstaad with proposal for partnership in a psychiatric clinic: "they went to the Swiss Alps for the Christmas holidays" (*Tender*, 224.6–7).

Summer 1927

Allowing time for the Divers' move from the Riviera to the clinic on the Zugersee after Christmas 1925, summer 1927 is the earliest possible date for Nicole's relapse at the Ägeri Fair: "Even this past year and a half on the Zugersee" (*Tender*, 236.18); "For eighteen months now he had lived at the clinic" (*Tender*, 238.3); "He was thirty-eight" (*Tender*, 238.1). It has been roughly six years since Nicole's collapse and recovery following Lanier's birth: "In these six years she had several times carried him over the line with her" (*Tender*, 246.22– 23). The summer dating for the Ägeri Fair episode is further supported by the open car ("they all stuck out of it" [*Tender*, 245.23–24]) and the "hot afternoon" (*Tender*, 247.8).

Early 1928

"For three months she had been all right" (*Tender*, 253.11): after Nicole's recovery from her summer breakdown, Diver goes to Munich where he learns of Abe North's death.

Early 1928

" 'I've wasted eight years teaching the rich the A B C's of human decency' " (*Tender*, 263.9–10): the Divers have been married about eight and one-half years when Dick, in Innsbruck, learns of his father's death.

March 1928

Returning from America after his father's burial, Diver encounters Rosemary in Rome. Spring has not yet arrived: "She plucked a twig and broke it, but she found no spring in it" (*Tender*, 276.32– 33). In March 1928 Rosemary is approaching her twenty-first birthday, and Diver is just short of his thirty-ninth. The coming June will mark the third anniversary of their initial meeting on the Riviera: "He guessed that she had had lovers and had loved them during the last three years. . . . He tried to collect all that might attract her—it was less than it had been three years ago. Eighteen might look at thirty-six through a rising mist of adolescence; but twenty-one would see thirty-nine with discerning clarity" (see Explanatory Notes, 271.7, 14). Fitzgerald stipulates that the Rome encounter between Diver and Rosemary occurs in 1928: " 'living in the year nineteen twenty-eight' " (*Tender*, 276.13). Since this is the latest date provided by the novel, it provides crucial evidence for working out the time scheme after 1925.

May 1928

After Diver returns to the clinic following the Rome beating, Gregorovious loses respect for him: "Yet it was May before Franz found an opportunity to insert the first wedge" (*Tender*, 313.18–19). In May of 1928 Diver is not yet forty but has begun his fortieth year; thus, he can appropriately meditate that "life during the forties seemed capable of being observed only in segments" (*Tender*, 317.2–4). This month Diver goes to Lausanne and encounters Devereux Warren.

May/June 1928

Following Diver's row with the Morris family, Gregorovious eases him out of the clinic partnership: "One morning a week later" (*Tender*, 326.1).

Summer 1928

The Divers travel "between German spas and French cathedral towns" (*Tender*, 331.3–4) until they can return to their home on the Riviera: "The Villa Diana had been rented again for the summer" (*Tender*, 331.2–3).

Fall? 1928

The Divers pay a truncated visit to Bozen: "Their hostess was the Contessa di Minghetti, lately Mary North" (*Tender*, 333.26–27).

February 1929

The Divers "return to the Villa Diana in February" (*Tender*, 342.6).

April 1929	Diver's altercation with the cook, as "the April sun shone pink" (*Tender*, 342.3), is immediately followed by the Golding yacht episode (*Tender*, 345.22–354.15), which reunites Nicole and Tommy Barban for the first time since June 1925, not quite "Four years" before (see Explanatory Notes, 347.17).
June 1929	During "the first hot blast of June" (*Tender*, 359.30), Barban writes to the Divers from Nice, and Rosemary wires them (*Tender*, 360.4–6) of her impending return to the Riviera. Dick and Rosemary's behavior on the beach recalls, three times, their first beach encounter in June 1925: "four years ago" (see Explanatory Notes, 364.5, 8, 14). Later in June Nicole sleeps with Tommy Barban; she has just passed her twenty-ninth birthday (*Tender*, 376.7, 14, 20).
15 July 1929	Barban and Diver have their confrontation over Nicole on the day that the Tour de France arrives in Cannes (see Explanatory Notes, 399.28).
Late July 1929	Nicole tells Baby Warren, " 'Dick was a good husband to me for six years' " (*Tender*, 403.29). The marriage endured for nine years and eight months to the time of Nicole's infidelity, but she recognizes that Diver's full emotional commitment to her terminated during the summer of Rosemary's first intrusion in 1925—in the sixth year of the Divers' marriage, four years before the July 1929 conclusion of the novel.

TENDER IS THE NIGHT
by F. SCOTT FITZGERALD

THIS is Mr. Fitzgerald's first novel since the publication of "The Great Gatsby." That fine novel was unanimously acclaimed, and, long after its publication, Rebecca West said: "It has not been superseded in the common mind by better books, simply by more books." In "The Autobiography of Alice V. Toklas" Gertrude Stein said it "really created for the public the new generation" and that Fitzgerald would be read when many of his well-known contemporaries were forgotten. T. S. Eliot called it "the first step forward in the American novel since Henry James."

Now, in "Tender Is the Night," Mr. Fitzgerald takes another step forward, and resumes his place among the leading American novelists of today, and supersedes "The Great Gatsby" with a book that is a complete departure from what has been the current fashion in novels.

The leading characters are Richard Diver, a young American psychiatrist, his rich and beautiful wife, Nicole, and Rosemary Hoyt, a young motion-picture star. The first quarter of the book is shown through Rosemary's eyes. It is all glitter and glamour, and nothing is more beautiful and satisfying than the opulent household of the Divers. But the reader soon senses that lurking behind the superficial beauty are horror and brutality. In the succeeding chapters the author savagely reveals the face of the life of rich Americans and "intellectuals" abroad.

Basically, the story belongs to Dick Diver, whose career was thwarted and his genius numbed through his marriage to Nicole, child of a raw and rich Middle-Western family. The cause and development of this marriage lie at the bottom of the plot, and "Tender Is the Night" is one of the few novels which is completely based upon abnormal psychology and reveals the strangeness of psychoses and their treatment.

The plot is closely knit, the characters superbly portrayed and developed, the drama indescribably tense and fraught with emotion, the writing the best that has yet come from Fitzgerald's pen.

CHARLES SCRIBNER'S SONS, NEW YORK

F. SCOTT FITZGERALD

TENDER IS THE NIGHT

F. SCOTT FITZGERALD

SCRIBNERS

$2.50

Tender Is the Night
A Romance by
F. SCOTT FITZGERALD

To the generation that was young when "This Side of Paradise" came out, the name Fitzgerald is still perhaps associated with adolescence, and with the Jazz Age to which he gave the name in his "Tales of the Jazz Age." The author was twenty-two when he wrote "This Side of Paradise." He had attained to full maturity when he wrote "The Great Gatsby." The estimates of his present position and promise are suggested by these more recent opinions:

T. S. Eliot: "I have been waiting impatiently for another book by Mr. Scott Fitzgerald; with more eagerness and curiosity than I should feel towards the work of any of his contemporaries, except, that of Mr. Ernest Hemingway."

H. L. Mencken: "His whole attitude has changed from that of a brilliant improvisateur to that of a painstaking and conscientious artist."

Paul Rosenfeld: "Not a contemporary American senses as thoroughly in every fiber the tempo of privileged post-adolescent America."

All who truly care about the future of American letters have awaited Mr. Fitzgerald's new novel with great expectations. Here these expectations are fulfilled.

A description of "Tender Is the Night" appears on the back of this jacket.

Appendix A
Dust-Jacket Illustration

Fitzgerald's concern for the impression his book would make on readers extended to the dust jacket. He had apparently approved a travel poster that provided the basis for the jacket art, but when he saw the preliminary jacket, he objected by telegram to Perkins:

> DECIDED REGRETFULLY DONT LIKE JACKET MUCH TOO ITALIANATE TOO RED AND YELLOW SKY DOES NOT GIVE WHITE AND BLUE SPARKLE OF FRENCH RIVIERA AM SENDING REAL RIVIERA POSTER SHOWING MAXFIELD PARRISH COLORS IF IMPRACTICAL WOULD PREFER SHENTON WOODCUT OR PLAIN JACKET WAIT FOR LETTER[1]

Perkins assuaged his concerns, but Fitzgerald asked him to try to change the yellow to white where possible.[2] The dust jacket is unsigned and the artist has not been identified.

Notes

1. 28 January 1934. *Correspondence*, p. 325.
2. 1 February 1934. *Correspondence*, 326–327.

Appendix B
Revisions in Fitzgerald's Marked Copy for "The Author's Final Version"

Front endpaper: This is the <u>final version</u> of the book as I would like it.

3.1   the shore] the pleasant shore

3.2   stood] stands

3.4   cooled] cool

3.4   stretched] stretches

3.5   Now] Lately

3.6   in 1925] a decade ago

3.7–8   April; in those days only] April. Now, many bunga-
           lows cluster near it, but when this story begins only

3.17   had come] came

4.8   this] one

24.19   Dick's] His

24.19–23   Shift this forward.] His eyes . . . more.

75   At the top of this page Fitzgerald drew a Greek key
           design.

120.1–   hour it had become] hour of standing. . . . It had
122.6   become

153.18   at (L.)] <u>in</u>

154.17   yourself. Once] yourself—once

154.24   subject. No good sense."] subject."

154.28   people—they were the illusions] people; illusions

154.7–9   *deleted*] Moreover . . . stranger

157.7   Kraepelin] Krapaelin

157.13–   You are still a carrot-top" Here insert description from
15   page 24 old numbering] You have the same stupid and
           unaging American face, except I know you're not stupid,
           Dick." *It is impossible to be sure what Fitzgerald intended
           here because he seems to have revised this passage twice.*

157.16   war" Dick said, "You] war—you

158.5   privates] private soldiers

158.10   "Toward] "—toward

159.6   plateau] eminence

159.12   Outside, some] Some

159.13   one] they

159.20   room. Pushing] room; pushing

159.24   first] first one

159.29   etc. etc.] etc, etc.

160.1   about the] about the time of the

160.16   [page] 2—Follow this form with the breaks here] (2)

160.23   [page] 3—(ect)] (3)

160   *This is my mark to say I have made final corrections
           up to this point.

178.19–   path; where, in a moment, a shadow cut across it—she
20   ] path—where in a moment a shadow cut across it. She

179.33   Bye-and-bye (?)] by and by

180.22   shoulder—then apart.] shoulder.

180.23   record,—Have] record," she said. "—Have

181.4   table, male eyes] table, eyes

193.15   Lester begin here + go to end of Chapter (2 pages)
193   *Probably a note to movie producer Lester Cowan, for whom
           Fitzgerald wrote a screenplay of "Babylon Revisited" in
           1940.*

212.9	Abe North] Tommy
212.23– 24	beach near my home above the Mediterranean with my husband and two children and our dear friends] beach with my husband and children.
362	This is DULL
362	You lay down the book + never pick it up—
369	Tiresome stuff! True but why?

Appendix C
Material Deleted between Magazine
Serialization and Book Publication

Fitzgerald made three substantial cuts between the serial
text and the book: 1) the extended account of Abe North's
day in the Ritz bar (second magazine installment, pp. 141–142,
144); 2) Diver's involvement with McKibben's mistress at Innsbruck (third magazine installment, pp. 217–218); and 3) the report of the young man who jumps from the ocean liner that is
taking Diver back to Europe (third magazine installment, pp.
219–220). These excisions were made because Fitzgerald felt that
they slowed the narrative; but the pruning of the Ritz bar material
is regrettable, for the writing is superb. The man-overboard material was based on an event that Fitzgerald did not witness: on 6
July 1928 Morton Hoyt jumped from the *Rochambeau* and was res-
cued. Fitzgerald almost certainly knew Hoyt, the brother of author
Elinor Wylie; he was married three times to Jean Bankhead—sister of actress Tallulah Bankhead—whom the Fitzgeralds knew.

(1)

The famous Paul, master of ceremonies, had not arrived, but
Claude, who was checking stock, broke off his work with no improper surprise to make Abe a pick-me-up. Abe sat on a bench
against a wall and examined the empty room more thoroughly
than ever he had before—the faded rose carpet, the olive frame

of a great mirror, the green upholstery, the yellow pillars matching the yellow walls, the clock, disregarded now as it ticked away the morning.

The drink Claude served him was a "Dashdeller," invented one day, years ago, for himself and Herman Dashdeller—it consisted of a jigger of gin shaken up with a jigger of cuantro with the addition of minor perfumes and charged water. Abe took two of them and began to feel better—so much better that he mounted to the barber's shop and was shaved. When he returned to the bar Paul had arrived—in his custom-built car, from which he had disembarked correctly at the Boulevard des Capucines. Paul liked Abe and came over to talk. . . .

Other clients had meanwhile drifted in to the bar: first came a huge Dane whom Abe had somewhere encountered. The Dane took a seat across the room, and Abe guessed he would be there all the day, drinking, lunching, talking or reading newspapers. He felt a desire to out-stay him.

It was eleven and the college boys had begun to drift in, stepping gingerly lest they tear one another bag from bag—Abe saw Collis Clay among them.

He watched Collis's conduct with amusement: Collis strode to the bar looking neither to left nor to right; he commanded a drink, and only then did he turn to search the room for friends. Out of the corner of his eye, he perceived Abe, but apparently decided that he did not know him well enough to come over; however an equivalent young man, who had entered with equivalent caution, was recognized as a pal, and with diffidence forgotten and confidence restored the pair of them sat down in the centre of the room—even bawled for a prominent barman to come and shake dice with them.

Many people were entering now. Meanwhile Abe was kept busy inventing excuses for the chasseur as to why he could not go to the phone to answer calls from a Mr. Crawshaw. Then he had the chasseur telephone to the Divers; by the time he was in touch with them he was in touch also with other friends—was feeling the bite of the "Dashdellers." His hunch was to put them all on the phone at once—the result was somewhat general. From time to time his mind reverted to the fact that he ought to go over and get Freeman out of jail but he shook off all facts as parts of the nightmare.

By one o'clock the bar was jammed; there were coteries of alcoholics, journalists, South Americans, innumerable collegians, a sprinkling of sponges; every table was occupied—clients stood in double ranks at the bar. An American gossip sheet was hawked through the room, but before the vender had completed his round, he was knifing through sardines; amidst the consequent mixture of voices the staff of waiters functioned, pinning down their clients to the facts of drink and money.

"That makes two stingers . . . and one more . . . two martinis and one . . . nothing for you, Mr. Quarterly . . . that makes three rounds. That makes seventy-five francs, Mr. Quarterly. Mr. Schaeffer said he had this—you had the last . . . I can only do what you say . . . thanks vera-much."

In the confusion Abe had lost his seat; now he stood gently swaying and talking to some of the people with whom he had involved himself. A terrier ran a leash around his legs but Abe managed to extricate himself without upsetting and became the recipient of profuse apologies. Presently he was invited to lunch, but declined. It was almost Briglith, he explained, and there was something he had to do at Briglith. A little later, with the exquisite manners of the alcoholic that are like the manners of a prisoner or a family servant, he said good-bye to an acquaintance, and turning around discovered that the bar's great moment was over as precipitately as it had begun.

Across from him the Dane and his companions had ordered luncheon. Abe followed the pattern except that he paid his check. After lunch—that he scarcely touched, though he envied the appetite of the correspondent Scandinavian—he watched the preparations for the afternoon. The glasses for champagne cocktails were banked in battalions on the bar—a majority of them destined for the women's side across the hall. At three-thirty the staff would begin to fill these glasses; a hundred could be served while another hundred was made up. The barman serving the women's side had an extraordinary face—hard and handsome.

Drifters came in the off hours, two to four, and there were a few business meetings. The Dane sat alone with his paper, deserted, speaking only to the waiters. Abe had not a paper; he sat, and each time he found a glass empty before him he ordered a new drink concocted from a brandy base that he called "L'Elixir Aux Nids d'Irondell." He was happy living in the past. The drink made past happy things contemporary with the present, as if they were still going on, contemporary even with the future as if they were about to happen again. . . .

He had been absent an hour, and during that time a change had taken place: the chatter from the women's side now reached out to the Rue Cambon, it roared into Abe's ears in the hall— and as he turned into the men's bar, he came upon its very personification: a woman, half concealed by the protecting screen, stood looking uncertainly toward the jam of males and wobbling an unconfident finger at it. She was conscious of being out of place; she could see the coldly disgusted looks in such eyes as she managed to meet; yet she was not able to muster the grace to quit. Only Claude's loud "Excuse *me!*" as he passed her with a tray served to discourage her—by the time Abe had collapsed on a bench she was gone.

A man had entered in a battered derby with a cane improvised from wire and was playing Charlie Chaplin; Paul gave orders that he was not to be served. After another pair of "Elixirs" Abe himself was in shining shape; he told his next companions an Odyssean version of how he had missed his ship. He was not having a good time but across the room his Danish antagonist was at his mellowest, telling stories and snickering aloud at them exactly as if he were a real person, instead of Hamlet's father in a few short minutes that approximated life.

A little before seven began the drift away. The chasseur was constantly on the telephone making last-minute engagements or consoling deserted wives. The blue, brown and slate had faded from the picture, and the tone was black and white. There was no further noise across the hall. The Dane, once more alone, had ordered dinner—a certain relation had sprung up between them, including some petulance on the part of the Dane about Abe's staying so long without even a newspaper. The Dane had read parts of his own newspapers many times over.

At eight an American came in, looked at Abe, and then at the Dane, and took a table as far as possible removed from either.

When, presently, another man joined him he arose and bowed. The acoustics were such that Abe overheard the beginning of the conversation:

"I asked you to meet me here because——"

"Cut out the preliminaries. What's it all about?" "Just this— I'll mix it up with you anywhere, at any time, with any weapons. But I didn't like it last night."

"Well, why didn't you say?"

"I'm not standing it any more. What you and Nancy do is——"

They saw simultaneously that they were overheard and their voices dropped back into obscurity.

It was dull in the bar—a few men in evening clothes came in wanting quick cocktails. Even the Dane was demanding a check, which he signed, and joked meanwhile with a not especially receptive waiter. He gave Abe a viking stare as he went out; after a few minutes Abe tried to leave but his legs would not support him, so he settled as inconspicuously as he could in the corner of his bench and fell asleep. Paul had long departed. The room was again a faded rose and two yellow pillars matching the walls. The one attendant was in the service room adjoining, so Abe was alone. [See Book I, Chapter 23.]

(2)

Neither of them moved. Her back was toward him as she faced the lights of the town. He scratched a match that she must have heard, but she remained motionless. He grinned—he was no longer Doctor Diver, gravely admonishing, rigidly paternal—he was Dick Diver at Yale, Dick Diver at Medical School, Dick Diver at Hopkins, Dick Diver Behind the Lines, Dick Diver on the Hunt . . .

She did not move—was it invitation? Or indication of obliviousness? He had long been outside of the world of simple desires and their fulfillments, and he was inept and uncertain. For all he knew there might be some code among the wanderers of obscure spas by which they found each other quickly.

—Perhaps the next gesture was his. That was neurotic thinking, born of too much enforced professional and domestic hypoc-

205

risy. Strange children should smile at each other and say, "Let's play." Who cared? . . .

After dinner and a bottle of heavy local wine in the deserted dining-room, Dick went out into the garden. He felt better, tired and tranquil.

There was a voice at his shoulder:

"Isn't it a lovely night? . . . I'll sit down here if you don't mind," the girl said. "The best view is from here. You're an Irishman, aren't you?"

"I'm an American."

"I thought you were Irish. I'm a Canadian. I've lived in the States a long time."

"Will you be here long?"

"That sounds like Hugo's 'All you want to know in German,' " the girl said, smiling. "Don't you know those questions, 'Are all your rooms taken?' and 'Is attendance included?' "

" 'Do not shut the windows entirely.' "

" 'We will finish up with black coffee, cigars and liqueurs.' I always liked that one."

"I used one of those pamphlets once in Italy," he confessed. "We're using one now. The people I'm travelling with can't speak German, and neither can I."

A wild memory struck him "—not exactly a governess."

"Are you by any chance with some people named McKibben?" he asked.

"Yes—do you know them? I'm taking care of their children, to get the trip."

"Is it difficult?"

"There you go again. And I thought you were an Irishman when I first saw you. Sometimes I think Americans always talk guide-book; 'cep' when they're tight."

She was close to him now, so sweet-faced as she brushed a ringlet of lovely hair away from her eye that there was nothing except to draw her up to him and taste unfamiliar lips. Their faces were little moons under the great white one that hovered . . .

Even as he drew away there was an interruption, quick steps and a voice wild with shock and anger.

"What's the idea? Alice! My God, what *is* this?"

It was McKibben and he scarcely recognized Dick, so upset was he by the discovery.

"Do you mean to say you've been kissing her?" he cried. "By God, do you mean to say——"

Dick was astounded. He and the young woman were on their feet now, the latter looking at McKibben with contempt. "Calm down, Barker—Calm down!" she advised him.

But McKibben grew more and more excited, and Dick felt his own muscles exercising for a mêlée.

"What business is this of yours?" he inquired.

"Plenty of my business!" cried McKibben. "What are you butting in for?"

"Butting into what?"

Nevertheless Dick was beginning to realize. The somewhat ambiguous lady who was "not exactly a governess" had worked herself into a state of indignation.

"You're acting like a maniac, Barker McKibben, and I refuse to listen. I've stood enough of this crazy jealousy and I'm going home tomorrow."

Haughtily she turned and swung toward the hotel.

McKibben was visibly moved by her last statement; once more his mustache quivered at Dick.

"What's the idea anyhow?"

"How was I supposed to know she was your girl?"

McKibben sat down on the bench and covered his face with his hands.

"All I've done for her—the dresses I've bought her, the jewels I've given her. She's had to tell my wife they're imitations." He sprang to his feet. "Do you suppose she has any real idea of going home? She's capable of it. She'd do it in a minute. She may be packing her trunk now."

They went up to the hotel.

"Come and join us if there isn't a row," urged McKibben. "You haven't met my wife." He looked at Dick hopefully.

Dick hesitated.

"I'll have to go to my room first," he said, tasting rouge on his lips. "I'll join you if everything seems calm."

On his bureau lay the telegram with which Nicole followed

his itinerary from place to place, but it seemed practically irreverent to open it in the midst of the ludicrous situation. He washed his face and went downstairs.

The trouble was not over—in fact, it had scarcely begun. Mrs. McKibben, a pretty woman of thirty, who had perceptibly been a pretty girl of eighteen, sat passive while Alice stood by the taproom table with the air of one about to take flight, using to its full advantage her key position in this *ménage à trois,* an opportunity she had obviously sought for some time.

"I want you to arrange for my ticket, I've stood enough."

McKibben's tone had changed—he was pleading as openly as he dared for forgiveness on any grounds.

"We'll think it over tomorrow," he said.

"No! This is the last time, Barker McKibben. I'm through. You arrange for my ticket or I'll go and do it myself."

Dick tried to make talk with Mrs. McKibben. His approach, feeble at best, was to compliment her on having a husband with such a sense of duty that he even looked after the morals of every one in the party; then, before this flimsy statement could be examined, Dick skipped quickly to broad generalities about the foolishness of quarrels, and of deciding things at night, and the poor woman, feeling very alone and grateful for anything to cling to, listened with pathetic eagerness. He wondered if she wanted Alice to carry out her threat; Dick knew that this would be of little profit, for it would be upon his wife that McKibben would take revenge.

"I feel responsible," he said insincerely, breaking into the other conversation.

"It's Barker's fault." Alice's mouth was so hard now that it was difficult to believe he had kissed it. Each time her temper rose, McKibben's wilted, with the exactitude of the liquids rising and falling in the jars of a gasoline station. Suddenly Alice realized how far she had gone, and as if at some invisible signal she and McKibben left the room together.

"I guess they are going to talk it over outside," Dick said.

"I guess they are," agreed Mrs. McKibben.

Ten minutes later McKibben returned, announcing with relief that Alice had gone to bed and nothing would be decided until tomorrow. They had a drink and Dick excused himself on the grounds of an early start tomorrow. He left them sitting at the table, so separated that such scenes were really of little significance; they were only pale reflections of what had been played many times and with much more poignancy in their hearts. [See Book II, Chapter 18.]

(3)

McKisco was interested in psychoanalysis and when Dick explained to him that it was only a small part of psychiatry, effective only in certain cases, he was disappointed. One day in the lounge his attention left Dick and his mouth fell open.

"I'll be damned," he said. "Look over there."

He was not the only writer on the ship—there was also a well-known woman novelist. Every day since leaving New York, McKisco was accustomed to come up to the lounge after luncheon to open his typewriter upon a desk in the main salon, and to go to work. He had chosen it as the most convenient place to work, but he was not unaware that considerable fluttering went on behind him as he typed away, passings-by, with attendant glances over his shoulder to see what he was doing; snickerings and grimacings, burlesquings of him upon imaginary typewriters. By functioning in public he had become the most noticeable figure on the ship. Now a rival apparition had appeared in the salon.

Preceded by a steward carrying her typewriter, the lady glanced over the heads of these people having coffee and signalled her porter to the desk opposite McKisco's.

"I'll be damned," repeated McKisco.

To distract him Dick treated him to a little medical sensationalism—

"See that young man? No, the one with all the girls. Watch his face."

"And why?" McKisco demanded.

The young man was tall and handsome; he had coffee-colored hair with a twinkle of gold in it.

"He's doomed," Dick said.

"How do you mean?"

"He'll commit a crime of violence. Look at those hands—look at that jaw. He wants to crush something—he doesn't care what it is—even himself."

"That's very interesting," said McKisco.

Leaving the delicate matter of the lady novelist to adjust itself Dick left him. He went along a corridor of the same deck, knocked at the door of a stateroom and went in. A woman was arranging her corn-colored hair at the mirror.

"Hello, Divah," she said. "Have the chair." She turned around smiling. "How do you like your night-blooming cereus now?"

"Wasn't it funny?"

"It was. Of caus I'm ruined with four of my best friends. But you were really so polite that I had to find out more about you."

"I hope it was all satisfactory," he said.

Turning from the mirror she smiled with flashing mock-intensity. Simultaneously Dick had a sense of change, of a new pulse that in a moment became a great silence. Far off in it there were voices calling. He stood up, shaking his head like a wet dog: "The engine's stopped. Something's happened."

On the deck the passengers were hurrying toward the stern. In a moment the engines started again, this time turning the ship almost on its own axis.

"A passenger jumped overboard."

"A young man jumped overboard."

"A guy jumped overboard."

Even the people on the highest deck could see nothing in all that great expanse of sea. A man with field glasses was shouting, "I see him—I see his head," immediately the head vanished, then, as the boat turned, the watchers lost their sense of direction.

At the stern a scene was taking place: two sailors were carrying the inert body of a girl through the second-class passengers into first-class. As the ship completed its revolution and slowly retraced its course, details of the catastrophe began to circulate.

"A young man from first-class."

"He must have been drunk."

"I'll bet he's sober now."

"It was a dare—the girl dared him."

"They were all in the bar. He ran to the stern and they followed him."

"They've got two boats ready to go off."

"Lucky it's calm."

"He dove fifty feet—good Lord!"

"They see him . . . Come on over to the other side . . . I can't see, can you see? That speck—the sun's in my eyes . . . look at them now . . . stroke, go to it, boys . . . They're fishing him in . . . he doesn't look dead. But he was in the water half an hour, and it's cold."

There was a cheer as the boat drew along side, but not for the limp bundle of exhaustion and confusion who had given thirty minutes of free entertainment. He had intruded his personal tragedies upon two thousand people, and the timidity he must have felt on returning to the living world was added to by the inappropriateness of his being saved; he had made his great gesture unsuccessfully, he had jumped into tragedy and been retrieved into farce . . .

In the lounge that evening Dick became aware of a whispering chorus: the young man had come in. The self-possession of his entrance was astounding; he returned all glances, strolled to a table, snapped his fingers at a waiter and glanced calmly about.

It was an excellent performance, but Dick saw the waiter return to the bar and hold a short colloquy with the bartender, then return to the young man and explain something, and the young man shrugged his shoulders. Presently the waiter brought him a bottle of mineral water.

Dick left the McKiscos, who were getting off in the morning at Gibraltar, and sat down at the young man's table.

"I am Doctor Diver," he said. "Can't help asking if I can help you."

"That's nice of you. Thing you can do—get me a drink some way. They've given orders that I can't be served anything, but when you've been on a bender you can't stop right off."

"I'll have a drink sent to my cabin and then I'll send it to yours."

Touched, the young man covered his eyes with his hands. "God! The sight of that ship—this ship—moving away is something I'll remember all my life. Those birds! A couple of birds tried to settle on my head—I suppose they wanted to pick my eyes out. The nearest I came to drowning was when I was trying to fight them off. Big white birds, bigger than gulls it seemed to me. God, I can feel them on my head."

"Why did you jump?"

"That's what I've got to explain to the captain tomorrow—that'll be fun. We were talking about jumping and for a moment life and death seemed just about the same, if you know what I mean. As if you wrote down the reasons and there were just as many reasons for dying as for living." He sighed, recovering some real confidence. "You were damn nice to do this for me. You know there's not much stuff on this boat. The last time I crossed, on the *Ile de France,* Boy did that boat rock with passion!"

"Well, I'm going to send you a drink," said Dick, getting up. "I'll see you tomorrow." [See Book II, Chapter 19.]

Appendix D
F. Scott Fitzgerald's Use of Story Strippings in *Tender Is the Night* by George Anderson

Although F. Scott Fitzgerald privately adopted the pose of a split man—half serious novelist, half slave to the commercial short story—the division between his novels and stories was never the chasm suggested by his famous remark to Ernest Hemingway likening himself to an "old whore" turning four-thousand-dollar tricks for *The Saturday Evening Post* (*Life in Letters* 169). In *The Composition of Tender Is the Night* (1963) Matthew J. Bruccoli argues that, apart from their interest as stories per se, Fitzgerald's stories "reveal themselves as the equivalent of a more orderly writer's notebooks," where the author "frequently experimented with themes, character, and settings that he subsequently developed in his novels." To suggest further the intimate relationship between Fitzgerald's stories and novels, Bruccoli notes that Fitzgerald often removed "Bits of description" from a story, which he "polished, and then inserted into a novel" (70)—a process the author called "stripping" (70).[1]

Subsequent critics have discussed the thematic connections between Fitzgerald's stories and novels and have in passing noted additional story strippings in *Tender Is the Night;* however, despite the long-term awareness among scholars and critics of Fitzgerald's practice, the extent to which he stripped his stories for his novels has not been thoroughly examined. No one has documented how much Fitzgerald recurred to his stories, nor has anyone considered the meaning of the practice in his development as a novelist or its effect on his novels. As tables 1 and 2 show, Fitzgerald's stripping of his stories is far more extensive than previously believed and opens an overlooked avenue to the understanding and appreciation of his craft and art.

As an artist and as a professional, Fitzgerald's ethic was to waste nothing. Every experience, every observation, every imaginative flight was material for his writing—no detail was too trivial, no revelation too intimate, no idea too intricate. As he implied when he wrote of Ring Lardner's death, Fitzgerald's aim as a writer was to put "himself on paper"—as much as possible to write down "what was in his mind and heart" ("Ring" 38, 40). Because of the nature of his career, then, Fitzgerald put some of his "mind and heart" into even his weakest stories, and he was loath to let the good pass with the mediocre into magazine morgues. Consequently, throughout his professional life Fitzgerald tried to salvage meaningful phrases and passages from his stories for use in his novels. From *This Side of Paradise* to *The Great Gatsby*, the importance of the stories in the creation and form of the novels is notable but not critical; however, in the writing of *Tender Is the Night* the role of the stories becomes crucial.

Table 1 lists thirty-seven stories which have strippings that appear in *Tender*. As Fitzgerald began the Diver version of the novel in 1932, he reviewed many, if not all, of his stories to cull out the phrases and passages he thought might be useful.[2] Of course, he made only slight use of many of these stories, but cumulatively the impact of the strippings on the texture of the novel is substantial. Fitzgerald uses strippings to characterize Dick and Nicole Diver and Rosemary Hoyt, as well as Tommy Barban, Albert McKisco, Collis Clay, Topsy Diver, and other minor characters. Short stories also provide descriptive details for scenes set in Switzerland, in Africa, and in America, for scenes set on the Riviera, in Paris, and in Gstaad, and for the scenes set at the fair where Nicole becomes hysterical and at the Hotel des Trois Mondes where Nicole's father nearly dies. Fitzgerald's use of even small strippings from minor stories indicate that the author, like Dick

Diver, depended on "the long ground-swell of imagination" (113) for his judgments.

Several stories were stripped of one or several long passages and are therefore of especial importance to the novel. "Jacob's Ladder" provides more significant strippings than any other story. Along with a passage from "First Blood" (83.25), strippings from "Jacob's Ladder" were used to show the beginning of Dick's infatuation with Rosemary as he kisses her in the "dark cave of the taxi" (83.12, 84.8). Passages from the story also capture the effect of Nicole's beauty on Dick, especially at the beginning of their relationship (43.17, 180.5, 205.8). And "Jacob's Ladder" is also the basis for much of the scene of Dick and Rosemary's quarrel over Nicotera (277.21, 285.5, 285.27).

"Magnetism" is another story heavily stripped by Fitzgerald to detail Dick's emotional involvements with Rosemary (90.2, 97.16, 138.15) and Nicole (262.13). A long, evocative passage from the story is used for Rosemary's visit to Brady's studio (29.7). Furthermore, "Magnetism" is clearly a story in which Fitzgerald was working out his theme of personal charm and its potentially deleterious effect upon personality (114.16).

"Indecision" provides much of the material for the Divers' Christmas trip to Gstaad in chapter 13 of book 2 (225.1, 226.30, 227.16, 228.12, 232.1, 234.15, 235.12). Like the story's Tommy McLane, who is torn by his attraction for two women—one an innocent eighteen, the other a mature twenty-five—Dick Diver is distracted by a "special girl" (228) whom he imagines listening in on his conversation with Franz Gregorovious. Although his attention is recalled to Nicole—"her beauty, tentatively nesting and posing, flowed into his love, ever braced to protect it" (231)—and he later finds the girl uninteresting, Dick, like Tommy McLane, is shown already to be a less-than-serious man. Given the similarity of the story to the chapter, it is clear that "Indecision" inspired this turning point in the novel.

"One Trip Abroad," a story Bruccoli asserts "might almost be called a miniature of *Tender Is the Night*" (*Composition* 69), contributes several important strippings to the novel. Three strippings occur in chapters 8 and 9 of book 2, the chapters in which Dick falls in love with Nicole in Switzerland, a country where "many things end" (54) in the story. By the Lake of Geneva, "the true centre of the Western World" (194), the storm that in the story signals the recognition by Nelson and Nicole Kelly of their own dissipation ironically marks the moment beginning Dick's reckless involvement with Nicole Warren (204.12). Later in the novel, strippings from the story are used in the scene set on T. F. Golding's yacht that depicts one of the last stages of Dick's decline (345.22, 349.26).

Fitzgerald also selects passages from "One Trip Abroad" along with strippings from "A Penny Spent" in the structurally crucial chapter 10 of book 2, where the years and details of Dick and Nicole's lives following their marriage pass through Nicole's stream of consciousness. Fitzgerald chooses at least two strippings from "A Penny Spent" to suggest the Divers' experiences in Italy (209.29); he uses four strippings from "One Trip Abroad" in a compressed paragraph to represent the Divers' travels in Africa (210.25). In each case Fitzgerald seems purposefully to be making private allusions to his short-story world, and though he could not expect his reader to catch his allusions, the fact that he chose to use strippings undoubtedly attests to a depth of meaning present for the author.

One of the most fascinating aspects of Fitzgerald's strippings is how he imbues story passages with new meanings and richer overtones in the novel context. The passages in "The Swimmers" that suggest the onset of Henry Marston's breakdown are used in the novel to portray a sharp change in mood (113.1) and to depict Dick's inability to control his feelings (119.8). Basil Duke Lee's transitory anxiety in "Basil and Cleopatra" over a story told of Minnie Bibble becomes a story told of Rosemary (115.10) that repeatedly haunts Dick with the sense of his old world passing away. The threatening ghost of "A Short Trip Home" becomes the sinister newsman (120.14) who appears twice in the novel, first as a harbinger and then as a seal of Dick's decline. The meaning of the father's funeral in "On Your Own" is enlarged as Dick says good-bye to the sense of self that had sustained him through the trying years with Nicole (267.14). The opening of "The Rough Crossing" becomes a meaningful transition as "the past, the continent" left behind is the old America of firmer values

216

"Here for long, Mr. Wales?"

"I'm here for four or five days to see my little girl."

"Oh-h! You have a little girl?"

Outside, the fire-red, gas-blue, ghost-green signs shone smokily through the tranquil rain. It was late afternoon and the streets were in movement; the *bistros* gleamed. At the corner of the Boulevard des Capucines he took a taxi. The Place de la Concorde moved by in pink majesty; they crossed the logical Seine, and Charlie felt the sudden provincial quality of the left bank.

Used in Tender

Charlie directed his taxi to the Avenue de l'Opera, which was out of his way. But he wanted to see the blue hour spread over the magnificent façade, and imagine that the cab horns, playing endlessly the first few bars of *Le Plus qu Lent,* were the trumpets of the Second Empire. They were closing the iron grill in front of Brentano's Book-store, and people were already at dinner behind the trim little bourgeois hedge of Duval's. He had never eaten at a really cheap restaurant in Paris. Five-course dinner, four francs fifty, eighteen cents, wine included. For some odd reason he wished that he had.

As they rolled on to the Left Bank and he felt its sudden provincialism, he thought, "I spoiled this city for myself. I didn't realize it, but the days came along one after another, and then two years were gone, and everything was gone, and I was gone."

He was thirty-five, and good to look at. The Irish mobility of his face was sobered by a deep wrinkle between his eyes. As he rang his brother-in-law's bell in the Rue Palatine, the wrinkle deepened till it pulled down his brows; he felt a cramping sensation in his belly. From behind the maid who opened the door darted a lovely little girl of nine who shrieked "Daddy!" and flew up, struggling like a fish, into his arms.

384

Fitzgerald noted the repetition of material in a copy of *Taps at Reveille* (Bruccoli Collection, University of South Carolina).

and larger dreams while Dick's future holds on unstable world of diminishing exectations (267.24).

It is important to realize that the stripping process, far from being a shortcut for Fitzgerald, actually cost him extra labor, first in the original culling process and then in the care he took to assure no stripped passages would appear in his story collections. Fitzgerald had learned early in his career that his reputation as a novelist would suffer if critics came to see him primarily as an entertaining short-story writer. He was careful, therefore, to keep his two careers as separate as possible. The author was adamant that he revise the stories he was to collect in *Taps at Reveille* (1935) so that they would not repeat any of the passages he had used in *Tender Is the Night,* even though, as he admitted to Maxwell Perkins, the effort would be arduous. Fitzgerald persisted even when Perkins tried to persuade him that such punctiliousness was unnecessary. "Each of us has his virtues," Fitzgerald responded, "and one of mine happens to be a great sense of exactitude about my work" (*Dear Scott/Dear Max* 207).[3]

For Fitzgerald as an artist, the single word mattered, and his practice of stripping his stories is an especially intriguing part of his craft. The world Fitzgerald created in *Tender Is the Night* is a world of echoes that readers feel *within* the work—the shots of the duel echoing in the shots fired at the railroad station, the echoing good-byes of many partings, the reverberation of Dick Diver twice being likened to Grant at Galena. This listing of the parallel passages between the stories and the novel allows readers to become aware of the echoes that exist *between* the author's works as well. By opening themselves to Fitzgerald's short-story world, readers can deepen their understanding not only of the writer in the marketplace, but also of Fitzgerald's sensibility as an artist.

Notes

1. This appendix presents the clearest examples of the strippings that appear in the text of the first edition of *Tender Is the Night.* My dissertation, *A Writer Wastes Nothing* (University of South Carolina, 1994), traces Fitzgerald's process of stripping in the Melarky and Kelly as well as the Diver versions of the

novel and analyzes fully the intimate relationship between the author's short stories and his fourth novel. In compiling this listing of stripped passages, I relied upon a working draft of a concordance to the novel generously supplied to me by Todd Stebbins, whose valuable dissertation, *Tender Is the Night: The Last Love Battle, With a Newly Generated Concordance*, is available through the University of South Carolina.

2. *After* he had consulted and selected passages from a story for his novel, Fitzgerald would collect unused as well as additional passages for his notebooks. The author would then designate the story as "stripped" and record it as "Permanently Buried" in his ledger, which meant that he had decided not to republish the story in a collection.

3. When he realized that he had missed the description of the threatening ghost of Joe Varland in "A Short Trip Home," Fitzgerald insisted that a footnote to the story be included in *Taps at Reveille*:

> In a moment of hasty misjudgement a whole paragraph of description was lifted out of this tale where it originated, and properly belongs, and applied to quite a different character in a novel of mine. I have ventured none the less to leave it here, even at the risk of seeming to serve warmed-over fare. (273)

Works Cited

Bruccoli, Matthew J. *The Composition of Tender Is the Night*. Pittsburgh: U of Pittsburgh P, 1963.

— and Judith S. Baughman, eds. *F. Scott Fitzgerald: A Life in Letters*. New York: Scribners, 1994.

Fitzgerald, F. Scott. "One Trip Abroad," *Saturday Evening Post* (11 October 1930), 6–7, 48, 51, 53–54, 56.

—. "Ring," *The Crack-Up*, ed. Edmund Wilson. New York: New Directions, 1945.

—. *Taps at Reveille*. New York: Scribners, 1935.

—. *Tender Is the Night*. New York: Scribners, 1934.

Kuehl, John and Jackson R. Bryer, eds. *Dear Scott/Dear Max: The Fitzgerald/Maxwell Perkins Correspondence.* New York: Scribners, 1971.

Table 1
STRIPPINGS CATEGORIZED BY STORY

Below, in an alphabetical listing of thirty-seven stories, the book (bold) and beginning page and line numbers of 125 selected strippings appearing in *Tender Is the Night* are given. These strippings can be examined by cross-referring to table 2. Fitzgerald's stripping a story in two or more places to create a particular novel passage is indicated in parentheses. Abbreviations: *American Mercury* (AM), *The Saturday Evening Post* (SEP), *Woman's Home Companion* (WHC).

Stripped Stories	Appearances in *Tender Is the Night*
"The Adolescent Marriage" SEP (6 March 1926)	**1** 4.21
"At Your Age" SEP (17 August 1929)	**1** 102.17, 137.23
"Babylon Revisited" SEP (21 February 1931)	**1** 97.23 **2** 175.27 **3** 331.11, 402.2
"Basil and Cleopatra" SEP (27 April 1929)	**1** 115.10
"The Bowl" SEP (21 January 1928)	**1** 41.1
"Crazy Sunday" AM (October 1932)	**1** 123.14 **2** 278.12
"Diagnosis" SEP (20 February 1932)	**2** 267.12

"Emotional Bankruptcy"   2 276.28
SEP (15 August 1931)

"First Blood"   1 83.25 2 252.6
SEP (5 April 1930)

"Flight and Pursuit"   2 180.18, 189.15, 204.1
SEP (14 May 1932)

"The Hotel Child"   1 4.16 2 195.21, 198.4, 200.10,
SEP (31 January 1931)   201.18 3 320.19, 320.23, 348.31,
                                350.2, 370.12

"I Got Shoes"   1 43.30
SEP (23 September 1933)

"Indecision"   2 225.1, 226.30, 227.16, 228.12
SEP (16 May 1931)   (2), 232.1 (3), 234.15, 235.12,
                                275.20

"Jacob's Ladder"   1 43.17, 83.12, 84.8 (3) 2 180.5,
SEP (20 August 1927)   205.8, 227.16, 277.21, 285.5 (4),
                                285.27 (2)

"The Love Boat"   1 48.19
SEP (8 October 1927)

"Love in the Night"   1 19.3, 103.22
SEP (14 March 1925)

"Magnetism"   1 29.7, 90.2 (2), 97.16, 114.16,
SEP (3 March 1928)   138.15 2 179.1, 262.13

"More Than Just a   3 372.27
House"
SEP (24 June 1933)

"A Nice Quiet Place"   2 177.8 (2)
SEP (31 May 1930)

"A Night at the Fair"   2 247.2
SEP (21 July 1928)

"Not in the Guidebook"   2 210.21
WHC (November 1925)

"One Interne"   2 178.11, 179.11 3 384.24 (2)
SEP (5 November 1932)

"One Trip Abroad"   2 203.29, 204.12, 210.25 (4)
SEP (11 October 1930)   3 345.22, 349.26

"On Schedule"   3 332.13 (2)
SEP (18 March 1933)

"On Your Own"   1 91.3 2 203.9, 267.7 (2), 267.14
Esquire (January 1979)   (3) 3 343.2

"A Penny Spent"   1 102.20 2 209.29 (2)
SEP (10 October 1925)

"The Popular Girl"   1 87.10
SEP (11 February 1922)

"The Rough Crossing"   2 205.5, 267.24 (2)
SEP (8 June 1929)

"The Rubber Check"   1 42.28, 102.24 (2), 106.23,
SEP (6 August 1932)   119.23 3 349.30

"The Scandal Detectives"   1 44.29
SEP (28 April 1928)

"A Short Trip Home"   1 4.12, 4.14, 4.22, 90.8, 120.14
SEP (17 December 1927)   (2)

"A Snobbish Story"   2 181.3 3 374.18
SEP (29 November 1930)

"The Swimmers"   **1** 94.1, 113.1, 119.8
SEP (19 October 1929)

"The Third Casket"   **2** 178.13
SEP (31 May 1924)

"Two Wrongs"   **2** 250.13 **3** 348.10, 349.1
SEP (18 January 1930)

"What a Handsome Pair!" **3** 398.24
SEP (27 August 1932)

"A Woman With a Past"   **2** 180.14, 181.13
SEP (6 September 1930)

TABLE 2
Comparison of Stripped Story Passages to Parallel Passages in Tender Is the Night

Below, the page and column number of story passages (left) and page and line numbers for the first edition of *Tender is the Night* strippings (right) are given. All ellipses are Fitzgerald's. Abbreviations: *The American Mercury* (AM), *The Price was High* (Price), and *The Saturday Evening Post* (Post).

"A Short Trip Home"
Post 6.1   4.12–14
    She had magic suddenly in   However, one's eyes moved on
her pink palms   quickly to her daughter, who
                              had magic in her pink palms

"A Short Trip Home"
Post 55.3   4.14–15
She had one of those exquisite   and her cheeks lit to a lovely
rose skins frequent in our part flame, like the thrilling flush of
of the country, and beautiful   children after their cold baths
until the little veins begin to in the evening.
break at about forty, and the

cold had lit it to a lovely flame, like the thrilling flush of children after their cold baths in the evening.

"The Hotel Child"
Post 8.1
An exquisitely, radiantly beautiful Jewess whose fine, high forehead sloped gently up to where her hair, bordering it like an armorial shield, burst into lovelocks and waves and curlicues of soft dark red. Her eyes were bright, big, clear, wet and shining; the color of her cheeks and lips was real, breaking close to the surface from the strong young pump of her heart.

4.16–21
Her fine forehead sloped gently up to where her hair, bordering it like an armorial shield, burst into lovelocks and waves and curlicues of ash blonde and gold. Her eyes were bright, big, clear, wet, and shining, the color of her cheeks was real, breaking close to the surface from the strong young pump of her heart.

"The Adolescent Marriage"
Post 7.1
a slender, dark-haired girl whose body hovered delicately on the last edge of childhood had come quietly into the room.

4.21–22
Her body hovered delicately on the last edge of childhood—

"A Short Trip Home"
Post 6.1
She was nearly complete, yet the dew was still on her.

4.22–23
she was almost eighteen, nearly complete, but the dew was still on her.

"Love in the Night"
Post 68.3–70.1
The Russian Orthodox Church was locked up and so were the bins of rarer wine, and the fash-

19.3–9
Most of all, there was the scent of the Russians along the coast—their closed book shops

ionable spring moonlight was put away, so to speak, to wait for their return.

"We'll be back next season," they said as a matter of course.

But this was premature, for they were never coming back any more.

and grocery stores. Ten years ago, when the season ended in April, the doors of the Orthodox Church were locked, and the sweet champagnes they favored were put away until their return. "We'll be back next season," they said, but this was premature, for they were never coming back any more.

"Magnetism"
Post 6.1

Together they walked out a back entrance, along a muddy walk, and opening a little door in the big blank wall of the studio building, entered into its half darkness.

Here and there figures spotted the dim twilight, figures that turned up white faces to George Hannaford, like souls in purgatory watching the passage of a half god through. Here and there were whispers and soft voices and, apparently from afar, the gentle tremolo of a small organ. Turning the corner made by some flats, they came upon the white crackling glow of a stage with two people motionless upon it.

An actor in evening clothes, his shirt front, collar and cuffs tinted a brilliant pink, made as though to get chairs for them, but they shook their heads and stood watching. For

29.7–27

The studio manager opened a small door in the blank wall of the stage building and with sudden glad familiarity Rosemary followed him into half darkness. Here and there figures spotted the twilight, turning up ashen faces to her like souls in purgatory watching the passage of a mortal through. There were whispers and soft voices and, apparently from afar, the gentle tremolo of a small organ. Turning the corner made by some flats, they came upon the white crackling glow of a stage, where a French actor—his shirt front, collar, and cuffs tinted a brilliant pink—and an American actress stood motionless face to face. They stared at each other with dogged eyes, as though they had been in the same position for hours; and still for a long time nothing happened, no one moved. A

a long while nothing happened on the stage—no one moved. A row of lights went off with a savage hiss, went on again. The plaintive tap of a hammer begged admission to nowhere in the distance; a blue face appeared among the blinding lights above and called something unintelligible into the upper blackness. Then the silence was broken by a low clear voice from the stage:

"If you want to know why I haven't got stockings on, look in my dressing room. I spoiled four pairs yesterday and two already this morning. . . . This dress weighs six pounds."

bank of lights went off with a savage hiss, went on again; the plaintive tap of a hammer begged admission to nowhere in the distance; a blue face appeared among the blinding lights above, called something unintelligible into the upper blackness. Then the silence was broken by a voice in front of Rosemary.

"Baby, you don't take off the stockings, you can spoil ten more pairs. That dress is fifteen pounds."

"The Bowl"

Post 7.2

Then he saw the two girls through the long hall, one dark and shining, like himself, and one with gold hair that was foaming and frothing in the firelight

41.1–3

In a pause Rosemary looked away and up the table where Nicole sat between Tommy Barban and Abe North, her chow's hair foaming and frothing in the candlelight.

"The Rubber Check"

Post 42.3

The conversation faded off whenever he entered it, giving him the impression of continually shaking hands with a glove from which the hand had been withdrawn.

42.28–30

He tried breaking into other dialogues, but it was like continually shaking hands with a glove from which the hand had been withdrawn—

"Jacob's Ladder"
Post 4.1–2

Her face, the face of a saint, an intense little Madonna, was lifted fragilely out of the mortal dust of the afternoon.

43.17–19

Her face, the face of a saint, a viking Madonna, shone through the faint motes that snowed across the candlelight,

"I Got Shoes"
Post 14.2

At these times it was a face so merry that it was impossible not to smile back into the white mirrors of her teeth—the whole area around her parted lips was a lovely little circle of delight.

43.30–33

Then Mary North with a face so merry that it was impossible not to smile back into the white mirrors of her teeth—the whole area around her parted lips was a lovely little circle of delight.

"The Scandal Detectives"
Post 4.3

The diffused magic of the summer afternoon withdrew into her suddenly—the soft air, the shadowy hedges and banks of flowers, the orange sunlight, the laughter and voices, the tinkle of a piano over the way—the magic left all these things and melted into Imogene as she sat there looking up at him with a smile.

44.29–33

But the diffused magic of the hot sweet South had withdrawn into them—the soft-pawed night and the ghostly wash of the Mediterranean far below—the magic left these things and melted into the two Divers and became part of them.

"The Love Boat"
Post 8.1

The boat floated down the river through the summer night like a Fourth of July balloon footloose in the heavens. The decks were brightly lit and restless with dancers, but bow and

48.19–22

They looked out over the Mediterranean. Far below, the last excursion boat from the Isles des Lerins floated across the bay like a Fourth-of-July balloon foot-loose in the heav-

stern were in darkness; so the boat had no more outline than an accidental cluster of stars. Between the black banks it floated, softly parting the mild dark tide from the sea

ens. Between the black isles it floated, softly parting the dark tide.

"Jacob's Ladder"
Post 4.3

Driving homeward through the soft night, she put up her face quietly to be kissed. Holding her in the hollow of his arm, Jacob rubbed his cheek against her cheek's softness and then looked down at her for a long moment.

"Such a lovely child," he said gravely.

She smiled back at him; her hands played conventionally with the lapels of his coat.

83.12–19

Rosemary put up her face quietly to be kissed. He looked at her for a moment as if he didn't understand. Then holding her in the hollow of his arm he rubbed his cheek against her cheek's softness, and then looked down at her for another long moment.

"Such a lovely child," he said gravely.

She smiled up at him; her hands playing conventionally with the lapels of his coat.

"First Blood"
Post 81.1

He saw all this and relaxed for a moment to pat her hand, and suddenly she came toward him, her youth vanishing as she passed inside the focus of his eyes, and he had kissed her breathlessly, as if she were thirty. She lay back against his arm.

"I've decided to give you up," she said astonishingly.

He started. For a moment he wondered if he had forgot-

83.25–84.5

Suddenly she came toward him, her youth vanishing as she passed inside the focus of his eyes and he had kissed her breathlessly as if she were any age at all. Then she lay back against his arm and sighed.

"I've decided to give you up," she said.

Dick started—had he said anything to imply that she possessed any part of him?

"But that's very mean," he

ten something—something he had said to her before—had he ever talked to her more than casually? Had he committed himself to be in some way possessed?

"But that's very mean," he managed to say lightly, "just when I was getting interested."

"Jacob's Ladder"
Post 4.3

"Not only are you beautiful," continued Jacob, "but you are somehow on the grand scale. Everything you do—yes, like reaching for that glass, or pretending to be self-conscious, or pretending to despair of me—gets across.

5.3
Afterward, in the dark cave of the taxi cab, fragrant with the perfume he had bought for her that day, Jenny came close to him, clung to him. He kissed her, without enjoying it. There was no shadow of passion in her eyes or on her mouth; there was a faint spray of champagne on her breath. She clung nearer, desperately. . . . Hesitating tentatively, he kissed her and again he was chilled by the innocence of her kiss, the eyes that at the moment of contact looked beyond him out into the darkness of the night, the dark-

managed to say lightly, "just when I was getting interested."

84.8–24
Then he should have laughed, but he heard himself saying, "Not only are you beautiful but you are somehow on the grand scale. Everything you do, like pretending to be in love or pretending to be shy gets across."

In the dark cave of the taxi, fragrant with the perfume Rosemary had bought with Nicole, she came close again, clinging to him. He kissed her without enjoying it. He knew that there was passion there, but there was no shadow of it in her eyes or on her mouth; there was a faint spray of champagne on her breath. She clung nearer desperately and once more he kissed her and was chilled by the innocence of her kiss, by the glance that at the moment of contact looked beyond him out into the darkness of the night, the darkness of the world. She did not know

ness of the world. She did not know yet that splendor was something in the heart; at the moment when she should realize that and melt into the passion of the universe he could take her without question or regret.

yet that splendor is something in the heart; at the moment when she realized that and melted into the passion of the universe he could take her without question or regret.

"The Popular Girl"
Post 89.2

She crept upstairs like a hurt child and sat before a mirror, brushing her luxurious hair to comfort herself. One hundred and fifty strokes she gave it, as it said in the treatment, and then a hundred and fifty more—she was too distraught to stop the nervous motion. She brushed it until her arm ached, then she changed arms and went on brushing.

87.10–14

When the door closed she got up and went to the mirror, where she began brushing her hair, sniffling a little. One hundred and fifty strokes Rosemary gave it, as usual, then a hundred and fifty more. She brushed it until her arm ached, then she changed arms and went on brushing. . . .

"Magnetism"
Post 6.2

She stood a long time with her back to him at one point, and when she turned at length, their eyes swept past each other's, brushing like bird wings.

Almost thankfully he felt the warm sap of emotion flow out of his heart and course through his body.

90.2–8

The day seemed different to Rosemary from the day before— When she saw him face to face their eyes met and brushed like birds' wings. After that everything was all right, everything was wonderful, she knew that he was beginning to fall in love with her. She felt wildly happy, felt the warm sap of emotion being pumped through her body.

"A Short Trip Home"

Post 6.1
[She had magic] in the sure, clear confidence that at about eighteen begins to deepen and sing in attractive American girls.

90.8–9
A cool, clear confidence deepened and sang in her.

"On Your Own"

Price 333
She felt fresh and young under the fresh young silk.

91.3–5
She remembered how she had felt in that dress, especially fresh and new under the fresh young silk.

"The Swimmers"

Post 12.2
Home was a fine high-ceiling apartment hewn from the palace of a Renaissance cardinal in the Rue Monsieur—the sort of thing Henry could not have afforded in America.

94.1–4
It was a house hewn from the frame of Cardinal de Retz's palace in the Rue Monsieur, but once inside the door there was nothing of the past, nor of any present that Rosemary knew.

"Magnetism"

Post 6.2
"Helen!"
She murmured "What?" in an awed voice.
"I feel terribly about this." His voice was shaking.
Suddenly she began to cry: painful, audible sobs shook her. "Have you got a handkerchief?" she asked.

97.16–20
"Rosemary?"
She murmured, "What?" in an awed voice.
"I feel terribly about this." She was shaken with audibly painful sobs. "Have you got a handkerchief?" she faltered.

"Babylon Revisited"

Post 4.1
Outside, the fire-red, gas-blue, ghost-green signs shone

97.23–26
and the fire-red, gas-blue, ghost-green signs began to

smokily through the tranquil rain. It was late afternoon and the streets were in movement: the *bistros* gleamed. At the corner of the Boulevard des Capucines he took a taxi. The Place de la Concorde moved by in pink majesty;

shine smokily through the tranquil rain. It was nearly six, the streets were in movement, the bistros gleamed, the Place de la Concorde moved by in pink majesty as the cab turned north.

"At Your Age"
Post 6.3
Her beauty sparkled bright against his strong, tall form, and they floated hoveringly, delicately, like two people in a nice, amusing dream.

102.17–20
The first time was when she and Dick danced together and she felt her beauty sparkling bright against his tall, strong form as they floated, hovering like people in an amusing dream—

"A Penny Spent"
Post 160.2
She was surprised to find how well he danced, as all tall, slender men should, with such a delicacy of suggestion that she felt as though she were being turned here and there as a bright bouquet or a piece of precious cloth before five hundred eyes.

102.20–22
he turned her here and there with such a delicacy of suggestion that she was like a bright bouquet, a piece of precious cloth being displayed before fifty eyes.

"The Rubber Check"
Post 7.3
Sometime in the early morning they were alone and her damp, powdery young body came up close to him in a crush of tired cloth, and he kissed

102.24–27
Some time in the early morning they were alone, and her damp powdery young body came up close to him in a crush of tired cloth, and stayed there,

her, trying not to think of the gap between them.

crushed against a background of other people's hats and wraps. . . .

41.1

she passed the door of the cloak room and saw them there crushed against a background of other people's hats and wraps, clinging together.

"Love in the Night"
Post 68.1
Two wan dark spots on her cheeks marked where the color was by day.

103.22–23
Two wan dark spots in her cheek marked where the color was by day.

"The Rubber Check"
Post 42.3
there was a rough nap on the velvet gloves with which she prepared to handle Val.

106.23–24
There was a rough nap on Nicole's velvet gloves as she slapped him back:

"The Swimmers"
Post 12.1
In the Place Benoit, a suspended mass of gasoline exhaust cooked slowly by the June sun. It was a terrible thing, for, unlike pure heat, it held no promise of rural escape, but suggested only roads choked with the same foul asthma.

113.1–5
In the square, as they came out, a suspended mass of gasoline exhaust cooked slowly in the July sun. It was a terrible thing—unlike pure heat it held no promise of rural escape but suggested only roads choked with the same foul asthma.

"Magnetism"
Post 76.2
"No, I know. You can't control charm. It's simply got to be used. You've got to keep

114.16–19
On the other hand, there was a pleasingness about him that simply had to be used—those

your hand in if you have it, and go through life attaching people to you that you don't want.

"Basil and Cleopatra"
Post 166.3–4

Basil's blood ran cold.

"It was funny afterward, but she was pretty scared for a while," continued Fat. "She had a compartment with Bessie Belle, but she and Littleboy wanted to be alone; so in the afternoon Bessie Belle came and played cards in ours. Well, after about two hours Bessie Belle and I went back, and there were Minnie and Littleboy standing in the vestibule arguing with the conductor; Minnie white as a sheet. Seems they locked the door and pulled down the blinds, and I guess there was a little petting going on. When he came along after the tickets and knocked on the door, they thought it was us kidding them, and wouldn't let him in at first, and when they did, he was pretty upset. He asked Littleboy if that was his compartment, and whether he and Minnie were married that they locked the door, and Littleboy lost his temper trying to explain that there was nothing wrong. He said the conductor had insulted Minnie and he

who possessed that pleasingness had to keep their hands in, and go along attaching people that they had no use to make of.

115.10–116.2

Suddenly his blood ran cold as he realized the content of Collis's confidential monologue.

"—she's not so cold as you'd probably think. I admit I thought she was cold for a long time. But she got into a jam with a friend of mine going from New York to Chicago at Easter—a boy named Hillis she thought was pretty nutsey at New Haven—she had a compartment with a cousin of mine but she and Hillis wanted to be alone, so in the afternoon my cousin came and played cards in our compartment. Well, after about two hours we went back and there was Rosemary and Bill Hillis standing in the vestibule arguing with the conductor—Rosemary white as a sheet. Seems they locked the door and pulled down the blinds and I guess there was some heavy stuff going on when the conductor came for the tickets and knocked on the door. They thought it was us kidding them and wouldn't let him in at first, and when they

wanted him to fight. But that conductor could have made trouble, and believe me, I had an awful time smoothing it all over."

With every detail imagined, with every refinement of jealousy beating in his mind, including even envy for their community of misfortune as they stood together in the vestibule, Basil went up to Miss Beecher's next day.

did, he was plenty sore. He asked Hillis if that was his compartment and whether he and Rosemary were married that they locked the door, and Hillis lost his temper trying to explain there was nothing wrong. He said the conductor had insulted Rosemary and he wanted him to fight, but that conductor could have made trouble—and believe me I had an awful time smoothing it over."

With every detail imagined, with even envy for the pair's community of misfortune in the vestibule, Dick felt a change taking place within him.

"The Swimmers"

Post 12.1

Through the washroom window his eyes fell upon a sign—1000 Chemises. The shirts in question filled the shop window, piled, cravated and stuffed, or else draped with shoddy grace on the show-case floor. 1000 Chemises—Count them! To the left he read Papeterie, Pâtisserie, Solde, Réclame, and Constance Talmadge in Déjeuner de Soleil; and his eye, escaping to the right, met yet more somber announcements: Vêtements Ecclésiastiques, Déclaration de Décès, and Pompes Funèbres. Life and Death.

119.8–17

It was a melancholy neighborhood. Next door to the place he saw a sign: "1000 chemises." The shirts filled the window, piled, cravated, stuffed, or draped with shoddy grace on the show-case floor: "1000 chemises"—count them! On either side he read: "Papeterie," "Pâtisserie," "Solde," "Réclame"— and Constance Talmadge in "Déjeuner de Soleil," and farther away there were more sombre announcements: "Vêtements Ecclésiastiques," "Déclaration de Décès" and "Pompes Funèbres." Life and death.

"The Rubber Check"

Post 44.2

He meets an American friend and shakes hands, and the friend notices how his shirt sleeve fits his wrist, and his coat sleeve incases his shirt sleeve like a sleeve valve; how his collar and tie are molded plastically to his neck.

119.23–27

But Dick's necessity of behaving as he did was a projection of some submerged reality: he was compelled to walk there, or stand there, his shirt-sleeve fitting his wrist and his coat sleeve encasing his shirt-sleeve like a sleeve valve, his collar molded plastically to his neck,

"A Short Trip Home"

Post 7.1

Seated in the coupe—he had not dismounted to help Ellen out—was a hard thin-faced man of about thirty-five with an air of being scarred, and a slight sinister smile.

Vaguely I placed him as one of the sort of men whom I had been conscious of from my earliest youth as "hanging around"—leaning with one elbow on the counters of tobacco stores, watching, through heaven knows what small chink of the mind, the people who hurried in and out. Intimate to garages, where he had vague business conducted in undertones, to barber shops and to the lobbies of theaters—in such places, anyhow, I placed the type, if type it was, that he reminded me of. Sometimes his face bobbed up in one of Tad's more savage cartoons, and I

120.14–27

As he paced the Rue des Saintes-Anges he was spoken to by a thin-faced American, perhaps thirty, with an air of being scarred and a slight but sinister smile. As Dick gave him the light he requested, he placed him as one of a type of which he had been conscious since early youth—a type that loafed about tobacco stores with one elbow on the counter and watched, through heaven knew what small chink of the mind, the people who came in and out. Intimate to garages, where he had vague business conducted in undertones, to barber shops, to the lobbies of theaters—in such places, at any rate, Dick placed him. Sometimes the face bobbed up in one of Tad's more savage cartoons—in boyhood Dick had often thrown an uneasy glance

236

had always from earliest boy-hood thrown a nervous glance toward the dim borderland where he stood, and seen him watching me and despising me.

at the dim borderland of crime on which he stood.

"Crazy Sunday"

AM 217.1
[Joel saw] the flash of a white face under his own, the arc of her shoulder.

123.14–15
there was the flash of a white face under his own, the arc of a shoulder.

"At Your Age"

Post 6.3
They came near and Tom ad-mired the faint dust of powder over her freshness, the guarded sweetness of her smile, the fra-gility of her body calculated by Nature to a millimeter to sug-gest a bud, yet guarantee a flower.

137.23–26
It took him a moment to re-spond to the unguarded sweet-ness of her smile, her body calculated to a millimeter to suggest a bud yet guarantee a flower.

"Magnetism"

Post 7.2
Suddenly she began to laugh:
    "Oh, we're such actors, George—you and I."

138.15–17
    Rosemary stood up and leaned down and said her most sincere thing to him:
    "Oh, we're such *actors*—you and I."

✳ "Babylon Revisited"

Post 84.1
They were not dull people, but they were very much in the grip of life and circumstances, and their gestures as they turned in a cramped space lacked large-ness and grace.

175.27–29
The domestic gestures of Franz and his wife as they turned in a cramped space lacked grace and adventure.

"A Nice Quiet Place"
Post 8.1

All that week there was much singing in her ears—summer songs of ardent skies and wild shade

the singing became so loud that Josephine's face was puckered and distorted, as with the pressure of strong sunshine.

177.8–11
She walked to a rhythm—all that week there had been singing in her ears, summer songs of ardent skies and wild shade, and with his arrival the singing had become so loud she could have joined in with it.

"One Interne"
Post 6.3

He stared at her, and the impression of her beauty grew until it suddenly welled up inside him in a compact little paroxysm of emotion.

178.11–13
Nicole took advantage of this to stand up and the impression of her youth and beauty grew on Dick until it welled up inside him in a compact paroxysm of emotion.

"The Third Casket"
Post 8.3

a gold-and-ivory little beauty with dark eyes and a moving, childish smile that was like all the lost youth in the world.

178.13–15
She smiled, a moving childish smile that was like all the lost youth in the world.

"Magnetism"
Post 6.3

There was that excitement about her that seemed to reflect the excitement of the world.

179.1–5
She thanked him for everything, rather as if he had taken her to some party, and as Dick became less and less certain of his relation to her, her confidence increased—there was that excitement about her that seemed to reflect all the excitement of the world.

"One Interne"
Post 6.2–3

Her hair, dark and drawn back of her ears, brushed her shoulders in such a way that her white, lovely face seemed to have just emerged from it, as if at this moment she were coming out from a forest into the clear moonlight. The unknown had yielded her up and Bill hoped suddenly that she had no background, that she was just a girl lost, with no address except the night from which she had come.

179.11–17

Her hair drawn back of her ears brushed her shoulders in such a way that the face seemed to have just emerged from it, as if this were the exact moment when she was coming from a wood into clear moonlight. The unknown yielded her up; Dick wished she had no background, that she was just a girl lost with no address save the night from which she had come.

"Jacob's Ladder"
Post 4.2

On the pure parting of her lips no breath hovered;

180.5

On the pure parting of her lips no breath hovered.

"A Woman with a Past"
Post 9.3–133.1

This time she made sure that smile gathered up everything inside her, directed it toward him in timeless appeal, making him a deep personal promise of her heart, herself, for so little, for the mere beat of a response, the mere assurance of a complementary vibration in him.

180.14–17

She smiled at him, making sure that the smile gathered up everything inside her and directed it toward him, making him a profound promise of herself for so little, for the beat of a response, the assurance of a complimentary vibration in him.

"Flight and Pursuit"
Post 16.1

all that he could do that night was to lie awake and remember

180.18–19

Minute by minute the sweetness drained down into her out

her waiting in the front yard, with the sweetness draining down into her out of the magnolia trees, out of the dark world

of the willow trees, out of the dark world.

"A Snobbish Story"
Post 6.2
Someone was staring at her from near by, someone whose eyes burned disturbingly, like an uncharted light.

181.3–6
when a stranger stared at her from a nearby table, eyes burning disturbingly like an uncharted light, he turned to the man with an urbane version of intimidation and broke the regard.

"A Woman with a Past"
Post 134.3
she paused in front of the mirror, fascinated as the uncorruptible quicksilver gave her back to herself—eternally, arrestingly, overwhelmingly beautiful.

181.13–16
He was enough older than Nicole to take pleasure in her youthful vanities and delights, the way she paused fractionally in front of the hall mirror on leaving the restaurant, so that the incorruptible quicksilver could give her back to herself.

"Flight and Pursuit"
Post 57.1
Dress stay crisp for him—button stay put—bloom magnolia—air stay still and sweet.

189.15–16
. . . Dress stay crisp for him, button stay put, bloom narcissus—air stay still and sweet.

"The Hotel Child"
Post 8.3
Among these was young Count Stanislas Borowki, with his handsome, shining brown eyes of a stuffed deer

195.21–23
The young man was a Latin with the eyes of a stuffed deer; the girl was Nicole.

"The Hotel Child"
Post 8.1

Watching the dancing there would be a gallery of Englishwomen of a certain age, with neckbands, dyed hair and faces powdered pinkish gray; a gallery of American women of a certain age, with snowy-white transformations, black dresses and lips of cherry red.

198.4–9

The salon of the hotel, a room of fabled acoustics, was stripped for dancing but there was a small gallery of Englishwomen of a certain age, with neckbands, dyed hair and faces powdered pinkish gray; and of American women of a certain age, with snowy-white transformations, black dresses and lips of cherry red.

"The Hotel Child"
Post 8.3

[Among these was young Count Stanislas Borowki, with] his black hair already dashed with distinguished streaks like the keyboard of a piano.

200.10–12

Listening, and watching Nicole's shoulders as she chattered to the elder Marmora, whose hair was dashed with white like a piano keyboard,

"The Hotel Child"
Post 75.1

He went past a flood of noise and song from the bar, past a window where two bus boys sat on a bunk and played cards over a bottle of Spanish wine.

201.18–19

Dick passed some cellar windows where bus boys sat on bunks and played cards over a litre of Spanish wine.

"On Your Own"
Price 332

Her bodice was stretched tight across her heart.

203.9–10

The voice fell low, sank into her breast and stretched the tight bodice over her heart as she came up close.

241

"One Trip Abroad"
Post 56.1

Below the hotel, where the terrace fell a thousand feet to the lake, stretched a necklace of lights that was Montreux and Vevey, and then, in a dim pendant, Lausanne; a blurred twinkling across the lake was Evian and France. From somewhere below—probably the *Kursaal*—came the sound of full-bodied dance music—

203.29–32

Two thousand feet below she saw the necklace and bracelet of lights that were Montreux and Vevey, beyond them a dim pendant of Lausanne. From down there somewhere ascended a faint sound of dance music.

"Flight and Pursuit"
Post 53.1

"No. I even have to think before I can really remember how I stood waiting for you in the garden that night, holding all my dreams and hopes in my arms like a lot of flowers—they were that to me, anyhow. I thought I was pretty sweet. I'd saved myself up for that—all ready to hand it all to you."

204.1–7

But she was still afraid of Dick, who stood near her, leaning, characteristically, against the iron fence that rimmed the horseshoe; and this prompted her to say: "I can remember how I stood waiting for you in the garden—holding all my self in my arms like a basket of flowers. It was that to me anyhow—I thought I was sweet—waiting to hand that basket to you."

"One Trip Abroad"
Post 54.2

And sometimes there was a booming from the vine-covered hills on the other side of the lake, which meant that cannons were shooting at hail-bearing clouds, to save the vineyards from an approaching

204.12–21

Suddenly there was a booming from the wine slopes across the lake; cannons were shooting at hail-bearing clouds in order to break them. The lights of the promenade went off, went on again. Then the storm; it came swiftly, first falling from the heavens and then falling again in torrents from the mountains, washing loudly down the roads and stone ditches; it came with a dark, frightening sky and savage filaments of lightning and crashing, world-splitting thunder, while ragged and destroyed clouds fled along before the wind past the hotel. The mountains and the lake disappeared completely; the hotel crouched alone amid tumult and chaos and darkness.

storm came swiftly, first falling from the heavens, then doubly falling in torrents from the mountains and washing loud down the roads and stone ditches; with it came a dark, frightening sky and savage filaments of lightning and world-splitting thunder, while ragged, destroying clouds fled along past the hotel. Mountains and lake disappeared—the hotel crouched amid tumult, chaos and darkness.

"The Rough Crossing"
Post 66.3

He could not remember when anything had felt so young and fresh as her lips. The rain lay, like tears shed for him, upon the softly shining porcelain cheeks.

205.5–8

Revolted by his harshness he made amends to Nicole, remembering that nothing had ever felt so young as her lips, remembering rain like tears shed for him that lay upon her softly shining porcelain cheeks. . . .

"Jacob's Ladder"
Post 63.1

He went to the window sometime toward three o'clock and stared out into the clear splendor of the California night. Her beauty rested outside on the grass, on the damp, gleaming roofs of the bungalows, all around him, borne up like music on the night. It was in the

205.8–11

the silence of the storm ceasing woke him about three o'clock and he went to the window. Her beauty climbed the rolling slope, it came into the room, rustling ghost-like through the curtains. . . .

room, on the white pillow, it rustled ghostlike in the curtains.

"A Penny Spent"
Post 164.4

"Good-by, Blue Grotte!" sang the boatman. "come again soo-oon!"

209.29–33

"Good-bye, Blue Grotte," sang the boatman, "come again soo-oon." And afterward tracing down the hot sinister shin of the Italian boot with the wind soughing around those eerie castles, the dead watching from up on those hills.

166.1

The city had disappeared behind a rise of ground, and now they were alone, tracing down the hot mysterious shin of the Italian boot where the Maffia sprang out of rank human weeds and the Black hand rose to throw its ominous shadow across two continents. There was something eerie in the sough of the wind over these gray mountains, crowned with the decayed castles. Hallie suddenly shivered.

"I'm glad I'm American," she said. "Here in Italy I feel that everybody's dead. So many people dead and all watching from up on those hills—

"Not in the Guidebook"
Price 163

all that the young woman could see was the agate-green, foliage-like spray, changing and complaining around the stern.

210.21–23

The waters are lapping in the public toilets and the agate green foliage of spray changes and complains about the stern.

244

"One Trip Abroad"

Post 6.1

Everyone talked; it would have been absurd not to talk after having been through a swarm of locusts on the edge of the Sahara.

Even the French chauffeur turned about and explained in a loud, clear voice: "Bumblebees"

7.3

"What is it?" Nicole asked her husband.

"Why, I believe—it appears that for a consideration the Ouled Nails dance in more or less—ah—Oriental style—in very little except jewelry."

6.3

They dined on the hotel veranda under a sky that was low and full of the presence of a strange and watchful God; around the corners of the hotel the night already stirred with the sounds of which they had so often read but that were even so hysterically unfamiliar—drums from Senegal, a native flute, the selfish, effeminate whine of a camel, the Arabs pattering past in shoes made of old automobile tires, the wail of Magian prayer.

210.25–31

On the edge of the Sahara we ran into a plague of locusts and the chauffeur explained kindly that they were bumble-bees. The sky was low at night, full of the presence of a strange and watchful God. Oh, the poor little naked Ouled Nail; the night was noisy with drums from Senegal and flutes and whining camels, and the natives pattering about in shoes made of old automobile tires.

"Indecision"
Post 12.1
With his hat, Tommy McLane slapped snow from his dark, convictlike costume.

225.1–2
With his cap, Dick slapped the snow from his dark blue ski-suit before going inside.

"Indecision"
Post 59.3
He began to feel like a man pushing a baby carriage. He took a dislike to her colonial costume, the wig of which sent gusts of powder up his nose. She even smelled young—of very pure baby soap and peppermint candy.

226.30–32
"I don't like ickle durls. They smell of castile soap and peppermint. When I dance with them, I feel as if I'm pushing a baby carriage."

"Indecision"
Post 12.2
It was a welcome blizzard and he inhaled damp snowflakes that he could no longer see against the darkening sky. Three flying kids on a sled startled him with a warning in some strange language and he just managed to jump out of their path. He heard them yell at the next bend, and then, a little farther on, he heard sleigh bells coming up the hill in the dark.

227.16–20
Outside he inhaled damp snowflakes that he could no longer see against the darkening sky. Three children sledding past shouted a warning in some strange language; he heard them yell at the next bend and a little farther on he heard sleigh-bells coming up the hill in the dark.

"Indecision"
Post 13.2
After meeting in the bar, they sledded down into the village to a large old-fashioned Swiss taproom, a thing of woodwork,

228.12–27
Their destination was a hotel with an old-fashioned Swiss tap-room, wooden and resounding, a room of clocks, kegs,

246

clocks, steins, kegs and antlers. There were other parties like their own, bound together by the common plan of eating *fondue*—a peculiarly indigestible form of Welsh rabbit—and drinking spiced wine, and then hitching on the backs of sleighs to Doldorn several miles away, where there was a townspeople's ball.

Some gray-haired men of the golden 90's sang ancient glees at the piano, the *fondue* was fun, the wine was pert and heady, and smoke swirled out of the brown walls and toned the bright costumes into the room. They were all on a ship going somewhere, with the port just ahead; the faces of girls and young men bore the same innocent and unlined expectations of the great possibilities inherent in the situation and the night.

steins, and antlers. Many parties at long tables blurred into one great party and ate fondue—a peculiarly indigestible form of Welsh rarebit, mitigated by hot spiced wine.

It was jolly in the big room; the younger Englishman remarked it and Dick conceded that there was no other word. With the pert heady wine he relaxed and pretended that the world was all put together again by the gray-haired men of the golden nineties who shouted old glees at the piano, by the young voices and the bright costumes toned into the room by the swirling smoke. For a moment he felt that they were in a ship with landfall just ahead; in the faces of all the girls was the same innocent expectation of the possibilities inherent in the situation and the night.

"Indecision"
Post 13.2
Then it was over and one hundred five-pound boots stamped toward the sleighs that waited at the door.

13.3
Outside in the crisp moonlight he saw her tying her sled to one of the sleighs ahead. The

232.1–16
One hundred pair of five-pound boots had begun to clump toward the door, and they joined the press. Outside in the crisp moonlight, Dick saw the girl tying her sled to one of the sleighs ahead. They piled into their own sleigh and at the crisp-cracking whips the

sleighs were moving off; he and Emily caught one, and at the crisp-cracking whips the horses pulled, breasting the dark air. Past them figures ran and scrambled, the younger people pushing one another off, landing in a cloud of soft snow, then panting after the horses to fling themselves exhausted on a sled, or else wail that they were being left behind. On either side the fields were tranquil; the space through which the cavalcade moved was high and limitless. After they were in the country there was less noise; perhaps ears were listening atavistically for wolves howling in the clumps of trees far across the snow.

The crowd was enormous—peasants, servants from the hotels, shopkeepers, guides, outlanders, cow herders, ski teachers and tourists.

horses strained, breasting the dark air. Past them figures ran and scrambled, the younger ones shoving each other from sleds and runners, landing in the soft snow, then panting after the horses to drop exhausted on a sled or wail that they were abandoned. On either side the fields were beneficently tranquil; the space through which the cavalcade moved was high and limitless. In the country there was less noise as though they were all listening atavistically for wolves in the wide snow.

In Saanen, they poured into the municipal dance, crowded with cow herders, hotel servants, shop-keepers, ski teachers, guides, tourists, peasants.

"Indecision"

Post 59.1–2

Probably very late, when the orchestra and what remained of the party—the youth and cream of it—would move into the bar, and Abdul, with Oriental delight in obscurity, would manipulate the illumination in a sort of counterpoint whose other tone was the flashing moon from the ice

234.15–23

The carnival spirit was strong and they went with the crowd into the grill, where a Tunisian barman manipulated the illumination in a counterpoint, whose other melody was the moon off the ice rink staring in the big windows. In that light, Dick found the girl devitalized, and uninteresting—he

rink, bouncing in the big windows. Tommy had danced with Rosemary in that light a few hours after their first meeting; he remembered the mysterious darkness with the cigarette points turning green or silver when the lights shone red . . . the sense of snow outside and the occasional band of white falling across the dancers as a door was opened and shut.

turned from her to enjoy the darkness, the cigarette points going green and silver when the lights shone red, the band of white that fell across the dancers as the door to the bar was opened and closed.

"Indecision"
Post 62.2
They were passing the crisp, pale green rink where Wiener waltzes blared all day and the blazing colors of many schools flashed against pale blue skies.

235.12–14
They passed the crisp green rinks where Wiener waltzes blared and the colors of many mountain schools flashed against the pale-blue skies.

"A Night at the Fair"
Post 8.1
[There were immense exhibits] and a whining, tinkling hoochi-coochie show.

247.2–3
There was the sound of a whining, tinkling hootchy-kootchy show.

"Two Wrongs"
Post 113.2
Grief presented itself in that terrible, dark, unfamiliar color.

250.13–14
Grief presented itself in its terrible, dark unfamiliar color.

"First Blood"
Post 8.2
Their eyes were like blazing windows across a court of the same house.

252.6–7
He and Nicole looked at each other directly, their eyes like blazing windows across a court of the same house.

"Magnetism"
Post 74.1

The grass was damp, and Kay came to him on hurried feet; her thin slippers were drenched with dew. She stood upon his shoes, nestling close to him, and held up her face as one shows a book open at a page.

"Think how you love me," she whispered. "I don't ask you to love me always like this, but I ask you to remember."

"You'll always be like this to me."

"Oh, no; but promise me you'll remember." Her tears were falling. "I'll be different, but somewhere lost inside of me there'll always be the person I am tonight."

262.13–20

He remembered once when the grass was damp and she came to him on hurried feet, her thin slippers drenched with dew. She stood upon his shoes nestling close and held up her face, showing it as a book open at a page.

"Think how you love me," she whispered. "I don't ask you to love me always like this, but I ask you to remember. Somewhere inside me there'll always be the person I am to-night."

"On Your Own"
Price 328

her train shambled down into the low-forested clayland of southern Maryland. . . .

She saw a star she, knew . . .

267.7–10

Only as the local train shambled into the low-forested clayland of Westmoreland County, did he feel once more identified with his surroundings; at the station he saw a star he knew,

"Diagnosis"
Post 90.3

the strange, sluggish, primeval rivers flowing softly under soft Indian names.

267.12–13

the sound of sluggish primeval rivers flowing softly under soft Indian names.

"On Your Own"

Price 328

[At the service next day in the Rocktown churchyard] the country doctor lay among a hundred Lovejoys and Dorseys and Crawshaws. It was very friendly leaving him there with all his relations around him.

329

The flowers scattered on the brown unsettled earth. She had no more ties here now and she did not know whether she would come back any more. She knelt down. All these dead, she knew them all, their weather-beaten faces with hard blue flashing eyes, their spare violent bodies, their souls made of new earth in the long forest-heavy darkness of the seventeenth century.

"I'm coming." And then, "Goodbye then Father, all my fathers."

267.14–23

Next day at the churchyard his father was laid among a hundred Divers, Dorseys, and Hunters. It was very friendly leaving him there with all his relations around him. Flowers were scattered on the brown unsettled earth. Dick had no more ties here now and did not believe he would come back. He knelt on the hard soil. These dead, he knew them all, their weather-beaten faces with blue flashing eyes, the spare violent bodies, the souls made of new earth in the forest-heavy darkness of the seventeenth century.

"Good-by, my father—good-by, all my fathers."

"The Rough Crossing"

Post 12.1

Once on the long, covered piers, you have come into a ghostly country that is no longer Here and not yet There. Especially at night. There is a hazy yellow vault full of shouting, echoing voices. There is the rumble of trucks and the clump of trunks, the strident

267.24–268.15

On the long-roofed steamship piers one is in a country that is no longer here and not yet there. The hazy yellow vault is full of echoing shouts. There are the rumble of trucks and the clump of trunks, the strident chatter of cranes, the first salt smell of the sea. One

chatter of a crane and the first salt smell of the sea. You hurry through, even though there's time. The past, the continent, is behind you; the future is that glowing mouth in the side of the ship; this dim turbulent alley is too confusedly the present.

Up the gangplank, and the vision of the world adjusts itself, narrows. One is a citizen of a commonwealth smaller than Andorra. One is no longer so sure of anything. Curiously unmoved the men at the purser's desk, cell-like the cabin, disdainful the eyes of voyagers and their friends, solemn the officer who stands on the deserted promenade deck thinking something of his own as he stares at the crowd below. A last odd idea that one didn't really have to come, then the loud, mournful whistles, and the thing—certainly not a boat, but rather a human idea, a frame of mind—pushes forth into the big dark night.

hurries through, even though there's time; the past, the continent, is behind; the future is the glowing mouth in the side of the ship; the dim, turbulent alley is too confusedly the present.

Up the gangplank and the vision of the world adjusts itself, narrows. One is a citizen of a commonwealth smaller than Andorra, no longer sure of anything. The men at the purser's desk are as oddly shaped as the cabins; disdainful are the eyes of voyagers and their friends. Next the loud mournful whistles, the portentous vibration and the boat, the human idea—is in motion. The pier and its faces slide by and for a moment the boat is a piece accidentally split off from them; the faces became remote, voiceless, the pier is one of many blurs along the water front. The harbor flows swiftly toward the sea.

12.3–13.1

The ship having swallowed him as impassively as though he were a missionary for Beirut, a low, portentous vibration began. The pier with its faces commenced to slide by, and for a moment the boat was just a piece accidentally split off from it; then the faces became remote, voiceless, and the pier was one among many yellow blurs along the waterfront. Now the harbor flowed swiftly toward the sea.

"Indecision"
Post 13.1
Her breathing was very young as she came close to him—young and eager and exciting. Her lips were faintly chapped, but soft in the corners.

275.20–21
Her breathing was young and eager and exciting. Her lips were faintly chapped but soft in the corners.

"Emotional Bankruptcy"
Post 8.3
She took his arm snugly, settling it in hers with a series of little readjustments, as if she wanted it right because it was going to be there forever.

276.28–32
Walking on the greensward between cherubs and philosophers, fauns and falling water, she took his arm snugly, settling into it with a series of little readjustments, as if she wanted it to be right because it was going to be there forever.

"Jacob's Ladder"
Post 58.3
At the second tea, young Raffino—he was an actor, one of innumerable hopeful Valentinos—appeared again

277.16–17
presently they were there and watched Nicotera, one of many hopeful Valentinos, strut and pose

"Jacob's Ladder"
Post 58.2
Everybody that's seen the rushes says it's the first one I've had sex appeal in."

277.21–26
"Everybody that's seen the rushes says——"
"What are the rushes?"

253

"What are the rushes?"

"When they run off what they took the day before. They say it's the first time I've had sex appeal."

"I don't notice it," he teased her.

"You wouldn't. But I have."

"When they run off what they took the day before. They say it's the first thing I've had sex appeal in."

"I don't notice it."

"You wouldn't! But I have."

"Crazy Sunday"
AM 211.1

he felt happy and friendly toward all the people gathered there, people of bravery and industry, superior to a *bourgeoisie* that outdid them in ignorance and loose living, risen to a position of the highest prominence in a nation that for a decade had wanted only to be entertained.

278.12–14

They were people of bravery and industry; they were risen to a position of prominence in a nation that for a decade had wanted only to be entertained.

"Jacob's Ladder"
Post 58.4

"Raffino's nothing but a baby."

He took her words as an invitation, but this time she relaxed wearily in his arms. He held her thus for the rest of the way, her eyes closed, her short hair falling straight back like a girl drowned.

Jenny watched this mood, which was more than jealousy and less than love, snow under, one by one, the qualities of consideration and understand-

285.5–15

"He's only a baby," she said, sniffling. "You know I'm yours first."

In reaction he put his arms about her but she relaxed wearily backward; he held her like that for a moment as in the end of an adagio, her eyes closed, her hair falling straight back like that of a girl drowned.

"Dick, let me go. I never felt so mixed up in my life."

He was a gruff red bird and instinctively she drew away from him as his unjustified jeal-

254

ing which she knew in him and with which she felt at home.

"H'm!" He was a gruff white bird now. He could scarcely credit his own unpleasantness, but something illogical as love itself urged him on. "An actor!"

"Oh Jake," she cried, "please lemme go. I never felt so terrible and mixed up in my life."

ousy began to snow over the qualities of consideration and understanding with which she felt at home.

"Jacob's Ladder"

Post 63.1

"I just feel comfortable and happy with you."

"I don't know. I guess I was young. You never know how you once felt, do you?"

She had become elusive to him, with that elusiveness that gives a hidden significance to the least significant remarks.

285.27–32

She had achieved the elusiveness that gives hidden significance to the least significant remarks.

"Is it like you felt toward me in Paris?"

"I feel comfortable and happy when I'm with you. In Paris it was different. But you never know how you once felt. Do you?"

"The Hotel Child"

Post 9.2

But the Hotel des Trois Mondes was full of people who were actually rich and noble, people who did fine embroidery or took cocaine in closed apartments and meanwhile laid claim to European thrones and half a dozen mediatized German principalities

320.19–22

throughout this hotel there were many chambers wherein rich ruins, fugitives from justice, claimants to the thrones of mediatized principalities, lived on the derivatives of opium or barbitol listening eternally as to an inescapable radio, to the coarse melodies of old sins.

"The Hotel Child"

Post 8.1

Failing that, you are faintly suspect, because this corner of Europe does not draw people; rather, it accepts them without too many inconvenient questions—live and let live. Routes cross here—people bound for private *cliniques* or tuberculosis resorts in the mountains, people who are no longer *persona grata* in Italy or France.

320.23–28

This corner of Europe does not so much draw people as accept them without inconvenient questions. Routes cross here— people bound for private sanitariums or tuberculosis resorts in the mountains, people who are no longer *persona gratis* in France or Italy.

"Babylon Revisited"

Post 4.2

Parents expected genius, or at least brilliance, and both the forcing of children and the fear of forcing them, the fear of warping natural abilities, were poor substitutes for that long, careful watchfulness, that checking and balancing and reckoning of accounts, the end of which was that there should be no slipping below a certain level of duty and integrity.

331.11–16

He managed to reach them over the heads of employees on the principle that both the forcing of children and the fear of forcing them were inadequate substitutes for the long, careful watchfulness, the checking and balancing and reckoning of accounts, to the end that there should be no slip below a certain level of duty.

"On Schedule"

Post 16.2

She was twelve, and very fair and exquisitely made, like his dead wife; and often in the past he had worried about that. Lately she had become as robust as any American child

332.13–22

Topsy was easier. She was nine and very fair and exquisitely made like Nicole, and in the past Dick had worried about that. Lately she had become as robust as any American child. He was satisfied with them

256

71.3

"Either one learns politeness at home," René said, "or the world teaches it with a whip— and many young people in America are ruined in that process. How do I care whether Noël 'adores' me or not, as they say? I am not bringing her up to be my wife."

both, but conveyed the fact to them only in a tacit way. They were not let off breaches of good conduct—"Either one learns politeness at home," Dick said, "or the world teaches it to you with a whip and you may get hurt in the process. What do I care whether Topsy 'adores' me or not? I'm not bringing her up to be my wife."

"On Your Own"

Price 325

Her mouth was made of two small intersecting cherries pointing off into a bright smile;

343.2–3

Her old mouth was made of two small intersecting cherries.

"One Trip Abroad"

Post 48.3

Nicole saw from her window the yacht of T. F. Golding, placid among the swells of the Monacon Bay, as if constantly bound on a romantic voyage not dependent upon actual motion.

345.22–25

It was the motor yacht of T. F. Golding lying placid among the little swells of the Nicean Bay, constantly bound upon a romantic voyage that was not dependent upon actual motion.

"Two Wrongs"

Post 109.2

Lady Caroline Sibly-Biers was a pale young woman with lovely metallic hair almost green in certain lights.

348.10–12

As she spoke, Nicole was aware of a small, pale, pretty young woman with lovely metallic hair, almost green in the deck lights,

257

The Hotel Child
Post 9.3
"The man is a scoundrel of some sort, but apparently he's a cat of the stripe; he's a great pal of Schenzi, in Vienna. I sat up till five the other night playing two-handed *chemin de fer* with him here in the bar and he owes me a mille Swiss."

348.31–33
"The man's a scoundrel, but he's a cat of the stripe. We sat up all night playing two-handed chemin-de-fer, and he owes me a mille Swiss."

"Two Wrongs"
Post 109.2
She was a member of that select sorority of the wickedest women in London, though another woman was at that moment considered the wickedest one.

349.1–5
Tommy laughed and said: "She is now the wickedest woman in London—whenever I come back to Europe there is a new crop of the wickedest women from London. She's the very latest—though I believe there is now one other who's considered almost as wicked."

"One Trip Abroad"
Post 51.1
"It's all right for the English," someone said, "because they're doing a sort of dance of death—you know, gaiety in the doomed fort, with the Sepoys at the gate. You can see it by their faces when they dance—the intensity. They know it and they want it, and they don't see any future. But you Americans, you're having a rotten time. If you want to wear the green hat or the crushed hat, or whatever

349.26–29
". . . It's all right for you English, you're doing a dance of death. . . . Sepoys in the ruined fort, I mean Sepoys at the gate and gaiety in the fort and all that. The green hat, the crushed hat, no future."

it is, you always have to get a little tipsy."

"The Rubber Check"
Post 42.3
Her manner had changed; it was interlaced with Anglicisms—the terminal "What?" the double-edged "Quite," the depressing "Cheerio" that always suggested imminent peril.

349.30–33
Lady Caroline answered him in short sentences spotted with the terminal "What?" the double-edged "Quite!" the depressing "Cheerio!" that always had a connotation of imminent peril,

"The Hotel Child"
Post 69.1
"After all," she protested, "a chep's a chep, and a chum's a chum"

350.2–4
she saw the young woman turn dark and sinewy, and heard her answer sharply:
"After all a chep's a chep and a chum's a chum."

"The Hotel Child"
Post 8.3–9.1
They were very Europeanized Americans; in fact, they had reached a position where they could hardly be said to belong to any nation at all; certainly not to any great power, but perhaps to a sort of Balkanlike state composed of people like themselves.

370.12–16
—Europeanized Americans who had reached a position where they could scarcely have been said to belong to any nation at all, at least not to any great power though perhaps to a Balkan-like state composed of similar citizens—

"More Than Just a House"
Post 30.4
The squirrel's flight on the branch, the wind nudging at the leaves, the cock splitting distant air, the creep of sun-

372.27–32
But as she turned into the road of arched pines and the atmosphere changed,—with a squirrel's flight on a branch, a wind

light transpiring through the immobility, lulled him into an adolescent trance, and he sprawled back against the leather for a moment without problems.

nudging at the leaves, a cock splitting distant air, with a creep of sunlight transpiring through the immobility, then the voices of the beach receded—Nicole relaxed and felt new and happy;

"A Snobbish Story"

Post 40.1

She felt her own lips' warmth in the mouthpiece of the phone.

374.18–19

She felt her lips' warmth in the receiver as she welcomed his coming.

"One Interne"

Post 86.2

Afterward, with their heads wet and their skins fresh and glowing, they sat side by side in his roadster, loath to start back.

It was very bright where they were, and as he kissed her he lost himself in the whiteness of her white cheeks and her white teeth and her cool brow and the hand that touched his face.

384.24–29

As they got into the car with their heads still damp, their skins fresh and glowing, they were loath to start back. It was very bright where they were and as Tommy kissed her she felt him losing himself in the whiteness of her cheeks and her white teeth and her cool brow and the hand that touched his face.

"What a Handsome Pair!"

Post 16.3

The two men regarded each other with a curious impotence of expression; there can be no communication between men in that position, for their relation is indirect and consists in how much each of them has possessed or will possess of the woman in question, so that

398.24–30

The two men regarded each other with a curious impotence of expression. There can be little communication between men in that position, for their relation is indirect, and consists of how much each of them has possessed or will possess of the woman in question, so that their emotions pass through her divided self as through a bad telephone connection.

their emotions pass through her divided self as through a bad telephone connection.

⚡"Babylon Revisited"

Post 84.3

He wasn't young any more, with a lot of nice thoughts and dreams to have by himself.

402.2–4

He was not young any more with a lot of nice thoughts and dreams to have about himself, so he wanted to remember them well.

Bibliography

Bruccoli, Matthew J. *The Composition of Tender Is the Night.* Pittsburgh: University of Pittsburgh Press, 1963.

Bruccoli, with the assistance of Jennifer Atkinson, ed. *As Ever, Scott Fitz——: Letters Between F. Scott Fitzgerald and His Literary Agent Harold Ober 1919–1940.* Philadelphia & New York: Lippincott, 1972.

Bruccoli. *F. Scott Fitzgerald: A Descriptive Bibliography,* rev. ed. Pittsburgh: University of Pittsburgh Press, 1987.

Bruccoli, ed. *The Short Stories of F. Scott Fitzgerald.* New York: Scribners, 1989.

Bruccoli. *Some Sort of Epic Grandeur: The Life of F. Scott Fitzgerald,* rev. ed. New York: Carroll & Graf, 1993.

Bruccoli, ed. *Tender Is the Night,* 5 vols.; Part 4 of *F. Scott Fitzgerald Manuscripts.* New York and London: Garland, 1991.

Bruccoli and Margaret M. Duggan, eds. *Correspondence of F. Scott Fitzgerald.* New York: Random House, 1980.

Bruccoli, with the assistance of Judith S. Baughman, ed. *F. Scott Fitzgerald: A Life in Letters.* New York: Scribners, 1994.

Kuehl, John, and Jackson R. Bryer, eds. *Dear Scott/Dear Max: The Fitzgerald-Perkins Correspondence.* New York: Scribners, 1971.

Smith, Scottie Fitzgerald, Bruccoli, and Joan P. Kerr, eds. *The Romantic Egoists.* New York: Scribners, 1974.

Stern, Milton R., ed. *Critical Essays on F. Scott Fitzgerald's Tender Is the Night.* Boston: Hall, 1986.

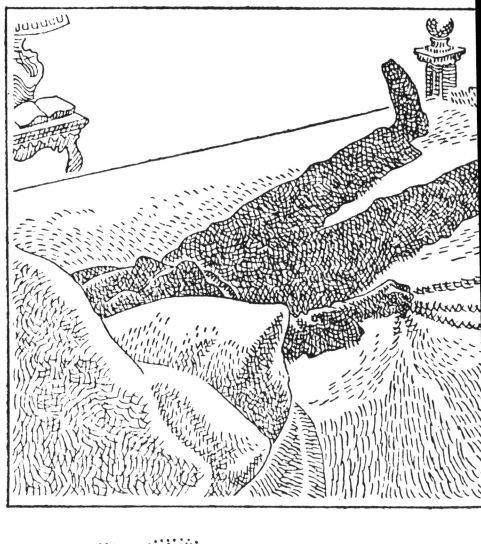